Cinema and Modernity

Frontispiece: The Lady from Shanghai: Rita Hayworth wears formal black attire to meet her fate.

Cinema and Modernity

John Orr

Polity Press

Firs published in 1993 by Polity Press
in association with Blackwell Publishers

Editorial office:
Polity Press
65 Bridge Street
Cambridge CB2 1UR, UK

Marketing and production:
Blackwell Publishers
108 Cowley Road
Oxford OX4 1JF, UK

238 Main Street
Cambridge, MA 02142, USA

ISBN 0 7456 0631 8
ISBN 0 7456 1186 9 (pbk)

A CIP catalogue record for this book is available from the British Library and from the
Library of Congress

Typeset in 10½ on 12 pt Palatino
by Photo·graphics, Honiton, Devon
Printed and bound in Great Britain by
Hartnolls Limited, Bodmin, Cornwall
This book is printed on acid-free paper.

Contents

List of Illustrations

All photographs are reproduced by courtesy of the British Film Institute

Frontispiece: The Lady from Shanghai: Rita Hayworth wears formal black attire to meet her fate. Columbia Productions, Paris.

1 *Marienbad*: the baroque interior as nuclear after-life. Robur Droits Audiovisuels, Paris.

2 *L'eclisse*: the cool apocalypse. Interopa Film.

3 *L'avventura*: the gaze as visual assault. Produzioni Cinematografiche Europee, Rome.

4 *L'avventura*: under the watchful eye of the absent Anna. Produzioni Cinematografiche Europee, Rome.

5 *Persona*: the camera as two-way mirror. Svensk Filmindustri, Stockholm.

6 *Le Genou de Claire*: eye-level shot/low-angle gaze. Films du Losange, Paris.

7 *Weekend*: the car as destroyer without qualities. Artificial Eye Film Company Ltd, London.

8 *Kings of the Road*: the driver's cab as home. The British Film Institute, London.

Preface

This book was prompted by a recent reading of a fervent debate in *Cahiers du Cinéma* over thirty years ago in 1959. Its subject was Alain Resnais's film of the moment, *Hiroshima, mon amour*, and the round table included Jean-Luc Godard, Jacques Rivette and Eric Rohmer, *Cahiers* critics about to embark on their own movie careers. Their response was one of excitement but also of puzzlement. They could not immediately place the film in the history of the cinema, for Resnais's narrative of a French actress in the peace movement of 1959 who visits Hiroshima to make a documentary of the new city risen from the ashes of the atomic bomb was unlike anything they had ever seen. Its interweaving of past and present and its refusal to name its central characters distanced it both from the American tradition of melodrama and the Italian cinema of neo-realism. The rapid cutting reminded them of Eisenstein but the long tracking shots had a fluidity and a freedom which was entirely contemporary. As written by Marguerite Duras, the voice-over was literary in its power and phrasing, but accompanied images which were dazzling and cinematic and a dialogue between the French and Japanese lovers which was precise and erotic. At the same time the documentary flavour of the film in which, for example, Resnais films Emmanuele Riva acting in a peace documentary in the streets of the city made it much more than just a love story in the nuclear age. It made felt what Pasolini has called 'the presence of the camera' and became a profound comment on the nature of cinema itself.

In the course of the discussion Rohmer and the others speculate on whether they are watching the beginnings of a truly modern cinema, where an art form still in its infancy has outgrown its classical phase to produce narratives and images of equal stature to the artworks of other modernists of the twentieth century. They also wonder if this will become the cinema of the future. Thirty years on, this study attempts to answer the question they had posed, at a time when their 'future' has finally become 'our past' and when as film-makers they themselves became part of the movement about which they speculated. Their sense of the modern fuses two vital questions we must ask about modern moves. It links Bazin's famous 'What is Cinema?' to the further and equally vital question 'What is significant in cinema?'

The problem posed by answering this double query is the two different planes of reading it demands. We need critical readings of movies in particular which never cease to question what is important about cinema in general. As such we must reject any 'scientific' study of cinema which tries to place itself above the feature film, or any quest to find a secret grammar of film similar to that of written language. Cinema is not displaced philosophy and at most theory or philosophy provides us with ways of seeing which the act of viewing may complete or refute as the case may be. How we see things is finally down to us. Yet we still need that kind of critique which is provided by structured ways of seeing. Without it there are movies, but no cinema.

Some readings for this study should be noted, specifically of Nietzsche, Freud and Sartre. None of the three has answers to what is important in the cinema, but indirectly, they have helped me to formulate mine. Thus the will-to-power and the eternal return, the uncanny, the oneiric and the compulsion to repeat, the look, the imaginary and bad faith, are all terms which reverberate through the text without nailing anything to the wall. All of them are modified by the movies discussed which turn them around, and the study singles out movies which are designed largely to turn them around, movies which challenge *us* to speak to them. Of Nietzsche whose inclusion is unusual, I would argue his vision of the will-to-power as art affirms film's nature as the product of dynamic and creative actions which are always individual and collective, an ensemble of creative actions which force themselves upon the raw data of our life-worlds and then transform them. Nietzschean 'return' emphasizes the power of all culture to repeat its forms under changing circumstances which in turn change the forms themselves, so that cinema is never to be viewed either as a pure state of being or as a pure state of becoming but as a form which constantly repeats itself in the process of changing. This is how I regard the neo-modern turn of the cinema over a period of twenty years between 1958 and 1978 in its relationship to Western modernity. For me that body of film-making remains the most vital connecting link between the cinema and modernity. Of course there are many more, but since it important to write about we feel is important, it is the one about which I shall largely write.

Acknowledgements

This study is a product of the collective enthusiasm shown for movies by my film classes at Edinburgh, but also of individual discussions with Duncan Petrie, Jim Hickey, Carmine Mezzacappa, Catherine Fellows, Brian Kirk and Paola Buonadonna, all of whom have helped me to be more precise in my thinking about the cinema. I very much hope the end result is worth it.

J. O.

1

Film and the Paradox of the Modern

In the cinema the modern is already history. But it has never been replaced. This is the paradox which confronts us in looking at film over the last fifty years. The reasons are complex. We can begin to understand them only if we view modern artworks, including narrative pictures, as processes which come into being in a Nietzschean sense by coming *back* into being, which move forward by echoing the past. Modern artworks are never exclusively 'modern' but also a multitude of other things. Their varied properties elude the abstract résumé of their honorific title, so that the word 'modern' never subsumes them. Faced with this local difficulty in film discourse, the temptation is to take short cuts. We ignore the constantly self-transforming nature of the modern, its inherent and ruthless dynamisms. Instead we fantasize its overthrow, see it as something already in the past. Spurred by a key design change in recent architecture, many critics now deem any new form 'postmodern' in the same manic yet reassuring way their predecessors lauded all things 'modernistic'. Labels patch over the gaps in thinking. Often the 'postmodern' reveals itself in part as the symptom of an ideology of consumerism, particularly in the United States, which preaches an uncritical pleasure. But the 'post' prefix now attached to many concepts in cultural theory generally bears witness to the impatient consumerism of our age. The prefix becomes a stand-in for concepts yet to be invented. Changes of form are commodified as absolute breaks with the past and prefixes become labels of convenience.

The cinema is not so easy to prefix. Moreover the terms used here, classical and modern, are themselves honorific short cuts which have finite use but no finality. They work tenuously in an art form which is merely a hundred years old. Our focus on the modern will be largely on the transformation of the cinema in the sound period between 1958 and 1978, a span of just two decades when, it is suggested, we reach the true moment of the modern in the Western cinema. Here, I wish to argue, the reflexive nature of the modern film, its capacity for irony, for pastiche, for constant self-reflection, and for putting everything in quotation marks, are not 'postmodern' at all, but on the contrary, have been an essential feature of the cinema's continuing encounter with modernity. Yet the term 'modern' also remains an enigma, if not a misnomer. In this period we call cinema 'modern' rather than 'classical' for two reasons. First, it can be seen as a critical and subversive rendering of modernity in Western societies. In the second place it can be seen as having made a decisive break with Hollywood narratives of the Studio system up to 1960. However, it would be more accurate to call this cinema 'neo-modern', not 'modernist' or 'postmodern', because it is also a Nietzschean *return* to the modern, to the earlier moment of high modernism between 1914 and 1925 when cinema was still in its technical infancy. Here cinema's first modern moment was short-lived. In Hollywood it was aborted by the cultural politics of the market place. In Europe it suffered the twin perils of censorship and dictatorship, hemmed in by the pincer movements of Hitler and Stalin. Thus one can really speak of two 'modern' cinemas, a silent cinema of Murnau, Dreyer, Lang, Buñuel, and Eisenstein and a sound cinema which crystallizes in the 1960s and early 1970s. How do we explain a gap of nearly three decades? The answer of course is that the 'gap' is a critical invention, but a necessary one. For two things coincided to frustrate the continuity of modern film, the fact of political repression and exile and the slow take-up of new technologies in the sound cinema. The use of sound by major European directors such as Eisenstein, Lang and Buñuel was overtaken and compromised by political developments. Lang's masterly fusion of Brecht and Expressionism in *M*, the movie which daringly combined serial killing with political allegory, was made two years before he fled Nazi Germany. During the war, Eisenstein's *Ivan the Terrible* moved the Soviet director forward into sound and colour, but some would also say *back* to political allegory and theatrical Expressionism. After Franco's triumph, Buñuel stayed in exile.

The great works of Lang and Eisenstein were thus only briefly linked to high modernism. Their work suggests Nietzschean return, artistic recurrence as well as cultural progression, a return to the modern in a more technically advanced form. The paradox of the modern cinema is recurrence as the *completion* of form. This paradox was not unique to the cinema but in the cinema as an industrial art it was at its strongest. The movement in film has been both linear and cyclical. The linear movement from Eisenstein onwards had been a movement, to use Kracauer's term, towards the greater physical redemption of reality, towards establishing, particularly in the cinema of Vigo and Renoir, the luminous validity of the image.[1] The cyclical movement, by contrast, stimulates the increasing *dislocation* of the image, the bracketing and the unmasking of its problematic nature in the modern capitalistic world. The history of cinematic artworks is thus the tension and contradiction between the two, between line and cycle, lineage and return, the aesthetics of Kracauer and the aesthetics of Adorno.[2] In this respect much current rhetoric of the 'postmodern' seems contrived and parochial. Indeed those features of style or narrative called postmodern – pastiche, self-conscious narrative, game-playing, polyvalence – which *are* undoubtedly present in contemporary culture are already there from the start as part of a modern departure from the *classical* narratives of sound cinema, a departure which takes place towards the end of the 1950s. Most are neo-modern inventions.

From 1910 onwards modernist revolt had targeted the romantic world-view of the artwork as a form of creative human struggle towards cosmic harmony. This utopian search for harmony in a divided, instrumental world was a quest through the suffering of the romantic artist for a new organic order. By contrast, modernism's mind-set was fragmentary, closer to the city than to nature, to technology than to tradition. But as Taylor points out, at a much more recent stage in our history the political revolts of 1968 effectively combined the two opposed movements.[3] The political style of Parisian contestation, its street revolts, its existential powers of invention, its self-conscious theatricality and obsession with cultural signs, all were modernist in their inspired dissonance. Yet the apocalyptic dream of a global industrial society based on equal participation of all was utopian and at times romantic. Despite the loss of utopia after 1968, and its intellectual replacement by a de-dramatized apocalyptics in French philosophy which Jay has called the enunciation of 'apocalypse for ever',[4] the quest to exorcise the attractions of the romantic has remained an important part of our culture. It is as true of the modern cinema as of any other art-form. The cinema uses both the narrative fragment and the play with the camera to break with the organic structure of the romantic world-view. It extends not only the subversions of form which Adorno detected in high modernism but also those forms of self-conscious play some critics wilfully pretend never existed in modernism at all. Yet this ceaseless invention and return of the modern needs another vital component. It needs the linear movement of cinema-as-technique which *enhances* the mimetic power of the image. If the romantic tradition has never truly left us, then neither has the imprint of the real, the urge among film-makers to open up the physical world to the lens of the camera. In the cinema it actually intensifies with the new technical properties of the medium. Jean Renoir's *La Règle du jeu* is now a classic, for example, because in 1939 it was both mimetic *and* modern. It boldly projects a filmic image of a given society, a given social milieu at a specific time and place – the French upper-middle classes in the city and the country just before Nazi invasion. At the same time Renoir's innovative filming proved technically indispensable for the neo-modern upsurge of the French New Wave in the 1960s. For its narrative lyricism was hailed a consecration of pure style, an inspiration for the whole modern movement. Renoir's 'realism' thus became the apotheosis of pure form for a future generation of neo-modern innovators.

Renoir's legacy is exemplified in François Truffaut's famous New Wave film *Jules et Jim* (1962). The latter's camera mobility, its fluid panning, its medium-long shots, its deep focus, its deft lyricisms are all indebted to the cinema of Renoir. Yet twenty years on it is much bolder in its tracking and panning shots, spatially more resonant in its use of wide-screen cinema while its tragicomic themes link the major decades of the modern in the cinema – the 1920s and the 1960s. Adapted from an autobiographical novel by Henri-Pierre Roche, it matches literary voice-over to lyrical editing, the written narrative to the moving image. It portrays a bohemian *menage à trois* of the high modern age throwing off the shackles of bourgeois constraint, but in doing so it conveys the more recent sensibility of the 1960s, existential and irreverent, the emergent structure of feeling of a critical younger generation in France. It is powerfully anachronistic, an image of *then*, but also of *now*. In *Jules et Jim* the New Wave is neo-modern, the rebirth of the modern at a later date.

With its stylized clothes and freedom of movement, it goes against the maturalistic clutter and wooden *mise-en-scène* of the British period movie but also avoids another seductive flaw in the movie treatment of the past, that of nostalgia. For Truffaut history is a movement of advance but also of return. The trio of Catherine, Jules and Jim survive the First World War and, in Truffaut's adaptation, their lives are taken through to the Nazi book-burnings which they watch disbelievingly on a cinema newsreel in Paris. But their lives are cyclical. Catherine cannot choose between husband and lover and can resolve her lack of choice only by taking other lovers, until tragedy breaks the circle. Raoul Coutard's fluid 360-degree pans reinforce the cyclical movement. As things move through time, as the trio gets older and Catherine fears old age, images and places repeat themselves. They visit the same houses, meet the same friends, have the same conversations and feel the same conflicting passions. The film stresses the difference of period between its setting and its making but also their affinities. We are distanced from the characters through the avoidance of melodrama and yet they could be us. Just as they 'are' then and now, modern cinema is then and now. In its lyrical embrace of advance and return, Truffaut's picture reflexively links its present to its past.

Our description of the New Wave as 'neo-modern' is clearly indebted to the neo-realist tag of post-war Italian cinema. yet, as we have stressed, by inheriting the complex legacies of Renoir, neo-realism, Lang and Eisenstein, the neo-moderns run parallel to the technical enhancement of the image. The more the power of the image is advanced, the more the neo-moderns transform it. Their innovation depends on that advance, on a history of technical and thematic advances which are absorbed and then displaced. The neo-moderns are both innovators and iconoclasts, achieving a special rank in twentieth-century art by combining pleasure and subversion, discomfort and fascination in equal measure. Theirs has been a cinema of challenge but also of affirmation, a cinema of dissonance but also of lyricism, a cinema of enigma but also of perspicacity. Above all it is a cinema of the reflexive will-to-power. Its narratives constantly speculate upon the power of the camera itself.

Since 1970, the scope of the modern film has been far broader. Like modernity itself, it has become global. In that period, the films of Akira Kurosawa, Satyajit Ray, Andrei Tarkovsky, Elem Klimov, Larisa Shepitko, Glauber Rocha, Andrzej Wajda, Chen Kaige, Zhang Yimou and Hou Hsiao-Hsien have been as powerful as any discussed here. But the neo-modern moment has its origin in the national cinemas of Western Europe and the United States where it engages with Western capitalist modernity. Here cinema is often at its most powerful in film-makers who emerge from distinctive *national* traditions. Jean-Luc Godard has asserted the existence of only four truly national cinemas, the Russian, the Italian, the German and the American.[5] Of these, claims Godard, the American cinema has always been in perpetuum mobile, a core of irresistible energy colonizing the world through the feature movie because as a country America lacks a firm sense of self. The German and Russian cinemas were by contrast pre-fascist, he suggests, products of the revolutionary turmoil of Europe after 1917. Since 1945 only Italy, a fascist country which overthrew fascism, has been for Godard a true national cinema. We can see the imbalance at once. Hollywood was and is the decentred energy of pure aggrandizement. The rest were specific and revolutionary and no longer exist.

Godard's formula is attractive but misleading. In global terms it is too narrow, and even in the West the national input of the neo-moderns can be taken in a different way. It comes out of the synergized interior subversions of Hollywood genre by American directors from Welles to Scorsese and out of the bleak threatening vision of film noir. Yet, more significantly, it emerges out of the neo-modern turn of European cinema in France, Italy and West Germany and individual film-makers in other countries, such as Ingmar Bergman in Sweden and Luis Buñuel in Spain. Nor can we understand the rise and fall of European cinema without the broader picture of financing and changing audiences. While the box-office value of European films in their own countries has declined relative to the global products of Hollywood, we have seen an extraordinary resurgence of film in

Eastern Europe during the decisive challenge to one particular ideology of modernity, that of communism. In years to come film-makers from communist countries in terminal crisis may be seen as making an equally vital input to the art-form as the neo-moderns. Tarkovsky, Klimov, Shepitko, Zanussi, Kieslowski, Kusterica and Abuladze are just some names here which should be conjured with *in the absence* of new film-makers in the United States or Western Europe of comparable power, and this includes David Lynch and Peter Greenaway. Communism in decline has, ironically, produced greater cinema than consumer capitalism in apparent ascendancy.

A vital difference still remains. In Asia and Eastern Europe the modern cinema has arisen out of the clash between the traditional and the modern, between myth and religion on the one hand and political ideology on the other. Where the Western cinema differs, it differs through its class-formation. Its images largely query the life-worlds of the upper middle classes. They are, in effect, profane images of the bourgeoisie. These images are always ambivalent in nature. They are images of frailty, not solidity, weakness not strength, anxiety not confidence, per-turbing images of a class which seems at times to have endured in spite of its enemies and its uncertainties. Without this key recognition, the whole discourse of cinema and modernity becomes vacuous. For the central problem of the post-war bour-geoisie lies in its profound crisis of value. Technology, wealth and pleasure not only challenge all firm values, they fail to fill the vacuum they often create. One of the crises of modernity, as Michelangelo Antonioni noted, lies in its failure to create new values which match the progress in technologies we use in every-day life.[6] While new technologies are bewildering in their implosive effect upon us, the improvements they offer often enhance our moral dilemmas. The difference with high modern-ism is instructive. In the 1920s the German Expressionist cinema had exposed an insecure middle class foundering on the verge of economic ruin. In the 1960s the neo-modern cinema challenged the complacencies of a European bourgeoisie spiritually wasting its new prosperity in the Cold War's climate of fear.

Here modern cinema is a vindication of much of Bourdieu's devastating critique of bourgeois taste.[7] Yet it is also a profound challenge to Bourdieu's critique. The bourgeois protagonists of neo-modern narratives live out the unease which Bourdieu detects in the relations between cultural and money capital. A more educated, prosperous world allows them to be ostentatiously cultured, to commodify the artworks and knowledge products of their own class. But they remain uneasy about the necessity of money and its loud vulgarity, its relentless knack of capitalizing cultural icons and reducing them to monetary artefacts, that is, to a market price. As Fellini and Buñuel have both shown in different ways, religious faith offers no consolation. This then is the spur for cinema's exploration of bourgeois modernity. It captures the self-critical and reflexive powers of the bourgeois psyche which Bourdieu often overlooks. It is querulous, puzzling, outrageous, enigmatic in its complex images of wealth and power, but equally in its explorations of risk and ontological insecurity. Here we see the crucial difference between high modern and neo-modern cinema. The first evolved out of an avant-garde culture which charted the growing threat of revolution in an age of war and depression. The neo-modern cinema, by contrast, is a cinema of the Cold War where liberal power has been largely reinstated, but without conviction.

One central theme, already touched upon, draws together all the different strands of modern film-making. The cinema had been part of a modern movement which embarked on a powerful quest to exorcize the romantic in art. Yet in the cinema of the neo-moderns this has been transformed into a love–hate quest where the traces of the romantic are never truly kicked over. The neo-moderns have challenged the conventions of love and marriage as fruitful forms of intimacy, as the most appropriate responses to the felt lack of harmony in the public realm, as a refuge from the guilt and dissatisfactions of renewed bourgeois privilege. In so doing, they have fleshed out the prescient critique a decade earlier in *The Second Sex*, where Simone de Beauvoir had powerfully outlined the formidable dilemmas facing independent and professional women in a post-war male-dominated world.[8] Here intimate relations between the sexes are put fiercely into question. They become the front line in a growing culture of mistrust which, as feminist critics have reminded us, the post-war American cinema of film noir had stereotypically portrayed as male paranoia and deep suspicion of any female power.[9] At the same time the growing crises of sexual identity and the ironies of disappointed love have renewed a source of romantic despair. The loss of romantic love often portrayed as irreversible has drawn responses in the cinema ranging from stoicism and acceptance to irony and despair. If there is little to replace absolute value in the modern world, desire does not replace love. Yet already love is a conception which belongs to the past.

The round table discussion of *Hiroshima, mon amour* by *Cahiers du Cinéma* is significant in recognizing the connection between the work of de Beauvoir and the new cinema of Resnais, Bergman and Antonioni. The film of Resnais and Duras is taken up as an example of de Beauvoir's existential feminism in action. Thus Godard remarks 'You could say that *Hiroshima* is Simone de Beauvoir that works', while Rivette sees Emmanuele Riva's performance in the role of the actress as an example of the new existential woman of post-war Europe challenging the constraints of her past.[10] Thus for the *Cahiers* group the new cinema is inseparable from its portrait of the 'new woman'. The portrayals of the modern woman by Riva, Jeanne Moreau, Anna Karina, Monica Vitti and Harriet Andersson, which go beyond the idealizations of Hollywood and its forms of stardom, are for them vital signs of the arrival of the modern cinema. While male roles often continue to display older forms of patriarchy and authority, the modern female persona challenges these conventions dramatically. Thus both modern cinema and its modern women spring from changing forms of modernity, but both subsequently challenge existing forms of modernity. It is a challenge later taken up and extended in the work of the woman directors of the neo-modern period such as Agnes Varda, Margarethe von Trotta, Claire Denis and Chantal Ackerman.

The challenge of the neo-moderns to the conventions of intimacy is inseparable from a challenge to the conventions of perception. For the neo-moderns the camera's powers of perception remain frail and partial. The greater power of the image cannot replace God, Marx, marriage or democracy but must question all of them. In the absence of absolute values lies a vision of the uncertainties of all knowledge. Through its vexing quest narratives modern cinema re-affirms Merleau-Ponty's assertion of the inherent ambiguity of the visual field of perception.[11] All filmmakers express on celluloid what they perceive in experience and, as Sobchack has shown in her phenomenology of film, spectators in a reversible movement perceive what is expressed, and express their perceptions of that expression.[12] The life-worlds of film-maker and spectator intersect through the medium of film which creates its own life-world as technical mediator. Yet the neo-moderns play reflexively on this process of mediation and test the binding chains of intersubjectivity to their limit. The more ambiguous the image, the greater the uncertainty of response. There are conventions of seeing but no absolute truths we can share amongst ourselves. All experience depends on context, on the positioning of the subject, the camera and the spectator. In that respect cinema is a changing medium which expresses changing conventions of how we view and how we are viewed.

Merleau-Ponty's emphasis on the intersubjective nature of experience as perception-expression gives weight to the view of the filmic image as an 'expression of experience by experience'. Narrative film is never omniscient, never completely detached from the subjective point-of-view. On the other hand it is technically difficult, as Robert Montgomery's *The Lady in the Lake* (1946) shows, to produce a narrative which is purely subjective, to persuade an audience that it can view an imaginary course of events exclusively from the eyes of one person's body. Film is a spatial medium which always shows the positioning of subjects in their life-worlds as a dynamic movement through space and time. In the cinema all human subjects, film-makers, actors and spectators alike, are both subject and object, viewed and viewing, looked upon and looking. There are no fixed points of experience, no absolute certainties in perception. Modern pictures forge imaginary narratives out of the life-worlds of everyday experience, expressing what is perceived, projecting on to a screen what the camera records. They seek revelation through images of the ordinary and like the modern novel from Joyce onwards, develop their own matrix of epiphanies not out of great events or melodramatic spectacle but out of the textures of everyday experience.[13]

Godard's advice to young film-makers has been to think about the course of their actual day and about how to capture that experience in images. This is not just a prescription for filming as pure observation. It may include that endorsement of the power of *cinema-vérité*, but it goes far beyond it. Film is a way of viewing action, but is itself also a form of action, both behind and in front of the camera. To film and to act in front of the camera are both forms of positioning with an integral relation to each other, and to human action in general. The neo-modern cinema plays reflexively upon this process, and in doing so highlights the frailty of all our cultural signs. It makes manifest what is inherent within the process of filming itself. How to judge the filmed objects of perception in any film is a puzzle shared by the characters within the film and the viewers who watch them, a puzzle which is never easily resolved. The neo-moderns thus seize on one key consequence of the many time–space transformations of modernity, the increasing gap that is felt by many between perception and expression and the anxieties of how they should respond to what they see imperfectly. Bergman, Buñuel and Fellini have questioned the power of religious devotion and authority, while Godard, Antonioni and Resnais have exposed the limitations of the vague, uneasy humanisms put forward as secular replacements. As Giddens has noted, the reflexive culture of modernity is one in which the searches for self-discovery, for new ways of seeing ourselves in the process of seeing, have all increased over the last thirty years as the certainties of absolute knowledge decline.[14] The neo-moderns sensed this from the start. Their cinema testifies to the paradox of that double acceleration, the increasing pace at which the search for self-discovery desperately tries to overcome our increasing sense of its impossibility.

If the moment of the neo-moderns is that of the 1960s and early 1970s, what, if anything, has since replaced them? First of all, their legacy has been absorbed back into all forms of cinema. All cinema is now modern. With a new generation of young directors and semi-independent producers, Hollywood from the 1970s onward commodified most dimensions of neo-modern style. The *mise-en-scène* of *Body Heat*, or, for example, the montage of *JFK*, are clear legacies of the modern turn of the cinema. But it is also clear that over the last decade two significant things have also happened to annul this process. First, the impressive technologies of 'special effects' has increased the vogue for big-budget science-fiction, horror and body-count movies. Meanwhile, American cinema continues to burn off its powerful energies on the elusive peripheries of Hollywood in the work of Lynch, Altman, the Coen brothers, Jim Jarmusch, Spike Lee and many others. Secondly, while Hollywood has absorbed the technical and stylistic features of the modern, it has also modified them. One premise of the 'postmodern' has been Eco's double reading which suggests the possibility of pleasurable highbrow and lowbrow readings of the same text.[15] But in Hollywood the double reading has become more ominous, and very different from what Eco suggests. It has become a strategy for dealing with the dissolution of the homogenous audience and the demands of segmented marketing.[16] The most powerful of those genre melodramas purporting to be moral statements now contain contradictory messages to appeal to both left and right, to black and white, to men and women, to those who defend human rights and those who deride them, to pacifists and practitioners of violence, to potential rapists and their potential victims. The most powerful Hollywood products are now schizoid, in a way which would in its classical period have been impossible. They are also great box office for being so.

American domination of world cinema, with its immense powers of marketing and synergy, means that the neo-moderns are unlikely to be superseded in terms of their artistic accomplishment. A second and momentous return of the modern seems unlikely. At the same time the multiple directions of the contemporary cinema in all its forms remain to be analysed. We have yet to understand them in their broader context and still lack the critical language for doing so. This applies even close to home where an obvious case in point is the work of David Lynch. Lynch has self-consciously recycled the outlaw and rebel themes of American genre cinema in the small-town ambience of the 1980s where nostalgia for sure tradition mingles with the daily horror of the unexpected and the inexplicable. Although Buñuel's name has been evoked in connection, for example, with the incident of the human ear in the garden in *Blue Velvet*, other influences are just as powerful. Lynch's brilliant and disturbing vision of contemporary mores is linked, somewhat incongruously, to a style of acting and static *mise-en-scène* which recall classic Hollywood melodrama and before that the exaggerated gestures of the Expressionist persona in silent film. Lynch is very contemporary precisely by returning to the past, the teller of parodic fables with endless echoes in his nation's film history. But the mocker of genre is also its prisoner, worshipping with a small town nostalgia the American dream which his films undercut. Thus it is that one of the most talented directors in the American cinema to inherit the neo-modern legacy is profoundly conservative in his mythic enslavement. It is a conservatism we have to move away from, by escaping, however briefly, from the seductive synergies of Hollywood genre and the American yearning for nostalgia which continue, now more than ever, to rule the cinema world. We must proceed to our main task in an earlier decade, namely to examine in detail the cinema's special questioning of modernity.

2

Tragicomedy and the Cool Apocalypse

The neo-moderns inherit four legacies from the high modern period, legacies which challenged not only naturalistic art but also the viability of the tragic sense in the age of modernity. They inherit the modernist architecture of the European city, the death of tragedy in modern drama, the inward turn of Expressionism in painting and the inward turn of narrative in fiction. Out of these legacies its cinema generates two distinctive structures of feeling which I intend to call the tragicomic and the cool apocalypse, that is to say structures within the text and within the movement which generate a new fusion of form and sensibility.[1] If we turn to the novel, we see that European cinema after 1945 inherits from it new narratives of survival amidst danger, the dangers, that is, of the modern city and modern war. We can see this struggle for survival most strongly in the work of Joyce, Proust, Woolf, Mann and Fitzgerald whose heroes, however flawed or weak, have the capacity to survive physical misfortune and complex disintegration of feeling. The prevailing structures of feeling in *Ulysses*, *Remembrance of Things Past*, *To the Lighthouse*, *The Magic Mountain*, and *Tender is the Night* are those in which madness, illness, the threat of death and failed intimacies are burdens to be stoically endured by their middle-class heroes. The risks and betrayals of everyday experience are to be resisted, never to be accepted with total resignation. Yet they are never to be conquered or transcended.

The mature industrial age can never be idealized as the age of heroic resistance or noble transcendence. It is fragmented, uncertain, painful and at times formless. Moreover, it is anti-romantic. Detached from God and nature life must go on, even as its moral structures deteriorate. The modernist hero is anti-heroic, an embattled survivor, often privileged in the material world but usually impoverished in the realm of the soul. This vision of modernity is part of the twentieth-century challenge to the nineteenth-century mind-set of optimism and progress. Towards the European bourgeoisie who are in the ascendancy, who are the beneficiaries of the age of progress, the modernists direct most of their ire. In fiction, it is largely a cultural critique from the inside, incestuous and bitter. Conceived in a new age of global warfare, the modernist text subverts the evolutionary vision of a perfectible world. Lawrence's organic 'wave which cannot halt', the onward wave which courses through *The Rainbow*, evokes a stream of living which endures beyond the novel's ending. But in *Women in Love* it is replaced by a cyclical and episodic movement where all advance is tempered by the recurrence of obstacles which cannot be transcended and which prompt the flight into exile. In Joyce's *Ulysses*, also written during the war, apocalypse is also imminent. As Stephen Dedalus prepares for exile, Bloom's Dublin cannot escape Ireland's past as a colonial nation or its future as a country of uprising and civil war. It is precisely this anti-heroic and displaced structure of feeling which modern film later inherits.

Yet the novel in turn was already paying attention to the moving image. After 1914, in the era of the new industrial city, the literary moderns were clearly influenced by the silent cinema in its use of fragmented imagistic narratives.[2] A succession of flickering images which told its own story was essential in the new fragmented narratives of Joyce, Proust and Dos Passos. The Expressionism of the German cinema was part of an art movement evoking the power of industrial technology, but despite this, despite Lang's extraordinary *Metropolis* (1926), the technical constraints of the silent cinema hindered a full breakthrough. Only with the location sequence and release from the studio stage does the cinema begin to capture the true impact of changing forms of modernity, to build on the relativities of space and time, the psychoanalytic 'uncovering' of the unconscious, the quickening rhythms and more complex topography of urban living. During the silent period, with the dynamic montage of Eisenstein, the distorted *mise-en-scène* of the German expressionists and the experiments of the surrealists, film had paraded its potential as a medium of fertile dissonance, as a new visual form of representation which could be culturally subversive. The imagistic poetry of Pound and Eliot had its correlative in the imagistic montage of an embryonic modern cinema. But only well into the sound era did the cinema begin to rival the narrative of the novel as a chronicle of modern destiny. It did so largely in Western Europe after the Second World War. European national cinemas were resurrected after the blight of fascism, in a period of Cold War where the wealth and power of the bourgeoisie had been quickly restored and its cultural capital accordingly boosted, but where its everyday existence intrigued the new film-makers, not because it was so heroic and visionary but because it was so fragile and banal.

Changes in twentieth-century drama are also vital to the cinema's changing structures of feeling. Chekhov, Shaw, O'Casey and Pirandello all produced a new form of tragicomedy which made reversal of fortune a matter of laughter as well as sorrow, of comic error as well as lament. Later, in Beckett, the change of mood is more abrupt, sorrow lightened by joy, laughter suddenly darkened by menace and fear. The nature of play, role and masquerade is increasingly reflexive, knowing, volatile, a property of the stage as much as of the soul.[3] Tragicomic heroes are helpless prisoners of performance, diminished by circumstance, prisoners of action, not its authorizers. Their world is circular and change of fortune merely moves them round a fixed circumference. These central structures of tragicomedy appear on cinema screens for the first time in Renoir's *La Règle du jeu* in 1939. The farce of amorous intrigue in the chateau at Sologne follows Beaumarchais and Marivaux in its classical separation of classes, of masters and servants, even where they intersect. But Renoir violates the class boundary and makes the respective fates of different classes totally interdependent. There is no hierarchy of importance. Life at all social levels, in all affairs of the heart, crosses over and is tragic and farcical at the same time.

In Renoir life and death, sorrow and laughter go hand-in-glove, but in his disgust in 1939 with the post-Munich vacillations of the French upper class, the emotional intensity and passion of Chekhov has disappeared. In Beckett or Pinter the dramatis personae are often marginal figures but in film the opposite happens. Modern tragiomedy focuses on the comic risk-taking of the bourgeoisie. Excessive risk, after all, undermines the pretensions of class dignity. This can be seen in Orson Welles's paranoia-parody *The Lady from Shanghai* in 1948, the volatile tragicomedies of the French New Wave in the 1960s, the chilling satire of Buñuel and the pastiche-nightmare of history in Bertolucci's *The Conformist* in 1970. The tragicomic generates images of fear, distrust, extravagance, desire and vanity. It points to the fragility of class power and the dubious morality of its cultural advantages, to gross mismatches of technology and culture, power and desire. Such contradictions cannot be easily resolved, in contrast to the easy contradictions of the classical American comedy, where the hilarious struggle against misfortune always reaps its due reward. Here the neo-modern tragicomedy differs sharply from the great romantic comedies of Frank Capra, Howard Hawks and Billy Wilder which make love the unlikely rescuer of harassed heroes floundering in unlikely circumstances. The comic mismatch of sexual opposites in *It Happened One Night*, *Ball of Fire*, *Bringing Up Baby* and *Some Like It Hot* is reversed into true love or what Cavell has called 'remarriage'.[4] In tragicomedy, there is no happy switching of partners, no 'remarriage', no resolution. Mismatch and sexual role-reveresal may start off as farce but end up as tragic stupidity and death.

Such tragicomic images of the bourgeoisie are not the product of an artistic elite but largely the product of a second and *non-elitist* cultural wave in the history of modernism[5] This second wave of the modern was acclaimed by a new generation of cineastes and by an expanding cinema audience in higher education and in the professions, growing fast during the Cold War and the move to mass consumerism. The neo-moderns are thus no avant garde. The 1960s are *their* decade of challenge but also a decade of the completion of something begun much earlier. It echoes the earlier subversions of the modern *without* its self-conscious elitism or fear of revolution.[6] Cinema, after all, has always had the potential of a mass audience for its iconoclasm. As an innovative form it challenges both the conventions of the modern artwork and modernity itself. It makes the challenge more accessible but does so without compromise. At the end of the 1950s the challenge begins with *L'avventura* (1959), *A bout de souffle* (1959), *Vertigo* (1958) and *Touch of Evil* (1958). It ends, but not abruptly, with *The Passenger* (1975), *Kings of the Road* (1976) and *Providence* (1977) in the mid-1970s. These two decades are in effect, the moment of the neo-modern.

In Europe, its main *auteurs* Antonioni, Bergman, Bertolucci, Bresson, Buñuel, Rohmer, Godard, Resnais, Herzog, Fassbinder and Wenders continued to make important films into the 1980s but usually without the same power of innovation, and often without equivalent funding. No new generation of film-makers replaces them. For their movement was born out of the renaissance of *national* cinemas, and by 1980 the European Community, with its supra-national powers, had prompted a crisis in national cultural identity which had significant knock-on effects. A similar rise and fall can be seen in the United States. Welles and Hitchcock were the two directors whose work foreshadowed the coming of the modern moment to Hollywood. In the 1970s that moment was absorbed and commodified by directors such as Malick, Rafelson, Scorsese, Coppola, Kubrick and Altman, only to be ground down into kitsch by lesser directors in the 1980s. Scorsese became unpopular, Malick and Rafelson disappeared from the cinema. Altman stopped making pictures. There was no new generation of subversive film-makers. With one or two exceptions, the modern movement drifted back into genre, sometimes as genuine innovation but more often as perversion, as mannerism or cliché, or else as narcissism, pastiche or kitsch.[7]

In Europe, the modern cinema had redefined bourgeois destiny as risk and survival in a nuclear age. But it did so in two separate ways, through two dominant structures of feeling. In tragicomedy the contradiction between an ideology of dignity and the resort to risk results in farcical mistrust. It is central to the desperate strategies of heroes willing their own destruction. But in the other dominant mode of the neo-modern we have the constrained apocalypse of the Cold War, an apocalyptic which challenges our perceptions of the world, and explores the increasing connections between the most intimate and most global forms of contemporary life. Whereas tragicomedy highlights a class culture which aspires to dignity yet is in danger of becoming mechanical and absurd, the cool apocalypse highlights the unspoken fears which lie behind the banalities of everyday life, the constrained anguish at the rapid fluctuation of unpredictable emotion. Here the neo-moderns are just as apocalyptic as their predecessors of the 1920s, but their tone is cooler and more ironic. This same tone has also prevailed in other neo-modern forms, in ludic drama, Beat poetry, abstract Expressionism, and the French New Novel. In cinema however, it is very specific. The great directors of the period, Godard, Bergman, Antonioni and Resnais, always emphasize the seeming lack of true connection between the public and the private, the incongruence of the intimate and the global. In doing so they confound our narrative expectations of space and time and break down our conventional ways of seeing. In their early films they use depth of field, long takes, exterior lighting and wide-screen ratios in monochrome to focus on the look of the intimate relationship at odds with its surroundings. The characteristic two-shot of Berman or Antonioni is one which separates out the faces of the characters from the vital social signs surrounding them. There is no distraction of colour here, no visual diversions from the intensity of the look. Monochrome dominates. Onscreen space contains arenas of separation, areas unfilled, areas *between* characters which intimate a shared loneliness.

Both structures of feeling share vital elements of tone and mood, common frailties of knowledge and memory. In both forms class power is implosive. It becomes a function of discontented sexuality and specifically the predicament of modern middle-class women. Here conscience and disaffection become the double-edged sword of sexual difference, and of the breakdown of trust between the sexes. In Godard, Resnais, Varda, von Trotta, Rohmer, Antonioni and above all Bergman, women who share in bourgeois prosperity and culture remain critical of bourgeois culture not as part of a collectivity but as isolated beings. They share in its wealth but not in worth, are disaffected with their social circles and with their partners in sex, love, work and marriage. In addition, by acting as the reluctant mediators of moral conscience in a purely material age, they reveal the lack of moral conscience of their class in general. Yet their efforts to overcome their marginality are a profound comment on the declining powers of patriarchy in their own class, and also a comment on what is to come in Western societies, the growing fragility of marriage as a modern institution, increasing divorce, separation, broken engagements, remarriage and no marriage at all.

The muted tone of the cool apocalypse is the product of a nuclear age in which mass destructiveness now has a potential for global genocide. Usually it is an oblique response. It does not tackle its subject head-on but prefers to explore its consequences. The sense of ruin and desolation in post-war Europe has been replaced by a reconstructed world. Life goes on, uncanny in its stillness, its deceptive tranquillity. The nuclear threat is remote, unseen, invisible. Alain Resnais's *Hiroshima, mon amour* (1959), set in Japan fifteen years after the end of the war which is the subject of the film's 'memory', links past and present in the demonstrations for world peace which pass through the streets of Hiroshima and the documentary film with the French actress the film itself 'films'. The past which cannot be fully reconstructed is a portent of a future too terrible to contemplate. The first atomic device contains the threat of those yet to come. Compromised by the past, and the failure of the actress to outlive her affair with a German soldier in Nevers during the war, the passion of the two nameless lovers, one French, the other Japanese, is put on ice.

This linking of the documentary, the apocalyptic and the modern is presaged in Resnais's remarkable retro study of the Nazi concentration camps, *Nuit et brouillard* (1955). Here the stylistic devices which mark his later feature films are all in place. The past is resurrected by documentary images in monochrome, the post-war present filmed in colour. The opening colour shot reveals a field of corn on a flat summer plain, pastoral, idyllic, but the camera pulls back to reveal the remaining barbed wire fences of a Polish camp now preserved as a museum. The glide of the tracking camera is a Bazinian opening-up of the image, yet more abstract and quizzical. It looks and probes, lyrically dissecting the unimaginable in unison with Jean Cayrol's screenplay, whose defining voice-over matches the inquisitive camera. The voice-over, the track, the ambiguous separation of past and present are also there in the corridors of the hospital at Hiroshima and the corridors of the baroque hotel in Marienbad: contrasting, polarized versions of the apocalyptic wasteland. Resnais thus moves from the documentary to the imaginary, but the one is the precondition of the other.

Deleuze has pointed out how in neo-realism the new open spaces of Europe's ruined cities opened up the cinematic space of the exterior location which did not have to define itself as a familiar locale. These filmed locations and images he calls 'any-space-whatevers'.[8] The use of architecture in the modern cinema goes further. It echoes both the post-war ruin and its replacements. Resnais juxtaposes the ruined and the rebuilt Hiroshima. In *Muriel* (1963) he places side by side the old city and the new post-war buildings of the reconstructed Boulogne, emphasizing their separate identities. The cityscapes of Antonioni are the modernist shapes and skylines replacing the any-space-what-evers of the previous decade of Italian film-making. The *mise-en-scène* of Milan in *La notte* (1960) or of the Roman suburb in *L'eclisse* (1962) are an ambivalent celebration of the new, a modern love–hate fascination with modernist architecture which at the same time damns its sterility. The same dialectic can be seen in Olmi's *Il posto* or more recently in Eric Rohmer's use of the new Parisian suburbs. As many critics have pointed out, the modern vision of the city is one which sees it without a centre, which not only deconstructs touristic badges of identity but can simply find no core to the metropolis. As Sorlin has noted, Godard, Wenders, Antonioni and others used disconnected locations within the city which bear no relation to its centre or to each other.[9] In particular, speed of movement in the car, the main instrument of time–space progression in the European city after 1960, is one which disconnects. In Godard the car and the space through which it travels generate a poetics of narrative mismatch. For Antonioni the car floats through space, and brackets inten-tionality. In Wenders the car simply passes by, rendering equal and equidistant both the trivial and the significant.

A brilliant sequence in *La notte* shows up the moral ambiguities of time–space travel in the modern city. Disturbed by the attempted coupling of her writer–husband with a desperate woman patient in the hospital where the married couple's best friend is dying, Lydia (Jeanne Moreau) strolls on her own throughout various sectors of the city. At one level, this is an indeterminate wandering through alien zones for which Antonioni is famous. But it is more. Lydia wanders alone and gazes at everything around her, including the men who gaze back at her. She is the challenging *flâneuse*, taking on the male role in the city, and revealing the hypocrisy which surrounds the presentation of gender in public places. This freedom of un-purposive wandering, and with it the freedom of the female gaze, brings a new freedom of the time–space image. Yet conven-tional signs would suggest the strategy of a prostitute, at whose role Lydia appears to be playing, and for whom, more than once, she appears to be mistaken by people she encounters. The sequence, however, is not just a play upon the sexual double-standards of the Italian city. It parallels the other central motif of the film, the commodifying of Giovanni (Marcello Mastroianni), the husband–writer, as a cultural property by the rich industrialist who wishes to use his literary reputation. Both spouses 'are' and 'are not' prostitutes. But this is not simply the prostituting of the 'self' for money in the modern metropolis. It is the discovery of the lack of any self as both body and soul to prostitute, so that even the temptation of the latter is undermined by physical and spiritual failure, by the absence of anything to offer. Indeed the deepest irony is that each entertains the thought of their 'prostitution' as a form of renewal for a dying marriage.

Later that night, the industrialist's garden party with its jazz band, swimming pool and guests in evening dress is a model of bourgeois decorum and posturing which Antonioni treats with the lightest of ironic touches. But the sudden storm, the comic hysteria of drenched and drunken partygoers throwing themselves headlong into the pool, and the power cut which reduces the modernist mansion to complete darkness, all break through the façade by breaking the mood. The posturing Milanese bourgeoisie are suddenly fatuous and vulnerable. Their pretensions are worthless. Against this sudden breakdown of order, both Lydia and Giovanni try without success to initiate adulteries. Resnais's *Last year at Marienbad* (1961) transforms the epiphanic moments of *La notte* into a fable of the nuclear age. With its characters in permanent evening dress and its endless tracking shots down the corridors of a baroque hotel, it already suggests a post-Holocaust afterlife for the rich of Europe, a living death of the spirit incarcerated in its ornate privileges, and frozen at the moment of its destruction. The formally composed, impressionistic shots of statuesque figures in the elaborate formal gardens are each like a freeze-frame capturing the last moment before annihilation. In *The Trial* (1962) the resemblances become explicit. The vast open spaces of the urban desert through which Welles's mobile camera tracks Joseph K. are dotted by the cowering survivors of an imaginary Auschwitz, and in the final scene the dynamite thrown down to K. in the ditch explodes, at his touch, into a mushroom cloud. To the nuclear threat, of course, we can now add, thirty years on with the benefit of hindsight, the apocalyptics of ecological disaster already in place in 1964 in

The Red Desert, those varied misapplications of technological rationality which threaten organic life on the planet. Here in Antonioni's cold neurasthenic colours of industrial Ravenna the mists of the river, the steam and chemical emissions of the factories and the vapours of the landfill sites all merge to obliterate the boundaries of nature and culture, the 'natural' landscape and its human pollution.

In the earlier 'hot' apocalypse of the German Expressionists there still existed a utopian distinction between war and peace, between a warlike, militaristic society and the possibility of a peaceful, just society, a distinction which after 1948 become increasingly more and more difficult to make. The fear of nuclear war, which reached its height with the building of the Berlin Wall and the Cuban Missile Crisis in 1962, provoked a due response in the cinema, not only in the commercially produced formulae of *On the Beach*, *Dr Strangelove* and *Fail Safe*, but in the subtle modulations of Bergman's *The Silence* and Antonioni's *L'eclisse*, in Welles's futuristic and baroque version of *The Trial*, in Resnais's post-Holocaust renditions of time and memory, in the orchestrated and calculated horror of Hitchcock's *The Birds*, and in the strip cartoon science fiction of Godard's *Alphaville* with its parodic use of streets named after nuclear scientists. The apocalyptic mood was shared and extended by later films of the same directors, by Antonioni's *The Red Desert*, *Zabriskie Point*, and the unmade *Technically Sweet*, by Godard's *Weekend* and Bergman's *Shame*. It is made the subject of wicked parody in Buñuel's *That Obscure Object of Desire* and Resnais's *Providence*.

The mood continues with the next generation of film-makers, but more thinly, in Wender's reflexive parody, *The State of Things*, in Peter Weir's Aboriginal mystery *The Last Wave*, in Coppola's *Apocalypse Now* and in the Soviet films of Andrei Tarkovsky and Elem Klimov. For the most part, film here has avoided the temptation against which Claude Chabrol once warned, of attempting to make The Big Film about The Bomb. Both, however, are still 'there', threatening to surface, often uncannily, the image more powerful because the ultimate referent is repressed. Thus the cinema has explored the pervasive undercurrents of despair and paralysis in an age of rational technology threatened by extinction, putting into images the emotional sub-text of an unarticulated climate of fear.[10] Pessimism and fear of the future, the impulse to live totally for the present and to forget the past are all cultural symptoms of forty years of Cold War. Material wealth has been inseparable from the sub-text of fear.

The cool apocalypse is a cinema of endurance, for both its heroes and its spectators, which thrives upon the imminence of an apocalypse which never comes. It does so both through memory – as in Munk's *Passenger*, Tarkovsky or much of Resnais – where the present is dominated by the past but also through the sense of a future which holds no redemption. In Hollywood from the end of the 1970s, the cool apocalypse is hotted up again and turned into a consumerist spectacle. It becomes commodified as miracle by the inventive science fiction of Steven Spielberg in *Close Encounters of the Third Kind* or as Expressionist horror by Ridley Scott in *Blade Runner* and *Alien*. It is spectacularized with great panache in Coppola's *Apocalypse Now*, or, at a low-budget British level, reduced to a barrage of sensory impacts in Derek Jarman's powerful but misguided *Last of England*. Melodramas of visceral immediacy have replaced the cool apocalypse. Perhaps such coolness is now too difficult to take. It is, after all, at the opposite extreme of the death camps and the Gulag, of the torture, terror, disease and starvation which has affected so much of the world's population. It charts the material excess of a bourgeois existence at some distance from all of these things, while knowledge of such global disasters remains its sub-text. It has been the European cinema's response to the waning of the tragic sense. Loss is no longer irreparable. It is resisted but accepted in the shadow of the Bomb. For even if the end of the world is near, it is not yet the end of the world. The cool apocalypse is thus the cinema's main response to the death of tragedy.

As we have noted, the story-telling speed of the cool apocalypse makes a mockery of our conventions of time. As modernity in the second half of this century has speeded up, its fractured narratives have slowed things down. Compared to the frantic pace of Hollywood melodrama which makes a virtue of the hyperactive, its diegesis seems to exist in limbo, a perennial form of slow motion. In Bergman, Bresson, Resnais, Antonioni, Wenders and Tarkovsky durational time is mesmeric, hypnotic, a magnet to the gaze even when its narrative appears endless, directionless, indeterminate. One is tempted to call it a visual approximation to the subjective experience of time as suspended, lingering, listless, waiting to be enlivened by spectacle, by the sudden, unexpected act. The first response to this turn in the cinema was to see it as non-dramatic. But Metz has argued that it should be seen as a new form of dramaturgy.[11] The 'dead' spaces of waiting for an event become in Antonioni's films as vital and vibrant as the 'event' itself. Thus 'Antonioni . . . was able to gather together within the skein of a more subtle dramaturgy all those lost *significations* of which our days are made'.[12] In Hollywood, lost significations are so much excess baggage.

Metz, however, is right. The dead spaces of waiting are dramatic. In this sense dead space is also dead time. Inactive action, which seems to add nothing to narrative, accumulates time past in the living world of the present. The lingering eye of Antonioni's camera which continues to gaze when all action ceases, or the unsignified return of Resnais's cut, where the absence of a fade or dissolve means we cannot identify the shot as 'past' at all – both are contrasting forms of the presence of the past in the present. Equally the cut can signal the 'elsewhere' of the imagination, images which are subjunctive or conditional, which show what might have been or might yet be. The inseparability of 'here' and 'elsewhere', past and present have been central to the apocalyptic vision, to the version of the nature of modernity that *Muriel* or *L'eclisse* re-present. Moreover, it is not merely that time passes slowly because the past cannot be eliminated. The modern world also tells no complete story. It has no obvious moral, beginning, or ending. Film becomes a Nietzschean narrative about the absence of narrative, a Sartean parable about the absence of parable. Here the presence of time is always unyielding. It hangs heavy because the *durée* of human existence is always open. Any closure would seem utopian. Nothing complete, nothing too tangible ever unfolds.

The cool apocalypse unmasks the narrative conventions of American cinema as forms of alchemy, magic potions which pass the time for spectators by making time pass more quickly on the screen, by making us forget time outside the cinema altogether. Apocalyptic film constantly reminds us of the nature of time where Hollywood tries to make us forget it. Deleuze argues in Bergsonian language that such a cinema is governed by a 'time-image' which he sets in opposition to the organic 'movement-image' of American cinema where dramatic situations have to be resolved by action.[13] The rhythms of neo-modern narratives are not a reversion to 'real' time but a corrective to Hollywood's neglect of time and its impulse to obliterate time in the darkness of the auditorium time and thus satisfy its paying customers. The neo-modern rhythms constantly question the nature of time itself. Resnais and Tarkovsky, for example, constantly re-echo the role of the past in the present but dispense with the signifying flashback which tells us where we are. While Antonioni makes time inseparable from the spatial composition of his *mise-en-scène*, Godard constantly interrupts his own narrative as if visibly taking scissors to his film in front of his audience.

Transformations of time are complemented by transformations of visual space. Modern uses of the long take or the wide-screen ratio are not simply those spatial advances of depth and diversity which Bazin advocated as the exemplars of movie realism.[14] They also dwell on instances of the everyday by framing them to appear significant in themselves, as well as in the development of the story-line. What is or is not important is what the spectator decides to make so. In *L'avventura* and *Kings of the Road*, Antonioni and Wenders produce visual epiphanies out of self-contained sequences of narrative as important to the history of the cinema as the epiphanies of Joyce are to the modern novel. Both films are supremely episodic as they move through space and time, uncanny approximations to the 'station dramas' of theatrical Expressionism. But they are still fluid narratives whose rhythms defy our usual expectations of story-telling. For they 'go' nowhere and their directors 'make them up' as they go along. Here establishing shots, scripted dialogue, continuity rules and plot resolutions often count for little as diegetic framing creates its own momentum.

The tragicomic structure of feeling dwells, by contrast, on the absurdities of duration and swallows up time, devouring it outrageously in huge narrative chunks. The swirl and puzzle of its rapid movement depend on the parodic effects of its style. It makes fun of its more vulnerable characters, drawing laughter out of their helplessness and folly, in effect creating its own holy fools. One of its most outrageous anti-heroes and some of its disturbing image-sequences are to be found in Werner Herzog's *Stroszek* (1977), the story of a diminutive and mentally disturbed Berliner, a petty criminal who escapes the sadism of local pimps, and departs for Wisconsin. As played by Bruno S, Stroszek is a contemporary version of the Dostoevskyan Holy Fool, a role the same actor played in Herzog's historical drama *The Enigma of Kasper Hauser*. His disturbed vision is one of a deceptive simplicity which renders absurd everything around him he cannot understand. Bruno escapes Berlin but cannot escape himself. Nor can he understand the American world of possessions and money in which he dismally fails. The comic failure is a return to degree-zero. Trying to rob a supermarket, the escaping outlaw with his truck, his shotgun and his stolen frozen turkey ends up penniless in a small tourist American Indian town. He abandons his truck at a gas station, engine still running, and leaves it to coast round in circles while he ascends the mountainside on a circulating chair-lift and shoots himself. Meanwhile in the amusement arcade where has fused the lights, he leaves a chicken dancing in perennial motion, the last image of the film as the slot-machine which governs its cage never cuts out. The superimpositions of circular motion, all futile, all absurd, are Herzog's ironic comment on a soulless consumerism which sells anything and everything to no purpose.

In spite of its residual darkness tragicomedy presents a world in which the bourgeois appear vain, cynical, endearing, egoistic, pretentious and only occasionally tragic. Here one of the most powerful texts is Buñuel's aptly named *The Discreet Charm of the Bourgeoisie* (1972). In their perpetual eating, their gross gastronomic self-indulgence, the bourgeoisie create their own class victims, but also become victims themselves. Earlier in *Belle de jour* (1967) Buñuel had self-consciously fabricated tragicomedy out of melodrama. His film is a European reprise of Hitchcock's *Marnie* (1964) in which the latter's frigid kleptomaniac is given a different double identity, the virgin working-class secretary and thief of Tippie Hedren replaced by the frigid bourgeois wife and sensual prostitute of Hedren's look-alike, Catherine Deneuve. The sado-masochism of Deneuve's fantasies is actualized in her encounters with grotesque clients whose ugliness contrasts with the handsome looks of her devoted husband. Thus Buñuel satirizes not only bourgeois morality but also its cult of beauty. He places himself at an ironic distance from the beauty-fetish of the cool blonde which Hitchcock had turned into psychic melodrama.

The coolness of Buñuel's camera, its refusal of moral judgement, highlights one of the comic dilemmas of the modern bourgeoisie which occurs again and again in the cinema. They are often so unsure of their status that the gap between aspiration and deed becomes ridiculous in those who go to great lengths to avoid the ridiculous. Above all, the bourgeoisie are not immune from what they dread most, reduction to the status of automata in the machine age, that mechanical quality which Bergson saw as the source of all laughter. Tragicomedy humorously undercuts the universal ideals of modernity, the rational models for living that are given to us all by the enlightened, professional bourgeois in a consumer age. In the cinema Welles, Renoir and Buñuel have bequeathed us, we live instead in an age without true moral exemplars. Power and self-interest lead to vanity and to suffering, and in the process they make fools of us all.

In European cinema, the tragicomic trades on social difference, on bemused heroes as commodities of the rich or the corrupt. Its weapon of ridicule works best in the realm of the hypocrisies of the wealthy. In Buñuel, Catherine Deneuve's ward-at-risk, Tristana, and Jeanne Moreau's Parisian chambermaid in a sterile Normandy mansion are both the cool laconic resisters of archaic values, especially the lechery of rich males who adhere to useless codes of honour and have become provincial and absurd. But *Tristana* and *Diary of a Chambermaid* go back to a pre-war period which marks for Buñuel's a return to an earlier history. Along with *Belle de jour* they expose the futility of a code of sexual morals *entre les deux guerres* which bears no relationship to the coming amorality of fascism, itself a grotesque travesty of all forms of tradition. With the advantage of hindsight which Renoir did not have, Buñuel, the exile, returns in the late 1960s to the scene of the crime. His icy humour is a function of that distance in time. In these films Deneuve and Moreau are thus not the 'modern women' of the present which Riva, Vitti and Ullmann are in the films of Resnais, Antonioni and Bergman. They are instead the modern women of the past, still socially and sexually subordinate, but challenging those archaic forms of authority which Western modernity will eventually destroy but only after fascism has murderously tried to conserve them.

Thus Buñuel's period films, his Nietzschean return, expose the deeply conservative face which often hides behind the liberal mask of Western culture, the fears and foibles of the bourgeoisie through which fascism briefly triumphed and on which the conservative spirit always thrives. The liberal mask is necessary because at times conservative values can longer be openly admitted to. Where they are, they appear as archaic and ridiculous. Two of the great modern film-makers constrained by censorship in their own countries, Buñuel and Andrzej Wajda have power-fully extended the tragicomic range of Renoir by ridiculing out-moded values of honour in societies which are ruthless and brutal. In *Ashes and Diamonds* (1957) Wajda is bitterly caustic about the outmoded romanticism of the remnants of the Polish Home Guard as it fights a tragicomic rearguard action against the ruthless post-war coup of the Polish Stalinists. Romanticism as a dying bourgeois value in a backward society is no more than a form of heroic failure. Having caved into Hitler, it caves into Stalin and the tragic end of the young nationalist dressed anachronistically in the James Dean look of the late 1950s, is a futile and absurd death. In his 1970s films, by contrast, Buñuel juxtaposes archaic notions of etiquette and honour to the nihil-istic values of a consumer society of the present and the future where casual sex, drugs and terrorism have become normalized as unremarkable features of everyday life. He thus charts the rapid descent from false values of the premodern into the 'no' values of modernity, where none the less the gluttonous bour-geoisie cling to a false sense of their own respectability whatever the cost.

Buñuel's cool anti-melodrama is in marked contrast to the Anglo-American 'justice' melodrama which commodifies mod-ernity as a working myth. The American films of Wyler, Kramer, Ritt, Kazan, Pakula, Stone and Costa-Gavras, the British films of Lean, Attenborough and Puttnam all force the heroic male resolution of agonizing liberal dilemmas, and reinstate the supremacy of an embattled Western reason. This forced marriage of the liberal and the heroic is the basic posture of an epic, rational maleness which uncovers and attempts to redress injus-tice in various forms throughout the world. Its central male figure is always the moral investigator. As opposed to Buñuel's laconic emphasis on the awkward and the ugly, we have the dashing handsome heroes of *All the President's Men*, *The Parallax View*, *Missing*, *Under Fire*, *The Killing Fields*, *Cry Freedom*, *Salvador*, and *JFK*. Where there is sexual variation of the formula, as in *The China Syndrome* with Jane Fonda playing female reporter to Michael Douglas's hippie photographer, the male–female bonding seems simply a copy of the male bonding of Robert Redford and Dustin Hoffman in Alan Pakula's film about the Watergate scandal. The liberal optimism implicit in the figure of the heroic reporter is crystallized through heroic images of enquiry in the age of the global village, images which overcome potential darkness by transcending the paranoid pathology which acts as the film's necessary motor. The reporter goes where we do not dare, uncovering what we instantly abhor, thus matching conscience to adventure. Such post-Vietnam films, from the mid-1970s onward, inform us that the historical moment of the neo-moderns has passed. Conscience is recuperated as a concrete value. The male ego is flawed but no longer in crisis. It tells us the world can redeemed from evil. It allows us to identify with the wronged investigator, the freelance forager who is maverick or self-right-eously eccentric but always 'under fire'.

Tragicomedy at times hovers on the edge of melodrama, but always pulls back. The narrative melodrama emerges organically from the structured ensemble of its different image-objects so that its ending seems a 'natural' outcome of its plot. In the neo-moderns narrative has to be recomposed by the spectator from images often with no obvious connection to one another. Tragi-comedy is at the boundary between the American and the Euro-pean but it still subverts the American impulse towards optimism and active resolution of the narrative. From 1970 onwards it feeds back into the post-classical American cinema. Tragicomedy is a central feature not only of *The Conformist* and *The Lady from Shanghai*, of *Belle de jour*, *Weekend* and *Jules et Jim* but also of *Chinatown*, *Five Easy Pieces*, *The King of Marvin Gardens*, Robert Altman's naturalistic Western, *McCabe and Mrs Miller* and of Terence Malick's two great anti-mythic Westerns, *Badlands* and *Days of Heaven*. But under the force of melodrama and genre, and the continuing power of the studios, the impetus is not sustained. The force of myth in American cinema is too powerful.

One of the great independent films of the American cinema, *Five Easy Pieces*, is thus a notable exception in its resistance to the power of genre. Bob Rafelson's offbeat 1970 study of American middle-class life during the period of Vietnam is much more than a laid-back parable of the homecoming of the prodigal son. It is a powerful satire on American life which ends in bleak and forbidding darkness. Anti-hero Bobby 'Eroica' Dupea drifts back to his North-West middle-class home after working in the oil-fields of southern California. Dupea (Jack Nicholson) dumps Rayette, his working-class Southern girlfriend (Karen Black) at the local motel before taking the ferry out to the family abode. Her style would be a liability, he assumes, to his anxious and reluctant return. But he himself is also a liability and the tragicomic absurdities of the family life he had previously abandoned are even more grotesque. His father is crippled by a stroke and cannot speak; the absent mother of the household is nowhere mentioned. Dupea's piano-playing brother wears a neck-brace after a freak accident and plays badly at table tennis. His piano-playing sister is involved in a masochistic relationship with her father's minder, and his brother's fiancée, Katherine, accepts the cheap excuse of Dupea's recital of Chopin – 'five easy pieces' – to go to bed with him. Failed pretension is the great equalizer. The end of the recital, which Dupea confesses to faking in the interests of seduction, provides the key connecting shot of the film. The long slow tracking shot with its 360-degree pan which starts with Bobby's fingers on the keys at the end of the recital moves through the framed photographs of the family room – the room *is* the family – before returning to the pianist, and captures with its gliding movement the arrested time in the still photographs of the family, setting the frozen images of the past – what members of the family were and might become – against what they have become, that is, what they are now, a motley collection of failures. It is a superb statement of loss, but also of the depreciation of cultural capital, of each solitary failure but also of the collective failure of the bourgeoisie, in microcosm, to renew itself.

The absence of the mother, traditionally the central figure of the American melodrama, the paralysis of the father-as-patriarch in the age of Vietnam, is a motif also on offer a few years later in *Badlands* (1974). In Rafelson's picture it is more distinctly middle-class. The offspring are failed classical musicians. The tragicomic pathos of failed achievement reaches its climax when Bobby breaks up the pseudo-intellectual soirée at which Rayette has been a 'class' embarrassment. In a reprise of the panning 'piano' shot, a hand-held camera follows the angered Dupea desperately searching for Katherine, his departing middle-class lover, through all the corridors and rooms in the house, only to discover his sister being tied up for sexual purposes by her father's minder. The shot ends in triple defeat for the outraged Nicholson. He is beaten up by the minder when he tries to assault him, rejected by the woman of his own class he craves and accepted back by the lower-class woman he has failed to shed. The gliding shot of the piano room which captures the frozen images of the past has been transformed into the walking shot of the corridor which jerkily uncovers the chaotic present and ends in violent bathos. As Dupea leaves home and neighbourhood with Rayette, a second, inevitable leaving, he also abandons her at a gas station with his car and money, hitching a ride in a logger's trucker and heading north to a cold, uncertain future.

With a brilliant, definitive screenplay by Carole Eastman, Rafelson's film absorbs the modern moment of the European cinema and deconstructs the classical narrative of the American dream. Dupea is recurrently moving down the scale, not up, tossing away his social advantages with a Heideggerian compulsion to repeat and constantly drifting with that existential quality of casual risk which Wenders later sentimentalized through the figure of Travis in *Paris, Texas*. While the homecoming of Travis, the return of the absent father to the motherless son, 'works' through the powerful performance of Hary Dean Stanton as a mythic recuperation of prodigality, *Five Easy Pieces* offers no such illusions. It brings home what previous American cinema had lacked, an enhancement of its profane images of the American bourgeois, not at the height of its power as in Welles but in humdrum, ordinary nemesis, not through that class's mythic fusion of money and passion as in film noir but through its historic failure in an age of disenchantment to renew its powers of culture and reason.

We end the chapter where we began, with the physical shape of the modernist landscape so vital to the modern cinema. The uneasy relationship of physical edifice and leading character is central to all modern films. As we saw, Deleuze has stated that the ruins, derelict buildings and deserted streets of post-war Europe created new cinematic spaces, 'any-space-whatevers', in which neo-realist cinema and its modernist successors could disrupt the organic unities of story and setting, sound and optical vision in the classical cinema. Not only could we take as starting points here Rossellini's bleak vision of a ruined Berlin in *Germany, Year Zero*, or later Resnais's documentary montage of atomic aftermath in *Hiroshima, mon amour* juxtaposed with the unyielding modernist city which had risen from the ashes, but also Welles's Xanadu, the hybrid monster of a dozen different architectures which the director brilliantly brings to life out of a matte painting in *Citizen Kane*. The dislocating of characters from their world in all three films is a sensory and spatial disorientation also imposed on the viewer, where buildings no longer give us the perspectives of the lived-in or the familiar, the certainty of a planned environment, where they are no longer easy labels of identity to cue the characters or tell us where they are. In the work of the two great directors of the period, Welles and Antonioni, cultural dislocation *is* spatial dislocation. The fractured relationship of modernisms and modernity is seen through the legacies of global war and the absurd heroic monuments of fascism, through the failures of the modern city and the lesions of the industrial landscape, and through the eclectic pastiche of the whole European heritage which in the contemporary age is going nowhere.

The wide-screen cinema of Orson Welles, after the studio productions of *Kane* and *The Magnificent Ambersons*, is above all an exterior cinema. It seems appropriate that, for *Touch of Evil*, Welles juxtaposes in his seedy border town Los Robles both the flaking arcades of a nocturnal Californian Venice which is a travesty of its European counterpart and the gaunt oil derricks nearby which are part of the landscape of Californian desert. In *The Trial*, in which Welles's vision of Kafkaesque dream logic has a distinctly post-war flavour, the bleak new tower blocks of Zagreb are juxtaposed to the vast derelict interiors of the disused Gare d'Orsay in Paris.[15] In Welles's film, there is little choice. Pastiche is decay and modernism a wasteland. In both films, Wellesian discontinuity is breathtaking in his audacity. Joseph K. walks out of the Gare d'Orsay to meet his cousin in the Palazzo di Giustizia in Rome and accompany her to a Milan factory before returning to his apartment in Zagreb.[16] Welles, the Expressionist magician, complements interior dislocation by topographical mismatches which are agoraphobic and terrifying. Filled out by the lacerating discords of dubbed sound, in Welles none the less, the totalitarian nightmare is mainly optical. Thus in his nightmare-reverie of the Italian past, *The Conformist*, Bertolucci echoes the pseudo-heroic world of Mussolini by replicating the tracking shots and the long shots of *The Trial*, his tight-suited anti-hero framed diminutively against high buildings and huge marble interiors which suggest in the same shot both the tightness of entrapment and the delirium of vast distances.

In contrast to Welles, Antonioni adheres to the neo-realist plane of physical continuity, of a literal topography of places. For this reason, the disconnections in his trilogy can be even more unnerving. For the camera deconstructs those very spaces it records with the enhanced power of wide angle and depth of field, as in the eerie visual silence of the fascist ghost town in *L'avventura* which Sandro and Claudia visit in their indeterminate searching for Anna, or the descending lift-shot from the Pirelli building which opens *La notte* with its geometrical vista of a Milan observed with sterile fixity through glass. In *L'eclisse* this is taken even further by an ending which re-treads the path of the lovers through a Roman suburb in their absence, and the absence of human beings in general. A brittle new cityscape, humanly made, which had earlier in the film appeared *a priori* to predate the presence of humans, becomes suddenly post-human, a deserted concrete desert. The modernist city signals here and elsewhere two things central to the modern cinema and its profane images of the bourgeoisie. It signals the end of that romanticism which suffused the first appearance of the moving image earlier in the century. In its place appears the cool apocalypse of the nuclear age in which monochrome, about to fall into disuse, becomes a supreme medium of twentieth-century art.

3

The Double and the Innocent

As a complete artwork, Coates suggests that film is the techno-industrial fulfilment of a romantic dream.[1] It is the fruition of Wagner's artistic vision, the *Gesamtkunstwerk* which combines story, song, music, dance, speech, movement and dramatic action. From its outset, however, the complete artwork has had a chequered career. Advocated by Heidegger as project of collective delirium of Nietzschean dimensions in the Third Reich,[2] in the reality the Third Reich had only Leni Riefenstahl left to implement the ideal in the German cinema. The rest of its great film-makers had migrated west and German cinema after 1933 effectively ceased to exist. It was Hollywood instead which appropriated the *Gesamtkunstwerk* for its own very ungermanic purposes. With the advent of sound, the Studio system provided continuous assembly-line spectacle, a series of genre dreamscapes which conquered the visual imagination of the world by consent while Hitler, the master of the political spectacle, tried in vain to conquer the world by physical force. Thereafter film technology outlived both the Third Reich and the Studio system. The camera nowadays is mobile and adaptable. It can use wide-screen ratios, deep-focus, soft-focus, zooms, scrims, slow-motion, telephoto shots of objects at great distances. But the film rushes are only the beginning. With sophisticated forms of dubbing, chemical processing, special effects, electronic sound mixing and musical scoring, film post-production is the re-embodiment of the disembodied into the existing image, the electronic transplant as an aesthetic fact, the completion of film after all filming is completed. In the darkened cinema, the finished product, a compilation of rushes and multiple sound tracks synchronized through editing, engages all the sensory functions. Such technical versatility the world of culture has seldom known.

The 'epic' Hollywood film still travesties the concept of a complete artwork, though never as much as the Third Reich. It convinces us of greatness by commodifying all the resources at its disposal. The totality of what money can buy produces the illusion of a total experience in the big-budget blockbuster. There are other reasons why the 'total' experience breaks down, reasons to be found within the cinematic apparatus itself. The cinema is an artefact masquerading as a live performance, technically prepared for a performing machine. Here projection must overcome the techno-spatial separation of maker and spectator. The camera records, the editor cuts, dubs and synchronizes. Only then does the projector initiate the act of consumption. As they watch, spectators are sporadically aware of the gulf between eye and screen. Yet because the power of the image is so strong, it is a distance which is seldom irksome. When film is at its most alluring, audiences view a spectacle which masquerades as magical. It is easy to forget that one sees a composite of images changing rapidly on a huge screen. Since film involves frames changing faster than the human eye can register, the continuity of the image is an illusion. Such 'continuous' images are part of an elaborate magic-show which seems to have a life of its own. The cinema attempts to rival the live performance of the stage through its magical abolition of the constraints of space and time. Yet the spectator always returns at some point to that sense of hiatus. The images towards which we are impelled are still, somehow, out there. If spectators hurl bottles at actors onscreen, they can break the screen, but not the image. The bottles will fail to knock the actors unconscious, and only in a Woody Allen movie will someone walk out of the screen and into the audience.

Film creates a dilemma which the modern impulse of the cinema has always exploited. It has its own technical reality, a hidden status of otherness. No matter how close we feel to them, screen images are tantalizingly other, apart. The complete artwork proclaims itself as a fruition of the nineteenth-century romantic longing for wholeness but instead film presents us with the image that got away. Among the neo-moderns the process of demolition becomes complete. The technical romance of the Hollywood screen is banished. The screen image is turned into a fragmented image, an incomplete sequence, an inaccessible figment of the imagination. Technically, its mimesis of the human figure and face echoes the romantic imaging of an alienated Other, a shadowing phantom. In the writings of Hoffmann, Hogg and Dostoevsky, the Other had been the ineffable of the romantic consciousness, the phantom which cannot finally be accommodated in the romantic utopia of an organic and pantheistic world. Instead the Other becomes an outcast in that competitive bourgeois world which tries to match evolution to moral progress. The Other is a hallucination of romantic disorder, an effigy of disintegration. The early horror film celebrates this through the figures of Dracula and Frankenstein. But this has a deeper import for the development of the cinema than Gothic horror alone. In film the Other is a technical fact. Lang shows this clearly in *Metropolis* where the false and decadent Maria emerges as a robot from an iron cast to impersonate the 'true' Maria who already exists as a virtuous and religious maiden, a sentimental carer for the worker-slaves of the underground city. The same actress thus 'plays' sexual decadence off against mystic purity in an allegorical rendering of the choice facing Weimar Germany. In *M* Peter Lorre, the serial killer, has no bodily double but still has a reflection and a shadow which doubles his screen image. It is these we see first, the phantom shadow falling across the advertising hoarding which at which his girl-victim innocently gazes. Later Lang cuts abruptly from a police official reading Lorre's letter to an unexpected shot of Lorre looking at himself in the mirror, the camera almost head-on to his reflection in the centre of the frame, while his gazing face is in oblique profile to the side.

The split image has a literary source. Otto Rank saw the double as an unacknowledged projection of the narcissistic self, troubled and perturbed in its relations with the external world. The external projection of the self-as-Other, or, in the fiction of Hoffmann and Dostoevsky, the Other-as-brother, can be the ego's anxious insurance against the prospect of an imminent death.[3] But it can also be the opposite, the creation of a hallucinatory figure which lures the self impellingly towards destruction. From narcissism there spring, therefore, two contrasting processes. The self can be externalized as a love-object in the person of the Other, or the Other can be a figure of evil, a mirror-image of the death-instinct the ego represses and cannot consciously recognize. This insight is fully contextualized by Freud in his work on the uncanny and the pleasure principle. For Freud, the unfamiliar always implies the repressed familiar. He plays on the etymological double-meaning of the German word *heimlich*, with its alternative senses of cosiness, familiarity on the one hand, and concealment on the other. The latter meaning, that of concealment, of being kept from sight, is very similar to its formal opposite, since *unheimlich* can mean weird, eerie or arousing fear. Following Schelling, Freud takes the uncanny to mean 'everything that has been hidden but ought to come to light',[4] and then links its paradox to the ambivalence of the familiar. The uncanny, on his analysis, is the familiar secret which has been repressed and now comes to light in altered form. It is literally and metaphorically a homecoming, a finding of the familiar in unfamiliar circumstances, of home within a strange country, of the self within the world of the Other. In broader terms, it is the return of the repressed.[5]

In the modern novel the use of doubling becomes highly self-conscious, but in Malcolm Lowry's *Under the Volcano* it becomes highly cinematic, nourished on the Expressionist cinema of the 1920s. Through its fractured and mirrored doubling, Lowry's novel becomes a modern and highly visual re-working of romantic conceit. One of Geoffrey Firmin's doubles in the novel, Jacques Laruelle, former teenage friend and now Hollywood director, occupies a house in Quauhnahuac with double towers which are joined together by a catwalk over the glassed-in gable of a studio. The tops of the towers are reached by spiral staircases in what is clearly a descriptive pastiche of the angular menacing set in Robert Wiene's Expressionist classic, *The Cabinet of Dr Caligari*. The Consul's drunken wandering is dogged by posters around the town advertising Peter Lorre in a remake of another Expressionist classic, *The Hands of Orlac*, while Lowry's story itself, of a hopelessly estranged married couple trying to overcome infidelity through the power of forgiveness, is fondly based on Friedrich Murnau's first American film, *Sunrise*. Lowry's highly visual text has in turn been through the hands of countless numbers of film-makers and actors, provoking over two hundred treatments and screenplays, before ending up sadly as a lame melodrama at the hands of John Huston,[6] where the double has no image and all Expressionist idioms have been eliminated.

The neo-moderns in the cinema follow Lowry in thematically transforming the early images of Expressionism out of low-life horror into epiphanies of modernism, into polyvalent, profane images of the bourgeoisie. They do so, it should be said, in a post-fascist and post-communist age, which marks them off from the cinema of the 1920s. As Siegfried Kracauer has pointed out in his famous study *From Caligari to Hitler*, the Weimar cinema had evoked both the existing fear of the hammer-and-sickle and the prophetic spectre of its antithesis, its reactive extreme, the swastika. If the slave-workers' revolt in *Metropolis* was a dystopian allegory of the former, then the underworld's illegal pursuit of the serial killer in *M* was clearly, in 1931, an immediate allegory of the latter. The themes and fears of Weimar Expressionism were clearly the underclass, the worker-slaves, the street, the outsider's threat, the monster-killer, themes which appealed at both conscious and pre-conscious levels to large sectors of an embattled German population after political revolt, economic depression and Versailles. As Lotte Eisner reminds us, however, the true horror of the Expressionist nightmare is not just the fear of the unknown, the monster, the social void.[7] It is more that the Expressionist demons populating this void would provoke a deeper desire for submission by the horrified subject, where revolt and submission are equally sources of fascination in a world beyond middle-class sanctuary.

In the neo-modern cinema, fear has become internal, psychic and not political; neurotic and narcissistic, not sado-masochistic. The power of doubling relates not to the threatening Other outside the bourgeois–liberal frame of discourse but to the Other *within* who debilitates. Here the decentred self lives out less the threat to civilization from the outside, more the contradiction between economic and cultural capital within, a conflict in bourgeois culture for which there can be no apocalyptic resolution, a conflict which is constant and unresolved. Here the dominant fear is the fear of being petrified into the fixed value of a commodity. The image of the double is the hope and lure of a multivalent desire which cannot congeal into a market price or a social stereotype stamping upon the weak and fearful ego its own death-sentence. The image of the double is an escape from fixity luring the ego towards destruction and death.

Returning to Lowry's novel we can see how the fate of Firmin presents an immediate challenge to the cinema. Doubled by his friend and by his brother, he tries in vain to live happily and soberly with the estranged spouse he has known sadly and drunkenly, and reveals the Freudian motif which has such filmic resonance – the compulsion to repeat. *Persona, Vertigo, The Conformist, The Passenger* and *Last Year at Marienbad* are all films about the events of past time haunting the present so intensely that the past is always liable to be 'present'. What starts as narcissism, the appropriation of the Other and the Other's gaze as self-love, ends as the pain of neurotic compulsion, the desire to repeat, a desire the past has thwarted in a dismal present where all has changed utterly. What the present appears to make easier, it also makes more difficult. Thwarted desire becomes, in the present, an impossible desire. The more impossible it becomes, the more neurotically it is craved. But the compulsion to repeat is also a compulsion *not* to repeat, a compulsion to escape impossible circumstance, to escape those destructive milieux of time past which have frustrated all hope. The neurosis of pain thus issues from the search for pleasure, from the pre-conscious determination never to give up the objects of pleasure while consciously refusing all evidence that such objects afford no pleasure at all.[8] Yet, as Sartre suggests, there is a further ontological dilemma. There is always a gap between past and present in which nothingness intercedes. This too is just as much part of the anguish of the past, that it can never be made over as part of the present nor can its relationship with the present be continuous.[9]

The figure of the double who cannot be incorporated also points to the hero's doubling of the spectator. As Metz has pointed out, the spectator's perception of diegetic film is akin at times to that of dreaming.[10] As a screen projection, the hero can be the dream double of the spectator. But the figure of the double points also to the crucial difference between dream and film, so that the dream strives after pleasure and suspends the principle of reality whereas film is always brought back to reality *in spite of* the pleasure principle. The double as exterior fact then eludes the hero much as the hero, in turn, eludes the spectator and much as film itself eludes the spectator's desire. We can take this assertion a stage further. In the image of the double, it can be suggested, spectators see refracted in a quasi-dream state their own idealized relationship to the figures they see on screen.

The hero is the double of the spectator, the villain the double of the hero. Both become dreamlike. Sexual boundaries are easily crossed and the double can change gender or be androgynous. In modern film the double's ubiquitous shadow usually signifies rebellion by the bourgeois hero against his middle-class role and its forms of sexual constraint. While the figure of the double often implies revolt, the double's face, or look, implies desire.

As a project with romantic origins, film projects the romantic division starkly on to a screen which is technically divided into two kinds of space. Screen space automatically doubles itself because any filmic image must exclude in order to contain. As Burch has suggested, these two kinds of cinematic space are vital to modern film from Renoir onwards.[11] One exists within the frame and the other exists outside its scope, out-of-field, off-screen, out-of-frame. It can intrude vertically or horizontally, from any side of the rectangle. Within this spatially bifurcated medium, the double can be present not only onscreen but also offscreen, a figure who lurks demonically 'out there', out-of-field, an absent presence liable to re-appear at any moment, as for example the figure of Klaus Kinski becomes in Herzog's 1978 remake of Murnau's *Nosferatu* (1921). Kinski, onscreen for only about twenty minutes as the diminutive vampire, seems to dominate the whole film because the audience always anticipates his re-appearance, which is a part of his melancholy 'horror'. And in Herzog's political allegory of fascism, which departs from Murnau's pre-Nazi film, it is quite clear that he is the double of his ostensible enemy, the respectable bourgeois Jonathan Harker, who is transformed at the end into a vampirish monster intent on returning to Transylvania in his place.

At one level Herzog's film is 'retro-homage' to Murnau's silent classic which echoes a familiar leitmotif of German cinema in the 1920s, the allegorical betrayal from the outside by the unseen intruder.[12] Dracula is the vampire disguised as a count who travels west to infect the 'body politic' of Germany, bringing plague to the Nordic townscape. Herzog consciously repeats many of Murnau's sequences, particularly that of the deserted, plague-ridden ship drifting slowly towards the civilization it will poison. But his ending is also allegorical in a way that is consistent with 1920s Expressionism. The substance of his ending also seems to avenge the ending of that other classic about which Kracauer was so bitter, *The Cabinet of Dr Caligari* (1919). Against the wishes of his screen-writers, Hans Janowitz and Carl Mayer, Wiene had opted to make Cesare's story of Caligari, the hypnotist who compels his victims to commit murder, the fantasy of a mental inmate nursing a grievance against his doctor.[13] The madness of authoritarian manipulation is then seen as a paranoid projection of a madman. Caligari is rendered sane, respectable, caring and responsible. If Wiene, responding to political pressure, normalized the mad tyrant as responsible bourgeois, Herzog in a post-censorship age, as well as a post-Nazi age, did the opposite. He demonized the normal where dubiously Wiene had tried to normalize the demonic. For Kracauer Wiene censored the premonition of Hitler which Mayer and Janowitz had elaborated. Herzog, as a champion of the Expressionist cinema the Nazis destroyed, has, it could be argued, taken a retro-revenge.

In what probably remains the best film by a British director other than Hitchcock, Carol Reed's *The Third Man* (1949), we also have a *mise-en-scène* like *Nosferatu* where the double dominates through absence as much as presence. Offscreen for much of the film, Orson Welles as the celebrated Harry Lime haunts the audience first with the anticipation of his entrance and then with his returning. As the American alter ego of Holly Martens, the pulp novelist, his absent presence haunts the empty nocturnal streets of occupied Vienna. We wait for him to appear out of the shadows, our sense of equilibrium, of perceptual balance already undermined by Carol Reed's tilted camera angles. When Lime steps out of the darkened doorway, preceded by a mewing kitten, he has metaphorically risen from the dead, and proved literally that he was always alive. His spectral haunting as the black marketeer who refuses to expire signifies, amidst the return to normality, the return of evil which did not die with the end of Nazism. As the hustler of doctored penicillin he is the naturalized vampire who preys on the ill amidst scarcity and ruin. When Holly Martens chases down his old friend amidst the endless labyrinth of the city sewers, it is almost as if he has chased down his own shadow, yet by comparison with Lime he is the weaker, the cryptic admirer, the ambivalent lover.

The spatial separation of Martens from Lime, his more powerful shadow, echoes the weak hero's separation from his more forbidding self which in romantic fiction threatens destruction and death.[14] But the double is also an 'absent Other' who provisionally represents the spectator on a screen from which he or she is excluded. In the modern cinema time and space are simultaneously displaced. The Sartrean gap between past and present, the Freudian separation of the figure and its double, the technical distance of screen and spectator all fuse in the poetics of displacement. We find that in the very act of viewing, heroes and their doubles both become doubles of the spectator. As divided figures on a screen divided in turn from its anterior space, its offscreen space, they seem to mirror in their separation from each other the estrangement of the screen figure's image from its audience in a darkened auditorium. One form of doubling, which is oblique to start with, reflexively mirrors another form of doubling which is even more so. It is no wonder that doubles onscreen obliquely divide the loyalties of the viewer, even when there are clear moral demarcations of hero and villain, and of good and evil. For they pose questions not only about the identity of the self onscreen but about the very act of identifying the spectator has to make. Screen doubles simultaneously repel and attract, and for that reason are the source of endless curiosity and fascination. In doing so, they deconstruct the boundaries of good and evil.

In the films of Resnais, Godard, Bergman, Bertolucci and Antonioni, otherness becomes the scenario for the doubling of the split self and the crisis in bourgeois identity. The modern bourgeois is the anti-heroic successor to the romantic hero of nineteenth-century melodrama. The decentred bourgeois self is narcissistic rather than romantic, uneasily at home in a world of wealth and power, the product of a desire to consume and manipulate rather than a craving for a new organic order of things. One central process unifies the very diverse films of Welles, Hitchcock, Altman, Weir, Antonioni, Bergman and Bertolucci. Doubling evokes the loss of selfhood more than the shadow of evil which torments its literal and romantic predecessors. Evil remains the supreme form of moral transgression but is no longer absolute. It is subsumed under fractured narratives. It becomes relative. It is naturalized as a feature of the everyday, of the necessity of the daily round. It generates banalities against which dreams and desires have to struggle. It is not merely a spectral haunting but also a social fact.

Film, here, is both romantic and anti-romantic. It deflates romantic intentions yet the figure of the double takes it beyond the mimetic nature of the camera into the schizophrenic visual field where there are two kinds of narrative space. As a medium, the cinema re-affirms human presencing through its power to re-present nature and culture. Despite its obvious powers of illusion, the camera still records 'nature' in the broadest anthropological sense. But the modern cinema of the double builds on that anthropology by transforming it. Representation becomes a form of the cinema's will-to-power and the figure of the double is one of its vital legacies. Refusal to recognize this is itself a romantic failing. In their obsession with eternal unsignifying, the Anglo-American neo-romantics who have made deconstruction and psychosemiology so fashionable forget one vital thing. The physical medium of film differs from other art forms. It has no formal grammar as language has, nor does it have the absolute capacity for the idealization of perspective on a piece of canvas which exists in painting. It is absurd to see the cinema as a laborious apparatus for the concealment of its own origins, to be endlessly deconstructed through the scholastic romance of language-games.[15]

In the classical cinema too the studious manufacturing of the 'star' has taken doubling to its simplified and melodramatic extreme. In this sense the 'star' serves to bind the spectator to the feature film. The Hollywood star, from Gable to Monroe, is an idealized figure who insinuates a fusion of the spectator's desired self and the love-object onscreen. Here the love-object is automatically doubled through the romantic matching of stars. As initially separate figures the star 'couple' onscreen conveniently marry, through their passion, the desired self to the object of desire, a process Hitchcock renders self-conscious in the famous long take of *Notorious* where the lips of Cary Grant and Ingrid Bergman seem glued together in unnatural embrace. Hitchcock's sequence is powerfully reflexive, a transformation of unnatural figures into the 'natural' star couple. In Hollywood melodrama, the popular form of the cinema inherited from the stage of the late nineteenth century becomes the ideal vehicle for stardom. It simplifies, it exaggerates, it intensifies. It is designed to put a stranglehold on the spectator's emotions. Above all, it shows the way to triumph and happiness through necessary sacrifice.[16] In Europe there was an alternative, a concern with the natural image which in the work of the neo-realists led to the vain hope of a different kind of popular cinema. It was an alternative, however, which Hollywood in the 1950s was unable to ignore.

Perkins has seen the key technical advances of film-making as a necessary condition for progress in the post-war cinema, one which gives it the capacity for a greater realism far beyond Bazin's seminal concern with deep focus and the long take.[17] Indeed the technical conditions for enhancing realism are *equally* crucial to the development of modern film-making which, paradoxically, has often called into question the validity of the real. Cinematic realisms and their modern subversions are not polar opposites but parallel events, symbiotic developments, closely intertextual. The stylistic advances of the modern have been made possible by the *simultaneous enhancement* of the mimetic image. In key shots of the interior of Xanadu in *Citizen Kane*, Welles happily combines matte projection with deep-focus photography, simultaneously expanding and undermining the conditions of the mimetic image. He thus confounds Bazin's much-touted assessment of him as a realist innovator and nudges us more in the direction of Renoir's view of him as a supreme magician.[18] Here film refuses to replicate the earlier chronologies of naturalism and modernism. From 1940 onwards when *Kane* first emerged, film modernisms and realisms have paralleled each other in their possibilities. Two of the greatest films in the history of the Italian cinema, Luchino Visconti's *Rocco and his Brothers* and Antonioni's *La notte* were set at the same time, 1960, in the same city, Milan. Conceptually, they can be placed at either side of the neo-realist/neo-modern divide. But made at the same time and in the same place in monochrome, both using long takes, extensive tracking and exterior locations, deep-focus and wide-screen ratios, they are both major testaments to the enhancement of the filmic image.

Post-Renoir realisms in directors as diverse as Rossellini, De Sica, Olmi, Pasolini, Rosi, Satyajit Ray, Wajda, and Rohmer all celebrate the triumph of the image, its luminous intensity, its priority over the spoken word. But they also demonstrate their closeness to the neo-modern impetus. The chronology of the mimetic image shows increasingly a debt to neo-modern style while developing what we can term the enduring thematic features of the realist paradigm – the epic and the innocent. The role of children in the work of Rossellini, De Sica, Ray, the Taviani brothers or Louis Malle's *Au revoir les enfants* demonstrates two vital features of the innocent. The naive gaze of the child or half-knowing gaze of the teenager illuminate the madness and hypocrisy of the adult world. Realist narrative here echoes the rites of passage in the *Bildungsroman* which mark the entry of the young into the perils of adult life. The young adopt strategies to ensure survival in the world of those who are materially strong, yet morally weak. But the actions of the young can seldom resolve dilemmas in the same way as adult heroes or villains. They learn fast, but their gaze is still that of the unsullied observer, which suggests at once freshness, innocence and helplessness as well as cunning and tenacity. Such features are found most succinctly in the teenagers of Rohmer's *Comedies and Proverbs* where knowledge and innocence are subtly combined. This innocent mode of the realists is highlighted by its dystopian opposite, the neo-modern transformation of the child in the psychic terrors of Bresson's *Mouchette*, Bergman's *The Silence*, and, more recently, Klimov's war epic *Come and See*, Tarkovsky's *The Sacrifice*, Kusterica's *Time of the Gypsies* or Ann Turner's *Celia*.

In truth neo-realism has itself been transformed by modern narrative. Nowhere is this more so than in Bill Douglas's Scottish trilogy (1972–8) which charts the horrors of childhood in a Lothian mining town at the end of the Second World War. The greatest work of British cinema of its decade, the trilogy, especially the middle section, *My Ain Folk*, recalls James Hogg in the strength of its Calvinist terror.[19] But in the wretched lives of his poor mining families there is simply no room for the luxury of a righteous belief in salvation. We are not in the world of the Elect but in the world of the Damned. The first stirrings of a child's consciousness are those of curse and doom. Eternal damnation begins on earth and proceeds apace. There is no innocence, justice or redemption. The world is too bleakly evil for the repentance of sins. In echoing the methods of neo-realism, the static shot, the still tableau, the fragmented episode, Douglas achieves the opposite effect. He renders growth as stasis, the sparse landscape of the mine and pit village as the living locus of hell. It is no wonder that Scottish cinema falls with immense relief a few years later into the welcoming arms of *Gregory's Girl*. In the trilogy the nightmare of the everyday life destroys the moral autonomy of the child's judgement in the instant that it becomes possible. Ten years on, in his nightmare vision of a child's experience of war in Byelorussia, a retro-vision of the same period, Klimov's swirling and lyrical camera does the same thing by opposite means. He dispenses with the certainties of the real. In extreme situations, there is no perceptual basis for the learning rites of childhood. All events are magical and threatening. Phantasmagoria replaces the grounded objects of the perceiving eye. In the cinema of the 1980s, innocence is aborted by the nightmares of magical realism. It never, in effect, has time to be born.

In the British cinema of the last twenty years the Douglas trilogy and the recent film of Terence Davies, *Distant Voices, Still Lives* (1988), stand out as two of its most powerful texts. Both are remarkable testimonies to the power of low-budget cinema. They are also part of an alternative strand in British film history to the studio legacy of Michael Powell which has clearly influenced Peter Greenaway and Neil Jordan. The films of Douglas and Davies use a realism whose style is thoroughly modern in their refusal of easy conventions of story-telling. Moreover as autobiographical memory films reconstructing the past they draw on the heritage of the British documentary, the highly charged poetic power of John Grierson and Humphrey Jennings. But they do so because they are part of the wider age of modern European cinema. It seems impossible to conceive of Douglas's work without the prior example of Bresson as well as Satyajit Ray. The delicate interwoven memories in Davies's picture of working-class Liverpool after the war, his bitter-sweet family chronicle, seem impossible to imagine without the emotional intimacy of Bergman or the complex memory narratives of Resnais and Fellini. The work of both directors builds on the modern cinema as such. The idea of a pristine 'realist' tradition hence becomes an unworkable fallacy.

Even if we return to those Catholicized films in Europe which proclaim the innocence of the real, we can see that 'innocence' must always be qualified. In Rohmer, despite the studied 'naturalness' of his young observers, often more important than what they see and say is what they fail to perceive, the gaps in realization which are never filled until it is too late. In *The Aviator's Wife* (1981) or *Full Moon in Paris* (1984) their compulsive talk is all about uncovering and controlling motive. But in the denouement of both films the exact opposite happens. The spectator finds out just how wrong the protagonists have been. Rohmer thus exposes the falseness of regarding simplicity as a natural attitude, and equally, perhaps, the limits of the neo-realist film which extols the purity of the simple gaze. Certainly in the world of the modern bourgeois there is no simple gaze. In the maze of uncertainties which afflict young people of all classes, the predicament of modernity begins to show its troub-ling face. It is too complex to warrant the detachment of a naive and pure simplicity which can 'expose' its hypocrisies. In *Jesus of Montreal* (1988) Denys Arcand turns this complexity into pathos when the natural attitude of Lothaire Bluteau, the Jesus of his Brechtian Passion play, becomes a recipe for unexpected disaster. The neo-realisms which had been visual hymns to the nobility of the young, the outcast, the poor and the unfortunate do not translate well into a polyvisual and polyphonic world which is spiritually impoverished and banal.

There is, however, a different cultural aspect to realism which is often overlooked. In the work of the great French critic André Bazin, the concern with the ontology of the image is not merely a philosophical position. It is also a moral one embedded in European Catholic culture, and in the Personalist philosophies of French Catholic intellectuals such as Pierre Teilhard de Chardin.[20] Bazin's affirmation of the 'isness' of existence prior to the making of moral judgements is itself a moral attitude. The natural atti-tudes of filming are piety, compassion and the celebration of the human in the everyday. Filming is a basic affirmation of human existence, not merely a reflection of reality but also an act of love. This, he argues, forms an essential part of the aesthetic of the neo-realist directors in post-war Italy, and from it he derives his concept of the 'image-fact'. The image-fact is the filmic sequence which uses the techniques at its disposal to linger in its *mise-en-scène* on the varied aspects of the human predicament.[21] Another attraction of the Italian directors for Bazin was their use of the collective. The crowd scenes, shot on location in *Ossessione*, *Rome, Open City, Bicycle Thieves* and *La strada*, mark the new cinema as one which films both openly and naturally the com-munity at large. It celebrates community which has undergone tyranny and which in the films of Rossellini and De Sica endures war, suffering and liberation. It is thus far removed from the subjectivity and isolation of the lone individual, or the images of the masses which dominate German Expressionism, either the robotic toilers of *Metropolis* or the malevolent underworld of *M*, where the collective symbolizes brute strength, rough justice and brutality.

Arguably, neo-realism reached its zenith when the legacy of the war had all but disappeared. As a truly national cinema built on the fundament of liberation, Italian film become epic and modern at the same time, so that *Rocco*, *La notte*, *8½* and *Accatone* all co-exist within the same time-scale, are all, in effect, part of the moment of the modern. Visconti and Pasolini crown the achievements of the neo-realist phase of Italian cinema at the very time it started to produce the new stylistics of the neo-modern. But the difference in form here was one of theme as much as style. The epic is proletarian, and runs counter to the neo-modern concern with the doubling of the split self. Visconti was the ultimate paradox in Italian film-making, an aristocratic Marxist who excelled in his movies of peasant, working-class and aristocratic life, yet stumbled disastrously in his latter obsessions with the spirit of the bourgeoisie fashioned self-consciously at times on the work of Thomas Mann. Pasolini, in his stunning debut in *Accatone* (1961) which deals with the peripheral world of the Roman underclass, and his adaptation of *The Gospel According to St Matthew* (1964) using Calabrian peasants, was a Catholic Marxist whose vision of hope and despair is as much Dantesque as it is communist. Visconti and Pasolini both place class politics at the centre of their vision of the world, eschewing religious sentimentality and the consensual vision of their predecessors.

The contemporary 'epic' is of course a contradiction in terms. But in *La terra trema* and *Rocco and his Brothers* Visconti turned it into an artistic unity. In both films the present has a timeless quality and its metonyms turn to myth. *Rocco* was a clear antidote to the rhetoric of the economic 'boom' of the time, a fragile vision of hope precisely metonymic in its focus on the southern peasant family in the northern industrial city, with its diurnal knack of enduring pain. In Visconti the epic qualities of human endurance are always operatic *and* diurnal. But the film is also profoundly Christian in its iconography. Simone's murder of Nadia, his prostitute-lover, her arms spread wide as she leans back against the tree-trunk awaiting the thrust of the knife, is one in which Visconti crucifies Mary Magdalene rather than Christ. For Christ is Rocco the supplicant suffering the pain of first her rape and then her murder. Despite his penitence the saintly Rocci is firmly of this harsh and pitiless world. He makes honest money as a boxing champion while turning the other cheek in everyday life and offering forgiveness to all the sinners around him. In the differing fates of the two brothers, the saint and the sinner, Visconti gives us a perfect fable of moral dilemma and class contradiction. Yet the film's luminous quality of the real works only through a fusion of the sacred and the profane in a world still profoundly Catholic. That same mixture of the sacred and the profane, of the necessary, acclaimed sins of poverty in the modern city and the lingering dream of salvation, echoes throughout *Accatone*. Franco Citti's brute portrait of the beggar pimp is vastly different from the radiant, still-innocent Rocco of Alain Delon but giving Citti in his powerful close-ups the haunting face of a fourteenth-century portrait, Pasolini figuratively evokes the iconography of the fallen angel and Dante's alternatives of the Inferno and Paradise. Moreover in citing the power the sacred, Pasolini mentions his use of 57 and 70 millimetre lens to add weight to matter and to highlight depth, light and shadow, a technique which for some critics gave the film a deeply aesthetic sense of death by hollowing out the eye sockets and the shadows on the face. Thus while acknowledging the religiosity of the film, Pasolini claimed that its religious nature lay 'in the technical sacredness of *seeing* that world'.[22]

The Catholic sensibility to which Bazin responded operated for him also at the level of the modern in Bresson and Fellini. Despite the formal rigour of *The Diary of a Country Priest* and the phantasmagoric vision of *La strada*, Bazin saw in Bresson a profoundly contingent vision of human suffering and in Fellini 'a phenomenology of the soul and perhaps even of the Communication of the Saints', all of which makes nonsense of the continual typecasting of Bazin as a 'realist' critic.[23] After the critic's death the impoverishment of the spirit was to work in a less operatic manner in the films of Bresson, Wajda, Rohmer, Arcand and Kieslowski, that is, through the complex fable or parable such as *Jesus of Montreal*, in which the spectator is forced to recognize an elemental moral dilemma. The choice the hero makes is one the spectator must judge. It relates not merely to the escape from suffering, or the search for happiness, but to the resolving of a situation in which justice and happiness cannot be made to coincide. Rohmer's *contes moraux* (Moral Tales) and Kieslowski's

Dekalogs (The Ten Commandments) are both of this order. Both evoke the uncompromising clarity of the real as a precondition for judgement. Yet their protagonists seek, however simply or tortuously, a state of grace which is constantly elusive, existential rather than theological. Realism, in this sense, is a radical and secular dimension of Catholicism which permeates French, Italian and Polish film culture, but at the same time acknowledges the persistence of faith and all its contradictions. In *Ma nuit chez Maud* Rohmer's prim Catholic protagonist, Jean-Louis Trintignant at his best, unwittingly choices to marry a woman who, it turns out, has previously 'betrayed' his outdated sexual morality. But the gaze of the camera, in casually observing the complex contortions of belief and action, of the realities of courtship and the ideology of love and marriage, brings us to one conclusion. The real and the moral are finally inseparable.

This shows us, perhaps, why the American cinema has never been a true cinema of realism. Only in the 1950s did American film start to achieve the naturalistic attention to sequence, detail and the human figure typical of Renoir and the neo-realists. Its debt to neo-realism was specially immense. But it did so as a means of reinforcing the leitmotif of American melodrama, the final triumph of the heroic figure over dark misfortune. In the period after 1955 American cinema did intensify our sense of the real. Film adaptations of the new poetic realism of Tennessee Williams, Arthur Miller and William Inge (all to become film writers themselves) were enhanced by the Stanislavskian work of the New York Actors Studio under Lee Strasburg. The absorption of the Method school of acting into movies was accompanied by a focus on working-class life, the marginal existence of the outcast, the delinquent, the disprivileged. William Wyler, Nicholas Ray, Robert Rossen, Martin Ritt and Elia Kazan all directed films whose psychosexual realities were not undermined by emotional excess or the studio's insistence on optimistic endings. No contradiction appears between social observation and mythic resolution. Accuracy of detail reinforces the power of mythic redemption so central to the American Dream. By mixing classic melodrama with new styles of filming and acting, the realism of the new 1950s cinema was enhanced. Location shooting, working-class neighbourhoods and social issues were linked to a storyline with a compulsion towards idealized closure, to a satisfying finale and the promise of redemption. *On the Water-*

front, *East of Eden* and *Rebel Without a Cause* incorporate the authentic location and the emotional realism of Method acting. Above all, in the acting of Dean, Brando and others they tap the emotional energies of the misunderstood and the afflicted, taking melodrama into a new dimension of psychic exposure.

The prime example is Kazan's anti-union epic, *On the Waterfront* (1954). Budd Schulberg, the scriptwriter, researched labour corruption on the New York waterfront before writing a screenplay based on real historical incident. Marlon Brando brought the idiom of contemporary youth and working-class life to the Hollywood screen in a manner which matched neo-realism to the psychological truth-seeking of the Actors Studio. But the basic structure is still melodramatic. As Terry Malone, the young docker trying to match loyalty to his racketeer brother with the defence of his brother's victims, Brando resolves the confusions of motive only through the clarity of decisive action. Against the odds, he forms an awareness of injustice and acts with courage to defeat evil. The film barely mentions the employer's collusion in corruption or the original 'insurgents'' desire for a committed union to fight for their rights rather than no union at all. It relapses into formula melodrama, echoing Kazan's renunciation of communism at the House Unamerican Activities Committee hearings.[24] Brando ends up as a contemporary version of an honourable Westerner who has come in from the cold, and Kazan resurrects one of Hollywood's most powerful myths, the redemptive powers of the lone Westerner, in its reverse locale, the East Coast city.

The simplicity of action demands a young, working-class hero but in melodrama's reversal of misfortune there have to be sacrificial victims – Harrison Ford's black partner in *Witness*, Sonny Corleone in *Godfather I*, Sal Mineo as the lonely teenager who idolizes James Dean in *Rebel Without a Cause*. Sacrifice of the nearest and dearest is the spur to triumph for those who survive. Melodrama has thus never had the openness, the detachment or the episodic fragmentation of the neo-realist film. The American stress on determinism is usually idealized as social uplift or redemption of the unfortunate. Action must always transform situation to create a new situation and move narrative forward.[25] In this way the initial situation must exhibit some degree of naturalist accuracy, the final situation little at all. The 1970s generation of Italian–American directors, Coppola, Scorsese and

Cimino, attempted to use the epic style of Visconti and Pasolini in their parables of modern American life. Thus the family rituals, the work setting, the boxing scenario and the proximity of the Church are all borrowed and turned back into full-blooded melodrama.

The great success here is *Raging Bull* (1980), Martin Scorsese's most powerful picture, in which he takes Hollywood melodrama for the first time beyond good and evil. Thus his boxing champion Jake La Motta does not follow in the footsteps of Brando's Terry Malone or Paul Newman's Rocky Graziano, as an exemplar of moral uplift through struggle and sacrifice. He is a mixture instead of Rocco and Simone, a demonic fusion of good boxer and evil boxer in Visconti's movie, determined and loyal, but also insecure, vicious and paranoid. Moreover his story is a period piece shot on location in black and white with souce sound. The period, the 1940s, is that of the Italian cinema of neo-realism. Later as the ageing paunchy La Motta falls on hard times, Robert De Niro has a night-club act in which he recites Brando's famous speech to Rod Steiger lamenting the failure of Terry's boxing career. Documentary, social history and the double referencing of film history are all intertwined. Through its neo-modern variations of neo-realist form, the legacy of Visconti and Pasolini, but also of the French New Wave and *cinema-vérité*, Scorsese brings a dimension to the naturalist melodrama it had lacked in the 1950s. But the success of the film depends very precisely on evoking the period in which neo-realism had flourished.

It is now easier to see why the European, not the American, cinema should be the source of the psychic labyrinth of the neo-modern. Not only does it owe more to the neo-realist, it has to surpass the limits which neo-realism sets it. In Italy the switch from neo-realist to neo-modern is often the *same* directors moving on to a new form of cinema. This is seen most clearly in the work of Roberto Rossellini and Federico Fellini. *Voyage to Italy* sets out, unsuccessfully, to create an entirely different cinematic form from *Paisa*. *La strada* gives little indication of the complex virtuosity that is to come in *8½*. Pasolini moves from the proletarian demi-monde of *Accatone* to the surreal bourgeois *Theorem*, where the figure of the angel is Terence Stamp not Franco Citti, no longer metonymic but firmly allegorical. Meanwhile Antonioni had moved through the whole period of neo-realism from documentary through the haunting yet still neo-realist quest narrative of *Il grido* to his great trilogy of the early 1960s. The 'moving on' here is also a moving forward and upward into the world of the bourgeoisie. In the work of Luis Buñuel it is topographical, moving on from the poverty and violence of the Mexican *Los Olvidados* and the mock religious pieties of the Spanish *Viridiana* to the Parisian upper-middle classes of *Belle de jour* and *The Discreet Charm of the Bourgeoisie*. This is a new, prosperous and outwardly stable bourgeoisie of the Cold War period. But the transition is fundamental. The profane image demands transitions in form and a new vision which neither the techniques of neo-realism nor the self-censored Hollywood cinema could register.

Neo-modernisms and the new prosperity of the Western middle classes combined to provide a new answer, in Europe through a cinema of spiritual and perceptual ambiguity, in America through the transformed myths of film noir themselves indebted to European ambiguities. The former was a further precondition of the noir renaissance from 1970 onwards. *Klute*, *Taxi Driver*, *Chinatown*, *American Gigolo* and *Body Heat* are mythic re-presentations of bourgeois dilemmas of wealth and sexuality, whose renovated style is heavily indebted to the modern images of the Europeans. Yet such myths remain, at the same time, within the mould of American melodrama. This is a feature of the new post-studio cinema which begins with Vietnam. *Mise-en-scène* in *Taxi Driver* or *Body Heat* would be impossible without the oneiric qualities of Bertolucci's *The Conformist*, while the existential conception of evil in Arthur Penn's *Bonnie and Clyde* or Terence Malick's *Badlands* is self-consciously borrowed from Godard's *A bout de souffle*. Modernisms are not therefore, identifiable as distinct, self-contained forms. They are intertextual. What they invent can be absorbed and taken back by melodrama, but often in a highly derivative form.

The new profane images of the bourgeoisie, which begin with *Touch of Evil*, *L'avventura* and *A bout de souffle* are evidence of the technical enhancement of the image we have spoken of in the previous chapter. The fast opening crane shot and intricate camera mobility in Welles's film, the 360-degree panning of Godard, the intimate exterior lighting of Antonioni, all open up the film image in new ways. Wide-screen ratios, such as those used by Antonioni in his trilogy, or by Andrjez Munk in the black and white Cinemascope format of his unfinished masterpiece, *Passenger*, or the 18.5 millimetre lens Welles uses for the first time in *Touch of Evil* and *The Trial*, all are equally important. But the complexities of bourgeois experience which come within the technical range of the 1960s cinema because of its enhanced powers of presencing are paradoxically possible only through a movement in the opposite direction. In the neo-modern idiom the enhancement of the image has also generated a *displacement* of the image. During this strange and powerful process, the image appears to double back on itself. It is nearer, more intimate, more ubiquitous.

Film takes us closer in further to figures and events, as in Douglas Slocombe's intimate interior photography for *The Servant* (1963). In Joseph Losey's oblique and brilliant dissection of English social manners the camera is an exploring eye which roams after its characters through the rooms and spaces of the elegant Chelsea town house. It shares the intimacy of place as if it were a fifth character to the ambiguous love quartet of master and fiancée, manservant and maid. But we feel removed and more distant from them by virtue of this very intimacy. The camera matches the glacial power of the spoken word in Harold Pinter's screenplay. As a visual medium it makes the distance between characters of different social classes spatial and emotional at the same time. The alienation of the image is visceral and cognitive because there is a process of spatial decentring within the narrative. Like Buñuel's, Losey's fascination lies in the sexual disintegration of the wealthy bourgeoisie. Likewise, the intimacy of his camera is not melodramatic. It lies not in the close-up or the reaction shot so much as in the presence of the camera which observes unnoticed, which exists within the spaces and the rooms it films, within the screen as well as in front of it.

This spatial decentring of intimacy can be brought about by various stylistic means, by the extremes of long shot, the absence of close-up and reaction shots, the jump-cut, the crossing of the 180-degree axis, the plastic modulations of offscreen space, so that decentring is not usually literal. Moving figures to the sides of the screen is less powerful than implying that the screen itself no longer occupies a fixed framework within space and time, that time is no longer sequential and continuous, that space is no longer bounded by the frame of the screen. The result is often a lack of connection between shots or between motive and action. The modern camera seems to film a story without telling it, to show action without obvious motive. The resulting puzzle is one that spectators have to piece together for themselves, since no narrative issues organically from the succession of moving images. The boldest and most daring of the modern innovators here is undoubtedly Godard. In her brilliant essay on the French director Sontag has shown his uncanny knack of combining B-movie melodrama with abstract forms of composition, making action movies with organic plot-lines which are then carved up by improvised sequences, offscreen interruptions, visual captions, voice-overs and finally analysis by the characters themselves posing as detached commentators. Ideas are formal elements not designed to illuminate meaning but to fracture narratives. Above all they 'lie at a tangent to the action'.[26]

Displacement of the image through enhancement of the image. The paradox is central. It shows the point at which the mimetic will-to-power signifies a loss of innocence. Stylistically, long takes, jump-cuts, hand-held cameras, the crossing of the line, the flashforward, the address to the camera, the unsignified flashback, the repeated shot have all transformed classical narrative. Neither *A bout de souffle* nor *L'avventura* narrates happenings in a conventional way: neither of them narrates conventional happenings. They play, instead, upon the alienation of the spectator from the image, and of bourgeois characters from bourgeois conventions. Such alienation effects are powerfully post-Brechtian. They enhance our perception of the frailties of class domination but force us to judge them without didactic guidelines. Film characters are no longer the stars of Hollywood melodrama. Hollywood asks its audiences to merge with the heavenly bodies of its stars, the neo-moderns challenge the audience to see the forms of human displacement that the image presents. It forces them not to identify personas but to judge events. The displaced image robs the bourgeoisie of its innocence. The alienation effect removes it from the moral centre of the universe.

For a time this polyvalent image of the new bourgeoisie had its 'stars', like popular melodrama. In the 1960s and 1970s Yves Montand, Jean-Paul Belmondo, Anna Karina, Jean-Claude Brialy, Monica Vitti, Jeanne Moreau, Marcello Mastroianni, Alain Delon, Anthony Perkins, Jean-Louis Trintignant, Dominique Sanda, Jack

Nicholson, Liv Ullmann, Max von Sydow and Bibi Andersson were all deemed by critics to be 'stars' of the new cinema. But they are figures of displacement, not icons of seduction. There is little crossing-over of the spectator into the image, into *their* image. Moreover displacement here should not be seen as divorce from the emotions, of complete emotional paralysis, a view fashionable in the critiques of alienation which pervaded the film criticism of the 1960s. Feelings *are* expressed, often without compromise. They are complex and volatile, fragile and unpredictable. The *durée* of ambivalent feeling cannot be reified into a fixed posture of alienation. Since nothing is obvious, the onus to generate emotion is upon the audience. Feeling must be discovered by the spectator.

As a *class* phenomenon the profane image now brings us back to the theme which began this chapter, the mechanics of doubling. This process is a double distancing, first of the bourgeois persona and secondly of the bourgeois spectator. Enhancement of the image, displacement of the image. This in no way entails emotional neutrality, the aesthetic illusion of being clinical and dispassionate. Instead it evokes a spectrum of changing emotional distances. Spectator and character touch many times, but their relationship remains, to use Adorno's term, one of nonidentity. Both characters and spectators have their 'absent Other' from which they are provisionally estranged. If the screen 'persona' is the absent Other of the spectator, the screen character can project an 'Other' version of self, or even multiple versions of potential personality, all of which become potential doubles. What the spectator sees here is often like a set of mirrors reflecting to infinity.

Profane images touch on the otherness of the bourgeois in two ways. Class privilege means wealth, glamour, sexuality, power. By doing so, it must call into question those authentic forms of self which belong to neo-realism and naturalistic melodrama, forms of self which are relatively innocent, which in varying degrees are child-like, adolescent, direct, heroic, unassuming, proletarian. In *L'avventura* Monica Vitti as Claudia watches with amusement the awkward wooing of a young Sicilian couple in a train compartment where the man shows off his new transistor radio to the woman with obvious intent. She turns in the corridor to see Sandro bearing down on her and instantly her voyeuristic fun is replaced by disquiet. But in her own situation, intent and consequence are less obvious. The simplicity of her gaze at the couple gives way to the complexity of the look between her and Sandro. The rituals of an unacceptable courtship so soon after Anna's vanishing are riddled with ambiguity and the stakes of betrayal are high. In Bergman's *Persona* Sister Alma wishes to become like Elizabet Vogler, the star actress under her care, but that desire is itself orchestrated by the mute Elizabet as a perversity, as a 'star' performance exercised as a form of domination.

As we shall see, all modern doubling plays on the displacement and the duplicity of the other, from *Lady from Shanghai* and *Vertigo* to *8½*, *The Conformist* and *The Year of Living Dangerously*. It uses the enhancement of the image in order to undermine it, the rational sophistication of the bourgeois personality in order to deconstruct the notion of the 'person'. One of its crucial weapons is the power of the gaze which, as we shall see, is fundamental to the modern cinema.

4

The Power of the Gaze

In a sense, all technologies of watching are an extension of the human eye.[1] In our own time when such technologies are so abundant we live in a truly ocular culture. Yet between eye and camera there is still an uneasy stand-off, a sense that neither can be assimilated to the other. The human gaze lacks the camera's powers of focus and depth of field, but it has no constricting rectangular frame.[2] More often eye and camera remain apart, at best facsimiles of one another. For the camera can be placed anywhere and be moved anywhere that is technically possible. The famous opening crane shot in *Touch of Evil* follows the trajectory of a predatory bird, swooping down and then hovering in front of its moving human prey, a curious vulture the eye could scarcely emulate. Yet Welles's camera remains intimately connected to the human gaze. The shot is one we enjoy witnessing, one of breathtaking pleasure. We wish to be there even though we are not and Welles's camera has shown us the wishful power of the gaze.

In societies at large the power of the gaze has been a central feature of what is called modernity. Here it is construed as the power of *surveillance*, a form of growing surveillance in the modern age by which all institutional powers acquire knowledge of their subjects in different habitats – in rooms, houses, factories, barracks, schools, hospitals, asylums.[3] Foucault has pointed to one of the key origins of surveillance in a daring invention of the Enlightenment, Bentham's Panopticon, a spatial model for incarceration whose circular transparency would allow for the continuous observation of all prisoners from a fixed point.[4] It matched enlightenment to utility in its functional utopia of a transparency which would enhance power through knowledge. It would see its subjects continuously without, it was assumed, provoking the forms of revolt which came in response to physical brutality. As a method, surveillance was thus an alternative to cruelty. Moreover as an observation machine at the inception of industrial society it paved the way for later forms of surveillance by other observation machines. Now, in the electronic age, these are almost too numerous to be counted – telescopes, telephones, computers, bugs, closed-circuit television, sound-recorders, cameras of all kinds and descriptions, satellites, sensors, infra-red and laser rays. In an age of information the cult of information worships to excess its own sophisticated technologies. As an instrument, the camera has grown up as part of a culture of surveillance whose possibilities it enhanced. Cinema, as a medium, was destined, therefore, to be highly self-conscious. In all the great modern film-makers there is a tendency to take issue with the power of the gaze, and to explore the sensitivity of the camera as its willing instrument.

At the very beginnings of the modern sound cinema the ambiguities of the camera eye are clearly etched in Renoir's *La Règle du jeu*. Renoir claimed his camera movements were intended to breach the normal convention of filming a precise set of integrated happenings.[5] Within the chateau his camera often wanders from one set of events to another without appearing to concentrate on any of them. In that way he hoped to escape the tyranny of the camera's gaze, which normally makes obvious what it is pointing at in the interest of its narrative. The movements of his camera thus seem random and undirected, not focused in any way with obvious intent. At times, the camera becomes an eye with no position, no platform, no centre. Yet perhaps also in that remarkable film he achieved something else. As the amorous intrigues and dramas break out in the halls and corridors of the chateau, the camera is less a decentred eye looking at nothing in particular than a curious gatecrasher happening on the scene, sometimes moving with the action to get a better view, at other times distracted by something even more outrageous out of eyeshot. Here camera style is perfectly matched to Renoir's theme.

The fluidity of the camera's eye thrives on the growing intensity of multiple events, of melodrama breaking down into farce as it simultaneously threatens to break through into tragedy. The composition within the single shot often changes so rapidly that at times the eye cannot fully grasp it. Renoir is right to stress the indeterminacy of the real here, the sense of one 'drama' being no more or less important than any other. Certainly, nothing is privileged. What he also does, though, is to alter the position of the human eye, transforming the gaze of the spectator through the altered gaze of the camera. At one level, his imaginary observer has a short concentration-span. At another, the non-identity of character and spectator, the failure of the audience to find any heroes is forged through bewildering transformations. We are breathless before the camera's displacement of frantic characters from one room to another, each action or gesture more ineffectual than the last. Renoir's camera makes a virtue of distraction and turns it into visual poetry.

This idle watching, speeded up to the point of frenzy, slows to a dilatory gaze in the work of Antonioni. At the start of an incidental shot in *The Passenger* (1975), the director parodies the difference between the camera and the human gaze when his camera idly 'watches' from a Spanish café as cars pass in the street outside. It is the gaze of no one in particular looking aimlessly into the street. It pans right as one car whizzes past, then changes course suddenly to pan left as another car comes from the other direction. The camera's movement seems to capture the way we might swivel our gaze back and forth in curiosity as we sat languidly with a drink watching the world go by. But the sudden swivel movement of the camera calls attention to itself as 'unnatural' in the way that the same movement of the human gaze would be perfectly 'natural'. In *Blow-Up* (1966), Antonioni shows even more clearly the differences between photographic reality and human perception. The blow-ups of a picture taken in the London park by Thomas, the professional photographer played by David Hemmings, appear to reveal the contours of an arm holding a gun in the bushes which the human eye could not see. But Thomas is also too busy taking photographs of the woman (Vanessa Redgrave) meeting her ostensible lover, to notice later what is more obvious, the lower half of the lover's body sticking out from behind a tree trunk. The audience cannot see the arm or gun in the bushes, but *can* see this segment of the body lying on the grass. But in yet another twist, it is unlikely to do so, since neither Thomas's photo-camera nor Antonioni's cine-camera, which is busy filming Thomas filming, directs attention to that bottom part of the frame in the shot. Our attention is directed to the top of the frame, the direction in which the woman has disappeared. Because the spectator is never cued in by either Thomas or the director to what is clearly visible, what is there for the seeing, the still legs of the corpse, remain unseen. The gaze has been directed elsewhere.

Eye and camera converge, then, diverge. The camera discovers both more and less than the human gaze. In this way it shows both its limitations and its power. In turn the desire and the vulnerability of the gaze is also exposed. In the bourgeois image the power of the gaze and its limits are central. The gaze becomes a form of cultural capital, of a symbolic power which secretly pursues the dream of material power. The bourgeois gaze cryptically surveys the world of Others in order that it can delight in the symbolic control promised by its look. It asserts symbolic power over inferiors and competes for with class equals. In gender relations the male gaze surveys the world of women and focuses on its chosen object of desire, scaling down its primal, objectless desire to a single point in which imaginary power enters the realm of the possible but proves, as in *The Lady from Shanghai*, to be a delusion. In all cases, the desire for control is inseparable from a quest for knowledge. If knowledge, along with money and force, is a form of power, then knowledge of the image becomes a form of potential capture, of the symbolic seizure of the image.

If the human gaze is part of the quest for knowledge, it is also part of the quest for self-knowledge. This explains the ubiquity of the double, and of the mirror and the reflection in modern cinema. Thus the gaze can also be turned back upon the subject. Federico Fellini's *8½* (1963) is an extended metonymic turning of the camera back on to its ostensible creator, a film about a director played by Marcello Mastroianni but clearly cast in the image of Fellini who cannot bring himself to make film number eight and a half, the very number *8½* was to become in Fellini's portfolio. As a successful orchestrator of the cinematic gaze Mastroianni is the temporary master of his surreal fantasies, which he always hopes he will translate into film. In the meantime, he compensates for the practical frustrations of film-making through fantasies of domination over women, fantasies which we sense are doomed to remain only in his imagination. The film films the residual fantasies of the film director which are destined never to become film. But through the process of location filming Mastroianni also hopes to escape from much of his disordered and unhappy life. As this 'extraneous' life of the personal predictably catches up on him, the gaze is turned upon his own doleful look. He is thus 'caught' in the act of preparing his film by all sorts of acolytes and hangers-on, by aspiring actresses, by his writer and his producer, by the media and finally by his mistress and his wife, all of whom, to his great unease, are 'watching out for him'. Thus the collective gaze is turned back on him, and he is unable to escape it. The director who aspires to film the world as a carousel which never escapes his panning camera is constantly being watched, hounded, questioned and assailed by those inhabiting the treacherous milieu his celebrity embraces. In one of the film's three endings, where all endings appear equal, he hides under a table at a press conference and shoots himself.

A more specific turning back of the gaze can be found in a telling shot in the middle sequence of Bergman's *Persona* (1966). The camera films a solitary Sister Alma (Bibi Andersson) in long shot framed against the sea-shore without, it appears, the presence of her patient, Elizabet Vogler, out of whose sight she has seldom been previously. But Vogler (Liv Ullmann) leaps up into the screen from a squatting position in medium close-up, holding a camera to take a photograph directly into Sven Nykvist's camera, as if, following the naturalist illusion, the filmmaker's camera was not there, as if she was photographing the opposite side of the deserted beach to that in which her companion walked. Offscreen space is given remarkable definition by the vertical movement. Ullmann shoots suddenly into view from the bottom of the frame, and as the audience locates the meaning of the movement in her abrupt change from a squatting to a standing position, it is photographed by the very figure it watches. It as if Ullmann's pressing of the switch captures the surprise of the gaze caused by the suddenness of her movement and records it for posterity. It is also the opportunist act of surveillance of someone formally under surveillance, the symbolic revenge of someone deemed in need of 'care'. In turning back the gaze, she reinforces the power of her silence (officially the symptom of her illness) in her relations with the talkative Alma. The absence of speech crystallizes the optical power of her look. But the power of her gaze is also strengthened by the film's theme of doubling. In 'looking' for the distant Alma, the audience is confronted by her double close to, the intimacy of an Elizabet with identical hair style and clothes. The illusion of distance from the figure of Alma as distance from the pathology of doubling is shattered by the surprise of Vogler's thrust, the ambushing of the camera which becomes an ambush of the spectator by the double of the gaze's object.

In different ways and with contrasting styles all four directors, Renoir, Antonioni, Bergman and Fellini, demonstrate the power of the gaze as a shared medium, something triangulated between film-maker, character and spectator. As a shared template of seeing, the gaze operates as a cinematic form of the will-to-power, of a restless struggle for spiritual domination in which the gaze is not a fleeting substitute for force but a force-field which, instead of committing a form of violence on its object, does violence instead to the conventions of cinematic framing.[6] It is a *reflexive* gaze in which struggle takes place simultaneously between the film's protagonists and between the director and the audience. The central expression of the will-to-power is mediated by the act of filming. The gaze is a creative act which can also be destructive, reactive and negative as well as active and positive. Through self-conscious commentary on the act of filming, many directors reflexively demonstrate their technical powers of manipulation, the power to film the nature of filming and alter the spectator's gaze, to attract or alienate it. In the opening montage of *Persona* Bergman takes this power to its literal extreme by showing the explosive contact of carbon and tungsten rods inside a 35 millimetre projector, by 'filming' the birth of his own film. Though it has a narrative autonomy, the interior power of the gaze within the film, as a source of an explosive contact between its major figures, its major characters, mirrors and doubles the exterior power of the gaze in the struggle for the film-maker's dominion over his audience. In *Vertigo* and many other Hitchcock films the power of the gaze is part of the technical romance of seduction. The optical withholding of the returned look from the woman who is the subject of the male gaze, the suspenseful turning away of Kim Novak from the penetrating blue eyes of James Stewart, is a neo-modern melo-drama which mirrors Hitchcock's persistent wooing of an audi-ence which can always have the final say by refusing to look at the images the screen presents them, but which he hopes will never do so. Thus the consent to return the gaze in full on screen, Novak's eventual looking into Stewart's eyes that is at first withheld in suspense, triggers in the audience a visceral (and unknowing) response to their own consenting to the image they see before them.

The gaze, however, can never be reduced to a formalist device. Equally, the director's reflexive gaze springs out of the auto-nomous struggle for power which takes place inside the film. In this kind of narrative, the will-to-power exists in its own right as a feature of fractured diegesis. Thomas's instinctive wish in *Blow-Up* is to establish domination, both sexual and cognitive, of the unnamed woman his film has exposed in the park. At one level his desire is a cheap, transient 1960s utopia, an orgasmic fusion of photographic and carnal knowledge. But as in all of Antonioni's best films, the consequences of action are more important than their origin in idle or desultory motive. Elusively, the woman slips away from his spasmodic surveillance, and just as mysteriously the blow-ups hanging up on the walls of his mews flat are ripped off and stolen in his brief absence. His gaze is torn apart and hangs in tatters.

In Peter Weir's *The Year of Living Dangerously* (1982), the same fragility of surveillance is treated as political melodrama in the tradition of Hitchcock.[7] The Chinese–Australian dwarf Billy Kwan (Linda Hunt) is also a photographer but equally a pup-petmaster in the land of Javanese puppets whose powers of manipulation belie his physical status. He brings together Guy Hamilton and Jill Bryant, Australian reporter and English spy, in the twilight of Sukarno's rule in Jakarta and orchestrates their dangerous affair until Guy, his investigating double, ignores the code of politics Kwan has set him and shatters the power of the tiny man's puppetry. By keeping files on both of them, by keep-ing them secretly under surveillance, Kwan's manipulative gaze constantly 'surveys' the lovers. What it does not literally see it hypothetically watches, as if its eyes are always there, penetrating through the walls of closed rooms. Moreover, both Welles in *Touch of Evil* and Coppola in *The Conversation* (1974) show us the power of the complex gaze which is as much aural as it is optical. In both films, the bugging of conversations on recording tape imperfectly captures that to which the hidden gaze has no direct access. It is an extension of the optical by the aural, of sight by sound so that the two merge into the surveying gaze almost as a single form. The cinematic gaze in that sense hears as much as it sees. Its limits are often revealed as much by what is out of earshot as by what is out of sight.

The gaze therefore is sonic as well as optical, a fusion of the visual and aural properties of surveillance. Such surveillance, as we shall see, can be discreet or indiscreet, visible or invisible. But it is not the function of a mythical omniscience operating out of a fixed camera. It is fluid, interchangeable, multidirectional, the source of constant struggle. In film modernisms it is not the gaze so much as the struggle for the gaze which defines the use of the camera. The figures within the film are defined by the reciprocity of the gaze. Sartre suggests that in concrete relations with others, as soon we direct our look upon the Other who is looking back, the look of the Other vanishes, and we no longer see anything but eyes.[8] It seems for a moment that the Other is a being that the subject now possesses. But in fact the whole structure of the relationship has collapsed. For Sartre what is possessed here is merely the being-as-object. In film what is possessed is merely the image of the being, that same experience of the possession of the image an audience will have in watching *Citizen Kane* where they come to possess a dazzling series of images of Kane but little sense of the person beyond the myth the film tempts them into seeking. Possession of the figure-as-image is at once a Faustian temptation and a source of existential dread, the dread of what can escape the look, the being which will never be possessed.

In the best of American film noir, the femme fatale looks without looking, constantly aware of the desiring gaze of the fall-guy, and all other men too, without showing obvious signs of awareness. Here the meaning of seduction becomes relative. It is impossible to say who seduces whom. The fall-guy lives under the illusion that his look leads naturally on to Renoir's 'contact of epidermises', that there is some intrinsic and necessary connection between gazing and touching. But in *The Lady from Shanghai*, *Vertigo* and *Body Heat*, the issue has already been decided in advance as a part of the woman's labyrinthine ploy. The gaze projects itself as part of the illusion of male power, just

as the absence of the gaze is part of the illusion of the absence
of female power. These films are an exception since they must
advance on the post-war convention of film noir that the femme
fatale as brassy, threatening dame fiercely returns the male look
in a gesture of sexual threat. This in turn, in films like *Double
Indemnity* and *Dead Reckoning*, was a radical departure from the
pre-war genre of historical romance. But though striking a new
pose in the history of Hollywood melodrama, the threat of the
returned look indicates a transparency of motive which tells us
in advance, and thus reassures us, that the femme fatale is
aggressive because she is also conspiring, conniving and deceit-
ful. Active female sexuality is thus identified with moral transgression. In Welles and Hitchcock the absence of the look evokes
mystery and wonder at the same time as it will come to signify,
in retrospect, concealment of intent. The woman is not then a
simple icon of threat-through-intent, an erotic embodiment of
malice aforethought. Rather she is the centre of conflicting
motives and discordant images, an icon of the unknowable rather
than the unknown, in which serenity is both posture and essence,
mask and nature.

The relationship of surveillance and the gaze is a complex one.
In *The Lady from Shanghai* all the men in sight look repeatedly
at Elsa Bannister and repeatedly spy on each other looking at
her, so that they are both purveyors and surveyors of the same
look, observing in others through sporadic voyeurism their secret
wish for desire-through-control. She in turn appears most of the
time to look at no one, to have no wish for power and no obvious
desire. But in order to fulfil her role credibly in an incredulous
plot as the orchestrator of murder most foul, she must have had
all her 'onlookers' under invisible surveillance all the time that
we have watched her display a seeming indifference to the events
around her. While the male gaze here is interchangeable, in
Touch of Evil it goes in different and bewildering directions at
the same time. As the corrupt Quinlan and the naive Vargas begin
their separate overlapping investigations of the same murder,
Grandi, the possible eventual suspect, has already set his
nephews to tail and terrorize Susan, Vargas's wife. Surveillance
is so triangulated that each watches the other watching back,
and Grandi also watches Vargas through his nephews' watching
of Susan. Unlike Vargas, Quinlan and Grandi who are spiritual
partners in corruption on opposite sides of the law, also watch

their backs – for each other. As a pawn in the power-game, Susan receives not the gaze of suspicious adoration common to the femme fatale but the look – which at first she refuses through racist arrogance to recognize – of gloating terror, surveillance by the makeshift terrorist crew in which the look is the portent of violation. If in Hitchcock's romances the lover's gaze is the prelude to a kiss, the group gaze of contempt in Welles's nightmare fable is a prelude to gang rape.

The denaturing confusions of surveillance in *Touch of Evil* become more apparent when we see the opposite form of denaturing in *Rear Window* (1954). Here Hitchcock uses the artifice of the fixed position, of a camera which never ventures outside the window of Jeffries's room, except for a single shot. Unlike Welles, Hitchcock reassuringly places us, but less reassuringly imprisons us in the fixed gaze. The immobile camera is in keeping with the injured Jeffries, immobilized by a plaster cast on his leg. We know therefore where most things are is in relation to Jeffries, his room and his own look across into all the apartments on the other side of the courtyard. But as we look voyeuristically with Jeffries through open windows in high summer, we see but hear only selectively, and Hitchcock shows us how deeply impaired the gaze becomes when the sound of voices is not high enough to capture the meaning of words. All the windows are like screens, but only in Thorwald's room are there concealed spaces the gaze cannot reveal. These are like the out-of-frame spaces of film, the offscreen space whose absent movements inform the presencing of what we see. Doubly impaired in our viewing, the arguments of different couples become fragmented mime-shows for our delectation but the mime-show of the Thorwalds becomes tantalizing in the absence of accompanying voices. As we become implicated in Jeffries's gaze, through first the naked eye, then the binoculars and finally the telephoto lens, our voyeurism stirs into active curiosity. The desire for the plenitude of full sound, instead of the selective sounds we hear, for room-length windows to unveil the movements which evade us, for light at all times, is akin to the desire for bodily wholeness that 'Jeff' lacks. The gaze becomes utopian, for Jeff a surrogate power which compensates for his disabled body, for us a recognition that in sharing his voyeurism we are diminished and need a solving of the murder mystery to be rescued. The shock of our gaze's intrusion comes when Thorwald, the 'murderer', sees

Grace Kelly gesturing across the courtyard to Jeff at the wedding ring on her finger. The camera pans from Thorwald's glance at the ring then to his sudden gaze back across the courtyard at Jeffries, whom he sees for the first time. At that point, the gaze is a weapon turned back upon its abuser.

In *Vertigo*, Hitchcock's masterpiece, the gaze is mirrored to infinity. It starts as the detective's downward look which fears and desires death, and then becomes a movement through space and time which is oneiric, all the more dream-like for Hitchcock's inspired use of Californian locations, and above all the steep streets of San Fransisco. As Scottie, not Jeff, James Stewart is mobile, stalking his mysterious prey in car and on foot. While the gaze of Scottie is on Madeleine the gaze of the camera is on him. At times, in key sequences, it is on both of them. The first sighting in Ernie's shows this in an almost perfect sequence. The camera glides back in a frontal crane shot from Scottie seated at the bar, pans gently across the adjoining restaurant, then moves forward again at a 45-degree angle to show Elster eating at a table with Madeleine. There is no frontal gaze by Scottie as there is by the camera, merely the slightest sideways glance. In the ensuing montage of point-of-view and reaction shots Scottie half-glances as they leave, but defers his glance as Madeleine walks towards him. She stops in front of Scottie to wait for her husband, then both walk the exit, leaving in front of a full-length mirror. In the montage are a set of ambiguous and fleeting eye-matches as Madeleine turns to look for Elster and Scottie discreetly turns away.

The second ambiguous sighting, where both face the camera in the same shot, occurs later in the flower-shop scene. Scottie follows Madeleine into a department store through the darkened back entrance with a glass-panelled door whose silhouette resembles a cinema screen in the darkness. In a startling reverse-angle we see Scottie open the inner door into a shop full of bright and colourful flowers, as if, in a *trompe d'œil*, that same screen had just burst into technicolour. In this point-of-view shot Scottie appears to see Madeleine walking towards him, towards, that is, the door he has pushed slightly ajar. A further reverse-angle, however, from inside the shop returns our gaze on to Scottie's peeping eye. The remarkable image in this shot, as Modleski has pointed out, is the fleeting appearance of Madeleine in the same frame through an ambiguous mirror positioned beside the door.[9] At this point the viewer is briefly lost in the duplicity of mirroring. Madeleine, who appeared to be walking *towards* the door, now appears to be walking past it, her gaze directed, like Scottie's, slightly to the side of the camera, hers to the left, his to the right. But a frame across the shot of Madeleine suggests the image is in a mirror panel on the wall beside the door. While the couple appear to be looking broadly in the *same* direction, in reality they must be looking *towards each other*. Madeleine must spy him head-on, while previously in Ernie's she had spied him from behind, glancing round at her. Crucially, the mirror here is the absent presence obliquely revealing to us her point-of-view shot – which Hitchcock openly forbids us.

As the narrative moves through space and time, gaze, image, mirror and desire all move towards infinity. The film is depthless, a series of surface images which cannot be penetrated. But it is also bottomless, a set of forward movements which cannot be held in check. All its images and characters are refracted in each other. In 'making over' Madeleine, Scottie becomes the double of Gavin Elster while the 'mad' Carlotta Valdes, the Hispanic ancestor whom Madeleine resembles and worships, is the dark shadow-double of the cool blonde Ferguson covets. In putting her bespectacled face on to the comic drawing of Carlotta's portrait, Midge becomes the parodic double of both women, the one who is dead and the one who is alive, who visits her ancestor's grave and wanders through the city like a ghost. Later Madeleine, in turn, is re-presented as the middle-class alias of Judy Barton, the working-class girl from Kansas made over by Gavin Elster. She is then persuaded by Scottie to double herself twice over, to turn back into the imaginary being who has more reality for him than the woman who has become his tentative partner. The male and female linkages are joined together, of course, by Scottie himself. His earlier attraction to Madeleine's apparent desire to die and 'be' the dead Carlotta is a mirror-image of his own vertigo, his desire to plunge headlong into another world. In the art gallery his distant gaze watches Madeleine watching the portrait of Carlotta. The camera first frames the posy on the seat beside her which is identical to the posy in the painting, and then frames the bun on Madeleine's hair in juxtaposition to the bun on Carlotta's hair, the hair tied in both cases in the image of the spiral which introduces the film's credits and later Scottie's dream sequence, a hair spiral which acts as a frozen tableau of that spiralling motion of vertigo contained in all doubling, of the vertiginous movement into the figure of the Other. In loving Madeleine, Scottie simultaneously loves her desire to be Other, and her apparent desire to die. But through her he also loves a projected version of his own desire to be Other and to die. In loving her, he wishes to be her. In loving her, he loves himself. The feminization of self through doubling, upon which he takes revenge at the end, fuses the male and female polarities the film sets up. Scottie and Judy can only love each other by sharing the same double, so that the masquerade becomes indefinite and can be ended, as it is, only by death.

Although it is a vital feature of film's reflexive being, the power of the gaze is not inimical to the realist image. If Antonioni proves this in one way, then Eric Rohmer proves it in another. If observation is often the key to the real, what is seen and what is missed can still assume metaphysical proportions. For Rohmer, to observe is to try to be sure of what one does not know, or to find out what is secluded from view. It can also be to pry and interfere, to make the act of perceiving one's adversary at close quarters an intervention in the adversary's destiny, especially when the adversary is a 'friend'. Thus Rohmer's significant achievement goes far beyond what he and others have said about his own work. It is to *naturalize* the power of the gaze. As a *Cahiers du Cinéma* critic who proved to be a Catholic interpreter, with Chabrol, of a Catholic Hitchcock, we should not be at all surprised. What starts out with great subtlety in the *Moral Tales* is made more explicit and humorous in the *Comedies and Proverbs*.

In *Ma nuit chez Maud* (1969) Rohmer contrasts the sensuous and open presence of Maud in her apartment with the fleeting appearances of the elusive Françoise. For his sanctimonious, yet unnamed Catholic hero (Jean-Louis Trintignant), Françoise seems to vindicate a Pascalian wager on the impossible, the virtuous attractive Catholic woman whom he loves and resolves to make his wife. But the real wager is on something else he cannot know, the repetition of a love triangle in which he blindly takes over one of the parts. Shot in Clermont-Ferrand in winter, Rohmer's monochrome feature film is also his *Vertigo*. While James Stewart follows the wraith-like Kim Novak to the church whose haunting graveyard contains the tomb of Carlotta Valdes,

Trintignant first spies Marie-Christine Barrault worshipping at morning Mass. Unlike Hitchcock's sleep-walking Madeleine, she is a real presence and returns the male gaze with cryptic yet equal force. Yet Rohmer takes the gaze out of melodrama altogether. Soundtrack strings are replaced by direct sound. The fanatic gaze is replaced by the subdued glance and the ambiguous look. While Stewart follows Novak's sleek Jaguar *down* the steep slopes of San Francisco, Trintignant tracks his blonde object of desire *up* the steep winding streets of Clermont-Ferrand, his car grinding slowly after her modest moped. The banality of driving up a winding narrow street after a local girl on a moped undercuts the melodrama of Hitchcock's oneiric chase, and is suitably captured in a series of bumpy, eye-level, back-seat shots. There are no reaction close-ups of Rohmer's pursuing hero to match the intensity of Stewart's stalking gaze. Yet, like Stewart, Trintignant loses his prey in the city streets, and like *Vertigo* this is a film of repetition. At the end we sense that Maud's absent husband has previously had an affair with Françoise, the devout student, and in retrospect we realize that Trintignant has forsaken Maud for the same girl, treading unwittingly in the footsteps of the ex-husband who becomes, therefore, the absent presence of the film. Embedded in the 'virtue' of Françoise is carnal knowledge of the unfaithful spouse.

The dark-haired Maud played by Françoise Fabian is a very material presence in the monochrome setting of her modern apartment. Divorced mother, hedonist and paediatrician, an agnostic woman with a sense of humour instead of a sense of sin, she has no illusions about love, religion or marriage. As spectators we share the embarrassed hero's ambiguous 'night' with Maud. Rohmer's naturalizing of talk and observation places us literally 'there' in the room. We see his hero crawl from the armchair on to the bed beside her as if he were no more than inches away from us, and early next morning we also watch him start to accept and then refuse her sexual advances, indecisive to the end. But glimpsing Françoise the next day there is no such indecision. He rushes coatless out of the café into the freezing cold to chase her moped as it speeds up the street to the church. The motion is amusing but, in its own way, as desperate as that of Scottie Ferguson. Unlike Scottie, Rohmer's hero is choosing between two very different women, not between two different versions of the same woman. Here his hypocrisy gets the reward it deserves. At one level her confession of an affair with an unnamed married man disqualifies her from his religious ideal. But having already made his 'choice' he accepts the betrayal of his absurd principles by falsely telling Françoise he has slept with Maud. He does not pursue her bleak hillside confession in the snow which he senses is little more than a half-truth.

Indeed she never tells him her lover's identity and he will not guess it until the end of the film, five years later during a chance meeting with Maud while on holiday. An unexpected voice-over only hints at the truth. What clinches it, however, is a repetition of the fearful look of the accompanying Françoise. Earlier Maud's ex-lover, Vidal, has recognized Françoise in the street as Trintignant introduces her. Maud's sea-shore look echoes the earlier look of recognition by Vidal. In returning the look, first to Vidal, then five years later to Maud, the expression of Françoise is identical. It is the fearful and haunted look of a woman desperate that no knowledge is imparted. Thus the double-look, as shot and reaction shot 'confirms' our suspicion of the insidious ways of chance. The Pascalian wager which had appeared to be on the chance meeting of the hero with his blonde of Catholic virtue is something less moral and much more sinister. It is the chance repetition of Maud's betrayal by her husband, the substitution of Trintignant as unwitting surrogate for the absent husband, who goes the same route so that Maud is betrayed twice over. Contained in this framework of repetition is yet another repetition, a mirroring of the look which echoes the previous look and the look which is yet to come. Thus Rohmer's camera becomes a 'natural' observer of the compulsion to repeat.

This comes at mid-point in the narrative. The hero 'repeats' his 'night with Maud' by engineering a night with Françoise which is just as ambiguous. Unconvincingly 'marooned' by a snowstorm in Françoise's student apartment, he sleeps in a separate room. When, cigarette in hand, he returns to her room to borrow matches, she makes no explicit effort to seduce him as Maud has done. But she still allows him to enter the room while in bed. Her silent look as she reads her bedtime book also suggests she might be prepared to allow him to share her bed. Safe in that secret knowledge, he is safe also in the knowledge of her virtue which consists in her making no obvious sign of her readiness. He can thus happily return to his room knowing that seduction is not necessary. For Rohmer, the hypocrisy which lies at the heart of bourgeois virtue is that of never making desire explicit. Maud's directness is not only a sensual but also a moral threat. Her moral strength contrasts with the weakness of Judy Barton. She is a woman apart, who cannot be made over into anything she is not. In that sense she is a constant threat to male power. The hero thus abandons her in order to 'make over' the devout Françoise as his virtuous future wife. Instead of the bonding of love and death in the relationship of Scottie and Madeleine, we have an ambiguous affirmation of the marital life to come. The wide-eyed couple stared devoutly at the priest at Mass, as he speaks with sombre conviction of the necessary human search for Grace.

In *Le Genou de Claire* (1970) Rohmer goes further in his dissection of the look. His plot subtly echoes the planned corruption of innocence in Laclos's *Les Liaisons dangereuses* on a more spiritual plane. At the same time, it is a fable worthy of Rousseau which turns into a Quixotic tale.[10] It starts with an air of pastoral innocence but the mischievous pact between Aurora, a novelist, and Jérome (Jean-Claude Brialy), a diplomat and old friend on holiday in Annecy, becomes a tale within a tale in which Aurora manipulates Jérome like a Quixotic character in one of her novels, nudging him as a myopic spoiler into the arena of mock-seduction and teenage romance. Thus Jérome is attracted in turn to Laura, the daughter of Aurora's friend and then to her half-sister, Claire, both of whom are happy with their steady boy friends. Rohmer plays on the metaphorical 'groping' of his middle-aged voyeur in two ways. Prompted by the clinical Aurora, his assessor and 'creator', Jérome watches the two girls obsessively but is spiritually blind to the vast difference of age between himself and them. Meanwhile his flirtatious reporting back to Aurora, in which his knowledge of their vulnerability holds the illusion of power, is merely the pleasure of sophisticated gossip masquerading as fate. Both 'gropings' in fact are surrogate pleasures where in each case the wish for sexual possession, never much more than an idle fancy, is in any case denied. Jérome's gaze of surveillance is that of a man groping in the dark.

The cinematography of Nestor Almendros emphasized this in a remarkable way.[11] Almendros filmed the Haute Savoie as a Gauguinesque setting of pure colours without texture, a place of objects which are two-dimensional, bright surfaces, a rich green landscape lit to suggest brilliance without jealous watching, of the limits to the power of the gaze. For despite his conscious interfering, Jérome is finally powerless to alter the course of events except as a voyeur. Through binoculars he sees Claire's boyfriend in town embracing another girl. As a malicious gossip, he tells Claire the bad news. As a jaded hedonist masquerading as a friend he comforts the girl he has upset by caressing her knee. His obsession with Claire's knee is a metaphor for the limit of his desire. It is also the fetish of his gaze. When he finally touches it at the end, the metaphor of groping becomes literal. He is no longer blind, but in an act of Freudian displacement Jérome touches only the part of her body he is allowed to see. Only the element of surprise his malice creates and his gesture of comfort give him the chance of doing so. The mimetic image naturalizes the fetish of the voyeur's gaze, which is finally rewarded by the briefest of caresses.

In *Comedies and Proverbs* it is often by contrast the young who watch the old, the innocents who observe the experienced. In *The Aviator's Wife*, François, a Paris law student moonlighting as a postman, dolefully tails the movements of his older girlfriend's real boyfriend, a married aviator who has recently jilted her. He is joined by a fifteen-year-old schoolgirl, Lucie, who appears to have got off the seame bus by chance to study in the park. For her amusement she watches Bernard watching the aviator with an unknown woman and clumsily pretending not to. If the older couple are furtive in their movements, Bernard is even more furtive about his watching until the girl, excited by the game, joins in, enlisting a Japanese-American couple to take her photograph in the hope that the aviator and his companion will appear in the background. The amusing and amused younger couple watch the older couple disappear into an apartment but cannot decide whether the woman is the aviator's sister or his wife, even though she may well be yet another girlfriend. Later it seems likely, though one is never sure, that she is yet another girlfriend. It also becomes obvious to Bernard at the very end that Lucie, whom he has begun to adore but who then disappears, is the girlfriend of his best friend in the post office. Hence she must have known who Bernard was when she 'accidentally' met him. In the end, nothing has been as it seemed but truth is still elusive. The act of watching becomes a tiresome and embarrassing way of suspecting the worst without ever being able to verify it.

In Rohmer's miniature masterpiece of the 1980s, *Pauline at the Beach* (1982), he extends the simple curiosity of adolescents towards the sexual behaviour of their elders in more complex ways. As well as the naturalistic tie between watching and social embarrassment. Rohmer explores here the ambiguous nature of idle curiosity. Waking one morning at the holiday villa she shares with Marion, her older cousin, Pauline casually seeks out her companion in the garden when she does not appear for breakfast. Glancing through a bedroom window she sees Marion in bed with Henri, the ethnologist they have both met the previous day. The revealing look through the window is repeated later when Pierre, Marion's jilted admirer, sees in passing the flower-girl naked in Henri's bedroom in his villa. Each look is a chance look of watchers 'happening by'. But each reveals things they might wish to know. The naked look here is mirrored in the deflected look of Sylvain, Pauline's teenage boyfriend, as Henri and the flower-girl go off to bed together. Pressed into going swimming with the couple and then returning to the villa, he never takes his eyes off the television set as they begin their lustful ascent of the stairs. Yet he remains in the house when he has no need to, and over-reacts swiftly when Marion returns early from Mont-Saint-Michel. Without appearing to look or observe, he is cast in the role of the look-out, and then allows himself to be cast as the lover when Marion sees the silhouette of the flower-girl through the frosted door of the bathroom. Thus in the comedy of errors which ensues the young win a Pyrrhic victory. While their freshness triumphs over the hypocrisy of their elders, both Pauline and Sylvain are forced to be accomplices in the sexual power-games of adults and thus 'grow up'.

At the same time Rohmer retains the corruption motif of *Le Genou de Claire*. Marion tries to persuade the virgin Pauline to go out with Pierre, her jilted ex-lover, and to persuade Pierre to seduce Pauline. Pierre, as a frustrated romantic, tails Pauline to ruin her innocent teenage romance. Henri ropes in Sylvain to witness his own promiscuity and crass two-timing of Marion. Later, after the fight between Pierre and Sylvain over Pauline, he persuades Pauline by acting like a surrogate caring father to stay the night at his own villa. In the morning however, before she wakes, he makes a botched, farcical attempt to seduce her, to assert not only the power of the body over the power of the gaze but the connection between them, to reaffirm that the gaze must end in seduction. In this Renoiresque comedy of errors in which moods and allegiances shift with casual rapidity, Rohmer explores not only the volatility and vanity of feeling but the act of watching as a natural attitude. The psychopathology of every-day life, in all its embarrassed detail, is truly comic. The watchful gaze in his cinema is not an extreme pathology or a distorting mirror. It is an eye-level glance, a muted expression which barely forms on the face. It is the casual flipping through a magazine by the seated Pauline in the left background of the frame, and her occasional glance up as Marion and Henri, in right fore-ground, begin to talk and flirt with obvious intent. Action and reaction are contained in the same still frame. The realism of the image fuses with the metaphysics of the gaze, the luminosity of Bazin's dream with the lingering traces of Hitchcock's nightmare.

The gaze is a weapon of limited power which often mimics the tired saying that looks can kill. As far as modern film is concerned, the metaphor has its origins in technology. Here the history of the camera is inseparable in the twentieth century from the history of war. For the camera has been developed as an instrument of military history and film has been one of the spoils of war. As Wollen reminds us, the real breakthroughs in film technology have been chemical and optical rather than mechanical.[12] The universalization of film as an instrument of recording came about at the end of the Second World War through the captured booty of the Allies in Germany, through the acquisition of magnetic tape, of reflex focusing, the hand-held Arriflex camera and the new colour stock, Agfacolor developed by IG Farben. But this merely pointed to the accelerated develop-ment of film through war. Thus the new competitive screen formats of Hollywood colour in the 1950s had their basis in military technology. The special sound-effects of the short-lived Cinerama derived from aerial gunnery simulation while Cinema-scope's successful wide-screen format and anamorphic ratios had their origin in tank gun sighting periscopes. Over twenty years later the techniques of a pilot-training system contributed to the renaissance of science-fiction movies in Hollywood. The resulting Dykstraflex camera was specially made for *Star Wars*, in which complex travelling movements were computer-controlled and no longer needed direct human guidance. Meanwhile, technical innovators in American cinema such as Stanley Kubrick and Francis Coppola began to programme their film recording like military planners through the aid of computers.

Recently, however, Virilio has gone beyond these elements of contingent relationship to suggest that war in our century has determined the very logistics of perception in the cinema, in fact in all audio-visual technologies as they exist today. The claim is huge, and perhaps overstated, but the crucial linkage at the level of perception is undeniable, right the way from the telescopic sight of the ordinary rifle to the high-definition cameras of spy satellites in space. The weapon–camera is an *'observation machine'*.[13] In war it records the terrain of the enemy as an abstract modernist landscape whose baffling fragments must be reconstituted through its negatives by military intelligence into an organic image, a picture of the 'whole' beyond the range and vision of the human eye. Moreover contemporary warfare has made huge qualitative jumps in harnessing the weapons of perception. The sightless firing of trench warfare in 1914 was a blindness of the pre-electronic age. It has been replaced by electronic combat in which weapons have eyes – video-cameras, infra-red or laser guidance systems. The audio-visual information they generate – vast, rapid, simultaneous – turns its human controllers on the ground and in the air into harassed interpreters. 'The fusion is complete, the confusion perfect' Virilio claims, 'Nothing now distinguishes the functions of the weapon and the eye. The projectile's image and the image's projectile form a single composite'.[14]

Modern battlegrounds from the vast aerial and searchlight battles of Berlin onwards have themselves become vast cinematic spectacles by which the Nuremberg Rally and Leni Riefenstahl's filming of it pale in comparison. Such vast explosions of sound and light and destruction raised almost insuperable problems for cinematic representation. The Hollywood response was to film patriotic war movies as historical epics in modern dress. When Coppola tried to confront the issue aesthetically in *Apocalypse Now* with huge production values to match his daunting theme, the result was eventually a grandiose disaster. We can see the fatal turning-point in the set-piece sequence which takes place two-thirds of the way through after Martin Sheen's journey upriver to find Kurtz. The filming of a nocturnal battle on the Cambodian border is a vast Expressionist firework display whose hallucinatory nature is affirmed through the drugged state of the front-line soldiers Sheen and his boat-crew discover. All this is a bold attempt to fuse subjective and objective point-of-view and suggest that war is the nightmare we have of it, that the two things, war and nightmare, are identical. Hallucinatory, dream-like, unreal, modern war is a narcotic experience and Vietnam is the first American drugs war in which the stimulant is a weapon of 'vision' as much as the gun is a weapon of destruction. Yet Coppola has a real dilemma. He wants to film through Expressionist modes of distortion a combat which in itself contained all the distorted modes of Expressionism. It was as if his style had been rendered superfluous by what it confronted. The distortion of distortion thus appears as self-indulgence, as over-emphasis. The sudden narrative turn in the film from Wellesian parodic-real to pastiche Expressionist nightmare collapses under the weight of its vaulting ambition and ends in the expensive shambles of filming three different endings, all of them apocalyptic and all of them arbitrary.[15] But ironically the nature of war itself is partly to blame. For Coppola, as he admitted, relived in the making of his war-movie in the Philippines the whole logistical nightmare, including the logistics of perception, which the American army had lived through in Vietnam.[16] The impossibility of the war had become, ten years later, the impossibility of filming it.

The notion that neo-moderns turn the gaze into a weapon is now less fanciful. For we now know that war technology has turned the weapon into a gaze. Coppola's film is at the extreme end of a spectrum. It starts as Wellesian parody but concludes as the distorted gaze of the hot apocalypse which tries to emulate its impossible subject. As the last great war movie, it immediately gives way to science fiction and slasher horror movies as Hollywood's new fantasy genres of hi-tech apocalypse. In Europe the cool apocalypse of the durational film has by this time also begun to vanish, but its parallel aesthetic tracking of the military observation machine until the end of the Vietnam war suggests the realms of the Freudian uncanny. Recent political events provide us with more direct examples of the gaze-as-weapon, in this case, an uncanny parallel to *Rear Window*'s 'turning back of the gaze'. The 1989 revolutions in central Europe have offered the spectre of former dissidents in new governments charged with the task of surveillance of the former secret police who were their tormentors under so-called lustration laws. We now know that the Stasi in the former German Democratic Republic and the STD in Czechoslovakia oversaw some the most thorough-going and sophisticated forms of surveillance over domestic populations in the world. These professional totalitarian watchers are now being closely watched themselves. In the denunciation of 'spies', 'informers' and 'collaborators' through the lustration process, the culture of surveillance perpetuates itself.

In the Western liberal democracies it would be naive to deny the existence of similar forms of surveillance to those of the communist police state. Technically speaking, surveillance must be justified by the law. Yet *de facto* it still remains, as a sophisti-cated form of electronic data-gathering, an indispensable element in our culture. It gets around the law where it can, veiled in a shroud of secrecy. Hence the paranoia of American film noir has had two great periods, that of the Macarthyite era and that of the Vietnam era culminating in Watergate. This is not simply because abuses in the power of watching were either alluded to allegorically or in the later case openly unmasked. Rather, their revelation in some form or other seemed at best partial, incom-plete. We sense for the first time what we still do not know. The paranoia of film noir suggests that, however much we come to know, we can never rid ourselves of the feeling there is more to know, because more has been withheld.

In a way the American cinema personalizes the politics of paranoia. On the wide screen the gaze has become personalized and hence to some extent pacified. For the cinematic form of the gaze is a form of pacification in which mystery, fear and mistrust are foregrounded while only in the background does there lie terror, death and destruction. What we have, then, is a partial pacification of the weapon-gaze in the ordered world of civil society, a world in which, none the less, for a privileged bour-geoisie, *surveillance is still destiny*. In *Hiroshima, mon amour* Resnais alluded to the vast blinding flash of the atomic explosion which at the moment of impact imprinted the shadows of its Japanese victims on the surviving fragments of wall which sur-rounded them. It is something any film could scarcely reconstruct within any veracity. Yet in his next film *Last Year at Marienbad*, the subliminal flash of the apocalyptic moment is echoed in a totally different context. It is the climactic shot of erotic seduction as Delphine Seyrig in the closed after-life of her baroque hotel is forced to imagine the bedroom of previous seduction by X, her would-be seducer, forced by him, that is, to share the instant of his burning vision of desire as already-having-been. The seducer's gaze succeeds in imprinting its fantasy upon his victim, since the victim submits by sharing the fantasy behind the gaze. The imaginary instant is a flare of radiant light, of a blinding whiteness in which her white dress, the white bedspread, her white face and the white windows of the room-image are all one uniform colour. As the shadows of atomic victims are imprinted on the walls of Hiroshima, so, it seems, the blinding image of the moment preceding seduction becomes a subliminal flash imprinted in the mind of the spectator, who shares the point-of-view of the seducer's victim. If it is imposed on her, perhaps, as the imaginary moment of a previous life in which she has submitted to the seducer's wish, it is equally the moment of a previous 'life' in which she is about to die.

Yet in *Marienbad* no one does die. Like *The Silence* or *L'eclisse* we have apocalypse without death. Instead Eros is a death which constantly repeats itself, and the erotic gaze is a weapon of spiritual destruction which Delphine Seyrig seeks in vain to evade. The gaze pacified in the bourgeois world is still destructive, but it is a continuation of war by other means. It is the expression of a will-to-power which has become confused, atrophied, indecisive. Here we must remember that Nietzsche never saw the will-to-power as a blind exercise of force[17]. If anything, that was its lower form. Its higher form, he insisted, was spiritual domination as a form of active creating. In cinema the hope of the watcher is to see the gaze transfigure the image, but the hope remains an illusion. But in the cinema of Resnais, Rohmer or Antonioni the will-to-power of the gaze is largely negative and reactive, a source of malaise. Confusion, atrophy, indecision are the sickness of the culture of the day. At the same time the gaze-as-creative-weapon is also *commodified*. Its purveyors are not usually the dominating figures of the elite but its professional servants who exercise it with a freedom which is deceptive. The detective, the telejournalist, the writer, the photographer, the architect, the surveillance expert, the film-maker – all inhabit commodified ways of seeing the world in which the apparent autonomy of their quest and the show of their skill is at odds with wider and often imperceptible structures of constraint. Thus the world of the rich and its various elites is the backdrop, the starting-point of the compromised quest of those by whom they are ideologically served.

Often the figures who populate that world of the elite are shadowy or invisible. But the *telos* of the 'free' investigator, for whom the gaze is a desultory weapon, becomes compromised by a more deterministic universe. The world of power may have a human face. But it still remains a world of shadow. In Welles the world of corrupt privilege is grotesquely tragicomic. In Resnais or Antonioni it is anonymous. In Wellesian film noir, Rita Hayworth is commodified by the rich as an object of female beauty upon which to gaze and desire. But Welles himself as Mike O'Hara, who gazes after and desires her, is equally commodified by the same world. He is the naive proletarian sailor recruited by the rich as a reluctant servant, a brainless confidante, a surrogate stud. His bemused progress is as much a subject for scrutiny as Hayworth's inscrutable languour. In *L'avventura*, with its seeming suspension of all *telos*, we appear to reach the extreme limit of indeterminacy. But the indecisive Sandro, wandering over the open volcanic landscape of a Sicilian island in search of Anna, his disappearing fiancée, is still a puppet, the willing architect of soulless modern buildings at the behest of unseen interests. While his search of the island allows us to forget that, his return to civilization once more reminds us of it. As the search for Anna evaporates, his gaze upon the world is peremptory, baffled by the architectural beauty of a Sicilian townscape he cannot hope to emulate but which he could potentially destroy.

The gaze active and creative, the gaze negative and reactive. In other words the gaze as creative power, the gaze pacified and commodified. Enhancement of the image, displacement of the image. The double contradiction spurs artistic synergy. The new uses of technology provide a new style, while the growing complexities of bourgeois life provide a new thematics. Together style and theme fuse into a new form, a new image, a new way of seeing. That complex world is one of prosperity and commodity, consumerism and sexual malaise, boredom and distant apocalypse. But it has no obvious grammar of signs. The neo-modern camera tries to decipher the indecipherable but actually deciphers nothing. As it moves closer to its subject, its subject evaporates. As it moves away its contours blur. Technique enhances the image. But thereby the image is displaced. The gaze is a weapon, but one no longer moral or villainous. It is beyond good and evil. It is a cryptic sign of the fight for spiritual domination which masquerades, from time to time, as the truth. Yet it is also an expression of the most powerful feeling, sign at times of the ineffable, of the anguish which informs all emotions and leaps the fragile boundaries between them. There, there is no truth. The sonic and the optical combined become, uncannily, the unspeakable. The image reaches a point beyond interpretation. The weapon-gaze of the camera, as we have stressed, is equally the gaze of the director, of any protagonist and any spectator. As such it is a shared experience of the depth of seeing which inadvertently uncovers the shallowness of the gaze, of its penetration through to the surface of the world. We know too that if it is the weapon of all of them, it can also turn out to be a weapon which can be turned against anyone who uses it. In the nature of the medium it can always be turned around, as Jack Nicholson discovers to his cost in *The Passenger* when the African subject of his 'in-depth' interview physically grabs the camera and points it back around at his invisible questioner. Nicholson is momentarily exposed, and his fear is ours.

A final example of the power of the absent gaze suggests itself in Orson Welles's version of the most powerful fable of surveillance written in this century, *The Trial*. The men who arrest Joseph K. are the visible emanation of an invisible power, the Law, which seems to observe him invisibly. Everywhere he acts as if he is watched but it seems he is watched by no one. Thus as K. moves closer to the law courts and the Law to try and uncover its fearful truth, we see no one furtively on his trail as we might in a common spy thriller. Welles makes his vain search for the Law which is persecuting him also a labyrinthine flight from the Law in which there are no pursuers except for the small girls who watch him through the bars of Titorelli's studio. The fast tracking images of search and flight are in a limbo. There are only lackeys of the Law, no masters who trail him. He thus flees from an abstraction and ends up running at the end into the arms of its concrete exemplars. Welles, forty years on, illustrates the systematic forms of surveillance-as-persecution which Kafka endowed with a prophetic dream logic. We might assign these complacently to the coming of the Stalinist police-state in central Europe. But Welles does not allow us this easy option. Joseph K. is a son of the bourgeoisie and shares complicity in his own damnation. Even as he flees it he knows power through the unseen gaze.

For Kafka, the unseen gaze was, as Citati points out, a total gaze, the gaze of the indestructible Being who cannot be named, the gaze of the transcendent God from which Joseph K. can never escape[18]. Welles's adaptation of Kafka's text reveals one crucial feature of the modern cinema. Its empowerment of the gaze takes place after the death of God in European philosophy. In Welles's film the invisible gaze cast upon K. becomes secular and totalitarian. Yet the trace of that ubiquitous gaze lingers on in the cinematic apparatus as a supra-human power. If the cinematic gaze can appear all-powerful and all-knowing it is for one very good reason. Transcendence, the sacred, the indestructible never finally die in the modern imagination. The camera becomes a replica of the divine gaze but is no longer transcendent and the human struggle for the gaze takes its place in the absence of the sacred. It operates, to use Bergman's phrase, amidst 'God's silence'. If neo-realism finds small miracles and a sense of wonder in its everyday objects, unacknowledged forms, perhaps, of an oblique divine compassion, the neo-modern camera is the opposite. It punishes the world with the severity of its gaze and it is no longer the gaze of a Being but the gaze of an instrument, brute, technical, factitious, without comforting transcendence.

5

The Absent Image and the Unreal Object

In his breathtaking essay on 'the imaginary', Sartre has set up one of the great challenges for the modern cinema – how to capture that which is absent from human perception.[1] If, as we suggested, the camera is somehow an analogue of the eye as a medium of perception, the innovating film-maker must also capture what is not there, what is out-of-frame, what exists beyond the perceptual horizon at any given moment. Hence it must go further than the precepts of Bazin and phenomenology in its representation of the present, the perceptual field and the Gestalt of experience. The planned dislocations of montage, in that sense, are a great liberating force. At the same time montage is a process and not a solution. The radical contiguity of presence and absence, being and nothingness, makes the relationship between images problematic, certainly more fluid than the technical abruptness of the cut allows for. There is always something *present* in existence which is out-of-frame, which for Sartre can be absent from perception but present in the imagination. Here the potential of the imaginary is never purely oneiric. The cinema cannot, as Metz almost but never quite suggests, be reduced to a technical field which objectifies the dream-work of its spectators.[2] The projected screen image and the cut are not merely analogues of condensation or displacement in the dream-work. They make the relationship of past and present, here and there, presence and absence a constant puzzle of all experience which is never resolved. The modern cinema 'exists' therefore somewhere between the respective theoretic and topographical spaces designated for it by Bazin and Metz. Its force-field oscillates between the immediacy of the image and an ensemble of disparate images which are 'not there', which the perceptual field cannot account for. In this instance Sartre, never the most 'visual' of philosophers, provides us, parardoxically, with an ontology for the displacement of the image in the modern cinema.

In everyday experience we can imagine things we do not see, hear, smell or touch. We imagine both imaginary objects and real objects in their absence, that is to say, real objects which the imagination evokes but simultaneously renders unreal. The absent object is both near and far, absent in space or in time or both. We can imagine what our friend is doing now in another town – Sartre's famous example of Pierre in Berlin – what he did yesterday, what he might do tomorrow. If she suddenly walks into the room, we can still continue imagining what she did or what she might do when we are not present. We can thus superimpose the unreal object of imagination upon the real object of perception, or in Sartre's terms displace it, the real by the unreal. For Sartre the imagining of the absent object as an object of possible desire is not the return of the repressed but a projecting of consciousness on to the unreal object. On this reckoning Hitchcockian obsession is not the involuntary neurosis of past trauma, not the Freudian return of the repressed, but willed compensation for the emptiness of present experience. It is an intentional haunting which negates the grounds for perceiving the real which is before us. Here nothingness intercedes between consciousness and its object. The void of the subject's present world is filled with absent images. For Sartre such images become 'reborn sensations'.[3]

Technically speaking modern film goes further than consciousness. It makes clear that presence and absence, the real and the imaginary co-exist within the cinematic frame. In effect, there is no absolute boundary between the real and the imaginary. In *Blow-Up* and *The Conversation* the vital meetings are seen but not heard by both onlooker and viewer. In *Rear Window* and *Touch of Evil*, by contrast, the hero hears the villain without seeing him in the narrative moment which precedes the film's climax. Yet in each case what is *not* heard or seen will be imagined by the hero to give sentient force to what *is* seen or heard. Still, despite this lack of a clear boundary the shift from the real to the imaginary is tangible, a form of apprehension akin to a Kierkegaardian anguish at the apprehension of nothingness.[4] In his secular reformulation of Kierkegaardian Angst Sartre too goes far beyond the pleasure principle. What can imagined as something to be desired is all the more painful for not being there, and is often desired because it is not there.

In general the imaginative leap of consciousness which tries to render partial experience more complete is, in Sartrean terms, an encounter with the void, an engagement with the nothingness which separates the real from the imaginary. The image is an unreal object which negates the real. For Sartre the 'imaginative act is at once *constitutive, isolating* and *annihilating*'.[5] It annihilates the present, as both space and time, in order to constitute its own presentness to the mind. In this context the modern film tends to the reflexive, at times to be self-conscious, in its technical use of the displacement of the image. In film any image is immediate whether it involves consciousness of the real-as-present for the perceiving subject or is an absent image posited by the imagination. This ontic equality of images, of real and unreal objects alike, mimics consciousness but at the same time subverts it, making the imaginary seem perceptual when it recasts the imaginary as immediate image and at times, with oneiric or surreal effects, doing the opposite, that is to say, making the perceptual seem imaginary through the instabilities of seeing. It thus profoundly acknowledges the Sartrean distinction and yet confounds it. The imaginary is clearly not the real, yet in filmic terms can be just as immediate as the real. Modern film plays endlessly and in different ways on this ambiguity. It knows the immediate image is questionable. It also knows the real is haunted by the imaginary.

It now becomes clear why the imaginary as a narrative element in film should be more problematic than in fiction. Merleau-Ponty, as we have seen, noted that film language was one of gesture and behaviour which did not lend itself easily to the interior mind-set or subjective point-of-view of the novel.[6] Despite the hard-boiled conventions of film noir, there is no equivalent of the Proustian narrator, that is to say, of a figure who dominates a movie discursively through reflective voice-over and yet iconically through immediate presence. The two most literary movies of the French New Wave, *Marienbad* and

Julies et Jim have unseeen narrators and an elegant abundance of dislocated images. To film thought, as Fellini's *8½* shows us, is to dissolve the boundaries of the perceived and the imagined. In modern film both the nature of the image and the composition of images break down Sartre's distinction between the imagined that is strictly nowhere outside of thought and its empirical analogues, the recollected moment of the past or the anticipated moment of the immediate future. Without special signifying all images can appear in the same locale and in the same tense and Sartre's categories do not appear to hold. Yet the key analogue, that of the out-of-frame and the imaginary, remains vital and enduring. It is the key to the modern cinema.

To film thought without voice-over turns it into pure image, and usually the image is thought of as past, signified in Hollywood by the flashback/dissolve. To be sure, in *Providence* and *La Guerre est finie* Resnais experiments just as intensively with the flash forward, the imagining of the future life. Yet just as important in consciousness is the lateral movement beyond the perceptual horizon, the imagining of the present as *elsewhere*. Between past, present and future, however, temporality refuses absolute boundaries. In film editing the refusal becomes even more intense. In Bertolucci's *The Spider's Stratagem* it becomes impossible to separate past and present, the imaginary and the recollected, the father and son both played by the same actor. In any case, all filming of the real (perceptual) and the imaginary (reflective) as simultaneous is practically impossible. Parallel editing, between what characters perceive and what they imagine, can be clumsy and often works better, as Buñuel demonstrates, as a comic or macabre device which plays on the artifice of the cut. Even here the ontological state of the image – past? present? future? real? imagined? anticipated? recollected? – is always in question and there is no final answer.

The ontological state of the image is deconstructed even further by Bertolucci in *The Conformist*. The film appears to be told in flashback sequences from the point-of-view of Marcello Clerici, a bourgeois opportunist craving 'normality' who has joined the fascists and agreed to undertake the assassination of a dissident Italian professor in Paris. We go back in time from the car journey of Clerici and his henchman, Mangiello, travelling to the rendezvous for the killing – not yet explicit for the audience – to Clerici's initial implication in the plot, his marriage and his childhood. After he agrees to their assignment, he appears to have two hallucinatory visions of Anna Quadri, the professor's wife with whom he later becomes infatuated in Paris. On one reading, it is an uncanny foreshadowing of the woman he has yet to meet. But if the narrative is retrospective, it may be not oneiric but imaginary. Anna in both scenes is dressed as a prostitute, first lying across the desk of a fascist minister Clerici has to visit about the assignment, the visit then being shot from a different angle without Anna present. The second time is after he breaks his journey to Paris – and honeymoon – to visit a brothel in Ventemiglia. Here he sees Anna, black-haired, dressed in a fetishistic fascist costume seducing his henchman Mangiello who describes her as 'wild'. Both images are visual contradictions of the anti-fascist Anna whom Clerici has yet to meet, but they can also be seen as projections of his imaginary, inserting Anna into his memories of the past, giving her an alternative persona. The blonde victim gives way to the dark-haired and dominant femme fatale, the political dance-instructor to the whore. And the scene where Clerici first tells Anna he has seen her in Italy in another incarnation may *also* on this reading be a retrospective imaginary. Clerici's imagining of the past is thus wishful and retroactive but for the audience it is retroactive in a different way. Only after they have seen the real Anna Quadri (Dominique Sanda) can they be reminded of the earlier double appearance of her lookalike. Because of the structure of Bertolucci's narrative, her apparition can still be read in two ways, as Clerici's dream of his future or as his retroactive imagining of an alternative past.

Often modern film thrives on the imaginary without the use of the temporal cut in its out-of-frame space, what we can call its immediate beyond. It thrives, that is, on the analogue between the out-of-frame becoming screen space, the absent becoming present, and the imaginary becoming perceptual. After the apparent suicide of Madeleine Elster in *Vertigo* Scottie Ferguson seems to see in every blonde in San Francisco a compulsive likeness to Madeleine. Repeatedly Hitchcock uses the rhetoric of melodrama to show Madeleine's lookalikes in long shot or with canceaaled faces suddenly turn towards the camera or approach it to the point at which the resemblance is broken. In Hitchcock's terms they are dramatic revelations which turn expectancy to disappointment. In Sartre's terms, they are images annihilated by becoming real. Hitchcock's haunting reprise of the romantic image as pure artefact is also the point at which American film melodrama becomes genuinely modern. But his impulse here is essentially to frame and hold the empty moment of the imaginary, to render explicit the disenchantment of that romantic impulse which earlier, in *Notorious* or *North by Northwest*, he had erotically consecrated. Thus Madeleine's disappearance and reappearance as Judy Barton is one where the altered image is the real person and the original persona is nothing more than a manufactured imaginary. In Hitchcock the imaginary precedes the real which as the female object of male desire is made over again and again into the imaginary. The neurosis of the Freudian compulsion to repeat is fused with the perverse Sartrean will to fill the void of the present world with absent images, but then to go further still and to make the image flesh. Presence and absence become the dramatic poles of melodrama between which spiral the recurring and repeating climaxes of Scottie's vertigo. In *Being and Nothingness* vertigo is the quintessential image of anguish, the envisaging of the fear of one's own actions and where, destructively, they might end.[7] In Hitchcock's movie Scottie's fear of falling captured in the simultaneous back-track and zoom shot is also the fear of jumping, of hurtling through space at one's own volition in the direction of one's apprehensive gaze.

In Hitchcock the haunting disappearance of the woman is oneiric but in Antonioni's *L'avventura* it is infuriatingly natural. As one of Anna's rich Roman friends remarks, people disappear every day. But Anna is never seen again. There is no reprise. The 'adventure' of the search for her is not an adventure at all, for by the end of the picture she has not yet been found, not known either to have escaped from the island and started a new life or been kidnapped, committed suicide or drowned. The story has no resolution, yet Anna's absence dominates the second half of the film, even after she ceases to be an obsession in the minds of her pursuers. There are no flashbacks to re-establish her, no images of recollection, no displaced images of the imaginary which show us how she might exist in flight in the minds of her friends. For Antonioni the sequences of pursuit are purely perceptual. We see Sandro questioning the shepherd in his hut on the island, and later in Sicily haranguing the smugglers in police custody, or talking to the jaundiced married couple in the chemist's shop. We see the worn worried exhaustion on the faces of both Sandro and Claudia as the search draws them closer together. We never seem to move out of the perceptual field of the searchers, to see anything they themselves could not see. Yet Anna in her absence is always there.

Here Antonioni's narrative inverts the significance of the Bazinian 'image-fact' in the long take and shows us the deeper ambiguity of the shot which casts doubt not only on what is seen but on who sees it. If Anna is out of sight, out-of-frame, none the less particular ways of framing her absence reinsert her as the unreal object become active observer. At one point in the search on the volcanic island Claudia sees a distant figure disappear out of sight. She runs forward expectantly, believing it to be her close friend. Instead it is Giulia. Antonioni frames the sequence so that at first the figure in the distant shot is unrecognizable. He cuts to a medium close-up reaction shot of Claudia looking at the disappearing figure, and then back to the initial long shot of the rocks above the sea which appears at first to be Claudia's point-of-view. Yet Claudia runs from the distant right of the frame into her own point-of-view only to discover that the figure on the rocks is not Anna but Giulia. The case of mistaken identity, coupled with the ambiguous framing of the cut – it is typical Antonioni for a protagonist to be doubled by walking unexpectedly into her own point-of-view – offers us a different option. The long shot of Claudia 'discovering' Giulia in a mixture of disappointment and contempt could then be the point-of-view shot of the furtive Anna watching both her friends from afar. The possibility is heightened by the repeated use of long shots of the pursuers stumbling across the volcanic rock. At one level these are omniscient shots, God-like, almost pitiless, of a Roman bourgeoisie dwarfed by a forbidding and barren southern landscape after the smugness of their banal gossip on board the yacht. Without doubt this could be viewed ironically as the bitter-sweet revenge of nature upon culture or of God upon the complacent rich. At another level however, which does not contradict the first, they are very credible point-of-view shots of the object of the pursuit looking back at her pursuers.

It is not just that Anna has to be 'imagined' as elsewhere, though often nearby, in the hunt for her by her friends. For Sandro and Claudia, as their affair precipitated by her vanishing develops in her absence, it is as if their particular imaginings of her are haunted by guilt. Their unspoken fear is that of being watched together unseen, knowing they are betraying her trust. For they end up trying to bring back the woman who would now in all likelihood disown them. Thus they imagine without obvious signifiers the hidden gaze of the unreal object. As opposed to Hitchcock's rhetoric of fractured melodrama, Antonioni plays naturalistically on such oblique transfers of imagining. His camera constantly observes and he is in that sense the authentic successor to Rossellini, whose *Stromboli* the island setting of the film echoes. In another sense he is the opposite. He is casual, not urgent, unassuming, indeterminate. His *trompe l'œil* is not an apparition of the other, as in Hitchcock, but the incidental impression which appears to be more than a digression. Remarkably the process of doubling here is just as strong as it is in Hitchcock. What is altered is the context of resemblance which has no cues. Back in Messina one of the first things Sandro witnesses is the local adulation of 'Gloria Perkins', a glamorous woman who attracts a swarm of eager male Sicilians. The organic and spontaneous crowd of neo-realism which flocks to a major event is here reduced to a ramshackle collection of 'fans' attracted to something sexually theatrical, artificial, fabricated. The pointlessness of the fans' enthusiasm and the seeming pointlessness of the sequence in the diegesis – it seems to have nothing to do with Anna's disappearance – doubly distract the viewer's attention. They distract attention, that is to say, from the uncanny resemblance between 'Gloria Perkins', dark-haired and Italian in looks but Anglo-Saxon in name and accent – clearly dubbed – and the vanishing Anna. If melodrama means excessively drawing attention to the camera's object, the diegesis of the moderns does the opposite. It presents the uncanny as incidental and irrelevant. It 'conceals' the unfamiliar familiar by refusing to pass comment on it.

Gloria Perkins is thus the ironic reincarnation of Sandro's fiancée as sexual celebrity. Yet she is an impure image of celebrity, not a genuine 'reincarnation'. She may be a model as she claims, or, as the journalist claims, an expensive prostitute outrageously advertising her wares. If she is Anna come back from the dead, she is also an unreal object, an imaginary being made flesh whose beauty is later to seduce the inconstant Sandro. Yet at first the connection between the two women seems purely contingent – Sandro is looking for a journalist interested in Anna's disappearance who also happens to be covering the Gloria

Perkins 'incident'. The link with Anna is then made clearer by the changing role of Claudia. Claudia is also 'standing in' for Anna by having an affair with Sandro in her absence – a point made strongly first when she wears Anna's blouse on the island and later when she playfully exchanges wigs in front of a bedroom mirror with the dark-haired Patricia, to become a momentary facsimile of her missing friend. The connection is made even stronger, again with no obvious signposting, in the later scene at a town square in Noto where Claudia is waiting for Sandro. Claudia is tailed by a drove of local males whose numberes increase as she wanders slowly through the square. This is rendered by a remarkable shot. In a slow lateral tracking movement, the camera captures Claudia moving through the moving swarm of watching males in a tripled motion which echoes the adulation of Gloria, but this time without urgency, idle, improvised, yet equally as pointless. What Gloria has seen as a triumph, however, Claudia experiences as a threat. Her anxious gaze past the camera suggests her sense of the bright-eyed faces around her, as if the camera were a mirror confirming her anxiety. Antonioni demythologizes the collective male gaze twice over, dissecting it as the foil of sexual celebrity and then as visual assault, as a shiftless threat which evaporates through its own lethargy. The responses of the two women are exactly opposite: Gloria commodifies the gaze as a source of sexual capital, Claudia resists it as an unwarranted imposition.

The lingering presence of Anna as the imaginary is suggested in a different way by an entirely unexpected shot. In their fruitless search Sandro and Claudia drive through the countryside to a deserted fascist ghost town, a set of pre-war buildings depopulated and without perspective which seem stuck in the siesta of the Mezzogiorno, where no one from within all the shuttered windows answers Claudia's echoing call. The film plays on their edgy response to such emptiness as Claudia in long shot calls through the windows and Sandro, foregrounded, moves in and out of the frame in front of her. Yet, as they prepare to leave a place which makes them once more intruders in a barren landscape, there is a slow tracking shot from one of the sidestreets towards their departing car. It suggests the human movement of someone coming out of hiding to watch the exit of their frustrated pursuers. It is thus potentially a point-of-view shot of the imaginary Anna. The context of the movement, at the end of a strange sequence of *nature morte*, is strengthened by what follows – an abrupt cut to a close-up of the couple's joyful love-making. The cut from the dolly to the close-up suggests the forward movement of the imaginary Anna's concealed gaze, as if the momentum carried her through to the primal scene of betrayal.

The film oscillates between isolation and density. On the one hand there is the barren island, the rock, wind and sea, the deserted shepherd's hut, the ghost town, the scene of the lovers on the bleak hillside by the coast. On the other hand the lover's idyll is broken by a goods train steaming out of nowhere on to a concealed track only yards away from them. And in the realm of the public. Heidegger's *Das Man* is never far away. There is the subtle claustrophobia of the yacht and its bored rich couples, the idle clustering males of Noto and the self-consciously over-dressed guests in the reception rooms of the baroque hotel in Taormina. If isolation suspends situation, social density returns it with a vengeance. Involuntarily the couple must return to 'civilization', to their social milieu and class, where the anguish of indeterminacy is replaced by the unwritten rules of norm and obligation. Yet that return is fraught with uncertainty. 'For the movies as for modern psychology', Merleau-Ponty claimed, 'dizziness, grief, love and hate are ways of behaving'.[8] Here in their ritual courtship, passion and marriage proposal, all shadowed by the imaginary Anna, there has been no grammar of signs. Gesture and gaze are unsure of themselves, invented on the spur of the moment only to evaporate a moment later, no more certain than language itself.

If Claudia, to her great despair, feels herself standing in for Anna, becoming the new fiancée to replace the old, Sandro predictably breaks the pattern of repetition by betrayal, itself a repetition of his 'betrayal' of Anna. His unwitnessed night with Gloria Perkins, Claudia's discovery of them as dawn breaks, has an uncanny ring. The compulsive movement on to the 'next' woman is also a return to Anna's lookalike, whose pointed stare at Sandro in the hotel foyer the previous evening had suggested two contradictory things – the bold soliciting of a confident prostitute or a look of recognition, of *déjà vu*. Thus the real act of betrayal is also an imaginary revenge by the vanished woman who may be still be present 'somewhere' but remains unseen, unfound. And 'Gloria Perkins' becomes what Antonioni makes her, an unreal object become flesh-and-blood. From his point-of-view Sandro may be betraying Claudia with just 'any woman', but equally possibly he is returning to an imaginary Anna just as Scottie Ferguson forsakes the real Judy Barton to return to the imaginary Madeleine Elster.

In Hitchcock the rhetoric of melodrama imposes its single reading as a visceral response. In *L'avventura*, by contrast, the double signifying in which nothing is imposed at all is part of the anguish of the imaginary in which consciousness is inverted. For if the real is always shadowed by the imaginary, here the imaginary becomes objectified in the real. The imaginary Anna returns as another woman, but the other woman is physically real and different – though culturally unreal – and is not the same woman. She returns, that is, as a projection of the imaginary, but unlike Madeleine Elster is an autonomous image. The scene of betrayal-as-revenge echoes the initial scene of Anna's seduction of Sandro in his Rome apartment, where she deliberately and spitefully lets her best friend wait in the street below. Claudia's waiting is a kind of witnessing. Except that she does not witness it. She stands outside in the square looking up at Sandro's apartment, waiting for the couple to come down as Sandro, with other intent, goes to draw the curtains. The high-angle long shot in deep focus has her distant figure looking up at the adjacent window in the apartment, as if her gaze were slightly off-centre. If she knows, she knows without seeing. Framed in the next shot leaning in shadow against the doorway of the apartment block, she is clearly bored waiting; but also, perhaps, idly imagining what she cannot see, what must have already dawned in her mind as she glances upwards. The sequence cuts between the waiting and the love-making. The narrative tension comes not only in the cross-cutting but in not knowing how much of the imaginary is objectified in the real. How much of what we see, which is brief and fragmented, is as it actually happens? How much of it is as Claudia imagines it? We assume it is the former, but cannot put from our minds the possibility that it is also the latter.

This ambiguity of seeing is more ruthlessly explored in Bergman's *The Silence* which moves the imaginary towards the realm of the oneiric, the absent image towards the world of dream. Like *L'avventura*, *The Silence* enters another country and a different culture. It deracinates its protagonists. But this world is even more distinctly alien, a foreign country with a foreign language, across a political frontier. Its strangeness incites the imaginary more than the familiar. The train journey of the two sisters and the young son through a foreign land sets up both strangeness and threat. In their hot, airless train compartment the claustrophobia of kin is pitted against the ominous outside, the train stopping in the middle of the night in the middle of nowhere, rows of tanks and armed trucks gliding past malevolently on the wagons of good trains. The dialectic of inside and outside is maintained in the city where they stop, in hot stuffy hotel rooms, their windows looking out on to silent streets peopled by silent inhabitants, the only sound that of shrieking newspaper sellers. The sense of the East European police-state under the shadow of Stalin is implied but no more. The imminence of war, war as permanent threat, is also implied, never more sharply than when Johan, Anna's son, gazes out of the window at night to see a solitary tank roll up and lurch to a halt in the dark narrow street.

This, however, is the objective correlative for the self-imprisonment of Esther, the elder sister, ill with tuberculosis and probably dying. Bergman saw the film as a dream chronicle shadowed by God's silence and there are obvious connections between the journey form and the dramas of the later Strindberg. But the power-relation between the two sisters is also a relation of images. The jealous, possessive Esther bedridden in her hotel room, confining herself to the forlorn pleasures of cognac and masturbation, can only imagine what happens on the outside, what 'adventures' Anna and her son might undergo. The 'adventure' of Johan in the hotel with the performing dwarfs who dress him on the stage in girl's clothing and then the erotic 'adventure' of Anna at the cabaret where she watches a couple in the audience making violent love can be seen as dream sequences signified by the respective awakenings of Anna and Johan from sleep. Equally, though, they can be seen as the projected wishes and fears of Esther, who remains behind, and equally they can be seen as objectified, real, disconcerting encounters in a foreign city with people speaking in a foreign tongue – a language invented by Bergman and mixed with Estonian phrases. In *The Silence* then we have the co-existence in the image of the oneiric, the imaginary and the real. The point of view is doubly subjective, the dream journeys of Anna and of Johan placed against the projective imaginary of Esther, and singly objective, Bergman's clinical exploration of the uncanny in a foreign country. But there are no multiple narratives here. All are fused into the continuous sequence, the identical image.

The equivalence of all three in the ontology of the image is Bergman's great modern achievement. He refuses the kitsch temptation of assigning one priority over the other, or of trying dramatically to switch track in the middle of his narrative, which is such a taxing problem, for example, in the films of Nicholas Roeg. In this Bergman is aided by the crepuscular interiors of Sven Nykvist's monochrome camera which fuses the harsh clear surfaces of the neo-realist image with high-contrast lighting suggesting the projective dream-work of film noir. The perceptual sequence is integral to the doubling of the split self, which like *Persona* defines both the claustrophobia of the relationship of the two women and their otherness, making them both identical and poles apart. Here the Sartrean ontology of the imaginary, far from contradicting the doubling of the Freudian uncanny, fills it out. Like the compulsion to repeat, the absent image of the unreal object goes beyond the pleasure principle. The modern cinema unifies the great opposition of twentieth century writing which become fused through the power of the displaced image. It is, above all, unity through displacement. Absence is reinstated through the displacement of narrative convention and a reimagining of space-time relations. Yet the absent image is impossible without the universe of presencing, the unreal object impossible without the existence of the real.

The paradox of unity-through-displacement, the key to the cinematic modern, is illustrated most lucidly in *The Passenger*. Antonioni's movie, along with Wenders's *Kings of the Road*, seems to conclude the high modernity of the Western cinema. Both films do so through the power of spatial extension as a continuous image. But it is a visible unfolding always subject to invisible constraint. What seems as journey, as 'passenger' to be free, arbitrary, unlimited is a movement which constantly closes back on itself. It is a ride which runs out of space and returns towards its starting-point, always a point of fragile origin. Thus the central figures of both movies pick up passengers, one female, the other male, who appear to go along for the ride and thus share the episodic movement as a form of destiny. Images of space and time always merge through contradiction. Time is fragmented and linear while space is continuous and circular.

As a transglobal movie *The Passenger* is also transcontinental and transcultural – North Africa versus Europe, the desert versus the city, the Islamic contrasted with the Christian. In that respect Antonioni finally surpasses his origins in the national Italian cinema which was so central to film narratives of modernity. With *Blow-Up* and *Zabriskie Point* the Italian is no longer just the chronicler of modern Italy but the chronicler of the modern West and its global power. Above all he chronicles relations between subjects, countries, nations, cultures. Here there may be a starting point but there is no longer any centre. Thus we do not start in London, the capital of Locke's own country, the centre of his media operations, but go there with him only when he has assumed the identity of another man. We start by contrast in the North African desert which disorients and humiliates him and then return to the familiar which he cannot re-enter because he has traded name and passport with a dead man, and declared himself dead. This space–time displacement is extraordinary. We start elsewhere and return 'here' when being-here, *dasein*, has been annulled by the change of a name. Locke thus starts as himself in a strange place and returns as someone else to a familiar one. The space–time topography echoes that of *L'avventura* but takes it beyond nation and continent. The earlier film starts in Rome, moves abruptly to the Aeolian islands then back to the mainland at Messina, going south with Sandro and Claudia in a circular inland movement to Noto before returning north along the coast to Taormina. It is thus poised for the further return north to Rome. *The Passenger* inverts this into the circuitous return south, from London via Munich and Barcelona to Andalusia poised for the crossing to Morocco which Locke and the girl plan but of course never make. Robertson's cryptic diary appointments keep him going along the points on the circuit, which is at once therefore arbitrary and predetermined, the appointments of someone else – a gun-runner – coded as girls' names which he feels free to keep or leave but point him back inevitably in the direction from which he has come. To use the film's own language the new code turns back into an old code. He has shed his skin only to tread anew over known territory. The attempt which as a journalist he surrendered, to make contact with the guerrilla army, he succeeds in achieving by different means.

Antonioni's endeavour here is to capture the fluctuating speed of real time as experienced. But this experience of duration as a quest, a movement towards, is spatial, just as much as the movement through space is temporal, that is to say constantly shadowed by the 'pastness' of what it has left behind. Deleuze is right here to suggest that the Bergsonian 'time-image' of the modern cinema can often incorporate space as the distance time has already travelled, but wrong to see this as invariant and to relegate space to a subordinate role in the construction of the image.[9] Rather the modern should be characterized by a 'time–space' image of displacement in which, unlike the American cinema up to 1970, action can no longer resolve the problematics of situation by transforming it, or moving it, narratively speaking, into a new situation. Deleuze is profoundly accurate and highly ingenious in seeing the switch of the neo-moderns as a switch in motor-sensory perception of the image away from the American 'movement-image'. But his view of the modern as a pure 'time-image' which incorporates space is also profoundly Francocentric, a search for straight lineage from Bergson and Proust to Resnais and Robbe-Grillet.[10]

In Sartre and phenomenology, by contrast, we find a recognition of the spatiality of the image which can be linked to the Deleuzean paradigm. The out-of-frame, for example, as a cinematic instance of the imaginary, evokes the time–space image as a potential movement of the camera which shifts the new image onscreen unexpectedly. By altering space and time simultaneously it alters narrative conventions of their unity. By changing position, that is to say by the act of repositioning, it alters our experience of duration. This can be done with or without the cut, by tracking or panning, or by the movement of people and objects in and out of the frame. Thus the dynamics of repositioning displace the sureties of narrative. What is crucial for the time–space image here is its need to combine four elements which have no absolute internal boundaries, the real and the oneiric, the recollected and the imaginary. The present image and the absent image, the real object and the unreal object, are all, therefore, potentially present in the experience of viewing.

The Passenger's famous penultimate shot, which is seven minutes long and took eleven days to film, is a supreme example of the time–space image, where the movement through time brings into play the change in space but conversely the movement through space brings time into play as time past, time present and time future.[11] As we have seen, the slow dolly out through the bars of the hotel room window is a hypothetical gaze, the forward-moving 'as-if' of the motionless Locke still lying on his bed. It sees what he has no longer has the curiosity to look at, because Locke does not want to see what he already knows – that his past is literally catching up with him. Thus the African secret agents arrive by car to assassinate him while his estranged spouse arrives too late with the Spanish police to try to 'reclaim' him as the person he used to be. In the same movement of the camera which dollies forward, pans, quickens and turns 180 degrees, in the single quickening movement through space, time past becomes time present. The illusion of a complete break with the past and the claiming of a new persona is shattered. Instead Locke is confronted by the nemesis of both personas, that of reporter he has shed and that of gun-runner he has adopted. At the end they converge in the sequential double movement of the arriving Others, captured by the camera at a brief interval within the same shot so that the split self is provisionally healed at the moment of the body's destruction.

Out-of-frame space here is concerned with capturing not just what moves into frame but also with what moves out of it. The time–space image is a continuous fragment which provokes the imaginary not only by what it sees but by what it does not see. The camera captures the girl seeming to wander aimlessly across the courtyard and out of shot left then the agents' car coming into shot right, stopping and moving out of shot left. In the brief moment before the girl and the white agent re-enter the frame and argue, there is the chance of some initial sign between them the viewer does not see. We share at the moment the frustrations of Locke earlier in Africa, the experience of a partial knowledge which remains ambiguous and is never completed, where the compulsive quest for the reading of signs ends in their mis-reading, their incompleteness or their inscrutability.

Moreover, Locke's death itself occurs out of shot before the turning camera can catch up with it, so that its motion links it not to the assassins but to the point-of-view of the rescuers who arrive too late and rush into the room to witness the dead body. Where at the beginning time seems to catch up with space as the past surges back into the present, at the end of the shot it goes beyond it. It moves out of frame to become time future so that the camera must catch up through accelerating movement with what it has yet to discover, with a time that seems to race ahead of it. Here Antonioni makes offscreen space three-dimensional. The assassins not only move out of range of the camera by entering the hotel: they also move *behind* it. The gaze of the camera having moved out from the room in idle curiosity becomes briefly stranded in the courtyard and cannot turn fast enough to reveal Locke's fate. But the spatial difficulty, that of the rapid turn, implies a further ontological difficulty, the turn of the subject's gaze upon himself. Since the camera has become Locke's 'as-if' gaze, it would be as if the camera, possessing the requisite speed, then became Locke witnessing – presumably – his own murder. Disembodied, his mind's eye would spy the fate of his relinquished body. The time–space image of the fusion of Locke's personas is subtly displaced in the process of its completion. While Locke's conflicting public identities are fused by the doubled look of the Other at the moment of death, first the assassins then spouse and police with the girl's presence ambiguously linking both of them, the healed subject is then split open again by the circular movement of the camera as mind-screen turning back upon its original starting-point. The mind-screen no longer is. We end with the point-of-view of the rescuers, of the estranged spouse who claims she never knew him and the mysterious girl who claims that she did.

The power of the time–space image is equally challenging in Wim Wenders's *Kings of the Road* (1976). On one reading this is a Germanized version of the American road-movie of the period, with its own brooding, strangely silent version of male bonding between strangers without women. But Wenders subtly alters all the conventions of movement. The journey of Bruno and Robert along a north–south axis by the West/East German border appears to have the free space of a road journey without limits. But though it appears, like the journey south of David Locke, to be open, it is in fact fixed. Bruno has a clear schedule for servicing cinema projectors on specific days at decaying border towns, and cannot deviate east. The border is a boundary not to be crossed. The constriction is a firm denial of transcendence which Wenders makes more apparent by further images of watching and crossing. The men meet when Robert, heading north after the break-up of his marriage, drives his Volkswagen full tilt into the Elbe. Later Bruno ascends a deserted observation-tower and looks, with a mixture of curiosity and longing, at the countryside on the other side of the frontier. Soon afterwards at a complex of deserted grain silos, Robert walks to the end of a broken platform suspended in space, leading upwards to a sheer drop where it suddenly stops. He stops too. Movement, the premiss of the movie, comes to a dead end. All three sequences act like concealed images of desire, images of yearning which never crystallize.

But the movement through space is a journey which goes simultaneously forwards and backwards in time. The provincial small-town cinemas, which Bruno services as a loving artisan, have been forced by distributors to take soft-porn movies as a condition of major features. The new proviso is clearly a break with the past. But the cinema is also a source of contact with the past. The opening scene with the ageing cinema owner reminiscing about the war years and National-Socialism is shot like *cinema-vérité* and echoed in the eerie night-time sequence in the countryside which pays homage to Fritz Lang. Robert goes to sleep in the back of the van under the glow of the full moon shining through the sunroof, and is then woken by a clanging noise outside. The culprit turns out to be a distraught man sitting in the grain chute of a deserted silo tossing stones down on to the echoing metal. The nocturnal sequence has the quality of an Expressionist nightmare, reinforced by Bruno awakening later when Robert has brought the man back to sleep in the van, and hearing their conversation through the partition between the cabin and the van. The man's story makes him Robert's double. His grief is the result of his wife's suicide in a car crash nearby, thus echoing and reversing Robert's own fate where he tries to kill himself in his own car after separating from his wife.

Wenders then naturalizes the nocturnal grief of the husband in the scene at dawn where Bruno goes to discover the wrecked car, its body twisted, mangled and crushed against a tree. It is a salutary experience. In the absence of any corpse it suggests what the farce of Robert's immersion in the river never did, the nearness of death. Yet of course we never see the crash or the death which results. The dead woman is not a character in the film. We see instead the consequence and are left to imagine its horror. The sequence ends Robert's confused imagining with the great horror of actual disaster, but again as imagined, as reconstructed by Bruno from his witnessing of the wreck. Bruno's action confirms Robert's nocturnal imagining as something real, the surreal incident in the wrecked silo as mimetic, the silo itself with strange angular contours not merely as an Expressionist device but as an *objet trouvé* which is appropriately bleak and menacing. At the same time Robert, who had found a newspaper clipping of Fritz Lang and associates in the back of the van on the previous night, now cuts out Lang's figure from the photo as if re-affirming the homage of Wenders in his imagination of disaster. Yet the self-conscious reference does not detract from the disturbing power of the incident. Desperately the man refuses to leave the back of the van until the wrecked car has been towed away. His wretched fate has triangulated the limpid road narrative of 'men without women' but it also adds genuine pathos through its involuntary nature. If Robert and Bruno have both made a choice, he has been denied one. If the road is a source of freedom, it is also a source of death.

When Robert leaves the road to visit his father the time–space image intensifies. The ageing editor with his printing press is a throwback to the 1930s, a fossil preserved out of a Fritz Lang movie and fixed in a time-warp. In travelling through space Robert has travelled backwards in time. As he enters the office he catches his father asleep wearing an old-fashioned eyeshade in front of an ancient typewriter. As he spends that night setting the type on the printing press his father sleeps once more at his desk, a model of order, decorum, sterility. But Robert himself cannot escape from the cult of the artisan. The difference between the generations is in the open and existential nature of the challenge. Wenders emphasizes this in the parallel cross-editing of the narrative between the two heroes. As Robert guiltily berates his father for mistreating his mother, having just left his own wife, Bruno tries with a dry irony to rescue the disappearing spirit of the cinema. That night he is busy helping out in the local picture house, tidying up the reels of a porn movie left by the masturbating projectionist to gather in a heap on the floor. Catching the amateur projectionist *in flagrante* is for Wenders a way of representing bad faith as dark comedy but also of capturing the forlorn fate of cinema itself. The dilemma for both travellers is the same, how to generate good intensions in a moral vacuum. Both men go lovingly through the artisan's motions but without total conviction. The broadsheet Robert produces on his father's new printing press merely denounces his father's marriage, while the garish repeating trailer which Bruno cuts and loops out of a discarded porn reel is equally a mere moment in the time–space of their trajectory along the road, existential, inspired but soon to be forgotten.

Yet something else is at work here. Wenders's movie is not strictly a *Heimat* film, that German tradition resurrected in the 1970s portraying the maverick outsider who has a fateful impact upon a close rural community.[12] The bleak border towns through which the van travels are nothing more than a series of bleak stops, disconnected. They are blank buildings, funfairs, half-deserted cafés, half-empty cinemas, empty streets. Bruno and Robert are not confronted by community as such. For Wenders it does not appear to exist. But the journey does contain a cryptic search for home, home as an absent image, a collage of unreal objects which can issue only in flawed realizations. At the very start, speeding along the flat plains in his car, Robert tears up a photograph of the home he has just left. On the road thereafter there is a complete absence of domestic signs. But it is a felt absence. We see the men eating and sleeping, but there are no kitchens and no bedrooms, only cafés and makeshift beds. They are no rooms, only places. The division of public and private has ceased to exist. Bereft of the romanticism of the American road-movie, the trivial discomforts of eating and sleeping rough call to mind the absence of home as the narrative's constant imaginary. In *Easy Rider* the road *is* home. But in Wenders's movie there is always a somewhere else beyond the distances to be travelled. This is heightened by the other central time–space image of the narrative, the journey by motorbike to the Rhineland as Bruno breaks his work-itinerary and returns to his mother's house, the house of his childhood on a secluded island in the river.

The house is a derelict mess, surrounded by trees and over-grown with creeper, unlived in and neglected. Despairing at the dereliction, Bruno hurls a brick through a window, but it does not add significantly to the mess. Wenders withholds any establishing shot of the place, so that it seems to have no shape, and as the two men snake in and out of the night shadows they seem unable to define where they are. When Robert asks if it is possible to sleep inside, Bruno, despairing, denies both of them the chance, as if the ruin were sacred territory. They spend the night outside, the ruin of 'home' withheld from them even in sleeping. Home is the ghost of itself, the absent image become unreal object. Here it cannot be 'realized' as home. The next morning, in an act of desperate nostalgia, Bruno finds a box of old comics under the porch steps, a sequence Wenders copies from the opening of Nicholas Ray's *The Lusty Men*.[13] But even the visual images of despair, of Bruno quietly weeping, are drowned out by the sound of passing trains and of dredgers in the river. The men's presence, like that of the two lovers in the hotel room in *Hiroshima, mon amour* with its open window, has no defence against the gross intrusions of external sounds, the moving machines of civilization. They hear what they cannot see and 'home' cannot insulate them. If home is the return of the repressed, a microcosm of the quashed history of a nation, its return is evanescent and cannot take root. Its identity lies in its lack. Identity lies in present motion. Thus Bruno claims the visit has made him realize that time is history.

The house bears comparison with the ruined house two years later in Fassbinder's historical movie *The Marriage of Maria Braun*. As her life improves after the war Maria makes periodic visits to her parents' ruined residence. The house, as an image of war-destruction in 1945, thus lingers on in its ruined state until the next decade, as Maria's fortunes, laced with a good dose of opportunism, change for the better with the times.[14] Fassbinder's film is a linear though episodic chronicle, in which as economic recovery begins we accept the house as constant reminder of the past. In Wenders the almost identical image is implosive. The ruin of the house has no clear origin. We can never tell from what date decay has set in. Yet uncannily we do associate it with destruction of the war. For, shot in black-and-white, Wenders's film makes subtle compositional use of 'any-space-whatevers' in the post-war neo-realist manner, as if the movie had bypassed the whole period of reconstruction. At the same time, the wide-screen format of the film's absent images, the dwelling on the vast spaces, the speeding and slowing of time, the absence of home and family, the absence of the economic miracle, the absence of the modern city, the absence of the rural community, mark it firmly in the modern idiom as a movie of the 1970s.

The film ends with a different fusion of the real and the unreal, the perceived and the imaginary. The pair's drunken showdown, in a deserted border post where they talk bluntly for the first time, makes us realize we have seen no border guards and no American service personnel throughout the course of the movie.

Instead we have the nearby presence of the like foe – German communists – and traces of the recent presence of the unlike ally, the American military, or 'bad ass from Georgia' as one of the graffiti on the wall puts it. At one point a solitary shot rings out across the valley but nothing comes of it. We are reminded of the conflict between West and East but it is Bruno and Robert who fight farcically over their respective taunts after they have downed a bottle of bourbon. Yet their fight is framed by the American outpost where they have shacked up for the night. The movie's most celebrated phrase, 'the Yanks have colonized our subconscious', leads on to the American lyric which colonizes Bruno's subconscious after, on his own confession, he has broken up with a girlfriend. 'I've got a woman, mean as she can be.' American lyrics define his emotions as well as his escape from them. The American lyrics which make life bearable on the road also define them as cultural surrogates. One of the songs they sing in unison, 'Just like Eddie', has a German singer, Heinz, using English lyrics to pay homage to Eddie Cochrane. Likewise, they themselves are stand-ins for the heroes of American road-movies, just as Belmondo in *A bout de souffle* is a stand-in for Bogart. Yet they are more than this. For they are not heroes at all.

This brings us to the central displacement in the movie. The absence of women is its central absence, as Bruno's brief encounter with the box-office girl makes clear. The reading which sees the relationship of the two men as homoerotic overlooks this. If anything, there is little male bonding at all. The most imposing images are of distance, reserve, awkwardness, otherness. To the American melodrama of tough and jokey loyalty Wenders poses frankness as something rare which occurs only as the relationship is about to end. Moving on and moving apart means moving back to the world of women from which they have escaped, in which they have failed and by which they are still scared. The failure of heterosexual relationships underlies the movie but there is no compensation in male bonding where trust is always fragile. For all their ability to extemporize and tough things out, Bruno and Robert do not connect. For all the light-hearted moments, 'the fear of fear' to which Rüdiger Vogler had confessed in *Alice in the Cities* is still the dominant structure of feeling here. In the road-movie whose Faustian sweep promises the exploration of everything in sight, the displacement of the image is still paramount. The dialectic of the time–space image, fluid, lingering, and lyrical, that is to say a lyricism of displacement, is what makes this Wenders's finest film. What deepens its sense of presence is the imaginary, its undying search for what is not there.

6

Commodified Demons I: The Machine and the Mask

Many of the great modern movies, *Vivra sa vie*, *Persona*, *The Conformist*, *The Passenger* among them, are about the self-creation of *subjects* as commodities. This is not an obvious coding of the romantic themes of literary alienation but a marked shift away from romantic sensibility, a subtle transforming of film narratives into fables of existential choice which confront the void of modern living and the invisible boundaries of its worldly constraint. The neo-moderns do not resurrect, therefore, the Expressionist *topoi* of robotic outcasts, of humans-as-deranged-machines, but raise instead the spectre of bad faith among the rational bourgeois for whom conscience is always an ontological presence even when it is abjured in practice. Bad faith, as Sartre has suggested, is self-deception, a limitless variety of self-betrayals in easy or difficult circumstance. It is a daily occurrence, part and parcel of commodifying everything in sight considered of value, of turning the material object into the magical symbol at the drop of a hat. The knack of commodifying material objects includes, of course, the knack of commodifying oneself. The marketable self, like Nana the Parisian prostitute in *Vivre sa vie*, is a central motif of the European moderns. Here classic heroic dilemmas of noble struggle against evil and the unjust, old romantic conceits, are replaced by spasmodic and anti-heroic efforts to resist bad faith. The choices are never simple, since we are almost never fully conscious of them. Yet marketable success of any kind can weaken our resistance to evil and the unjust in our daily lives. Here the Faustian temptations of world-mastery are never really an option, or a problem. Bad faith is always mean, trivial and close-to-hand, in a word banal.

Sartre notes the paradox at the centre of a bad faith based on the model of deceiving others: 'I must know in my capacity as deceiver the truth which is hidden from me in my capacity as the one deceived'.[1] The problem is in the nature of being 'hidden' and Sartre rejects a Freudian unconscious in which the censor repressing knowledge is placed outside the purposive activities of the self. But he also posits different planes of self-deception which arise from the multiple nature of selfhood. Bad faith is not so much the denial of self as the placing of one of our multiple selves over all others, the positing of a false priority where one persona rules at the expense of another. Equally, bad faith can entail the positing of a false ideal of personality, the wilful construction of an ideal persona at the expense of all our contingent ones. It is seeking false coherence on one plane of selfhood at the expense of others which are conveniently ignored. Here Sartre has been miscast as the earth-father of existential *dasein* when he is fact the supreme detective of modernity, the unraveller of the decentred modern self which masquerades as the source of its own cohesion. He thus dispenses with the romantic conceit of personality as a potential refuge from the corruptions of the public domain, and, sure enough, the public domain is the nexus of bad faith in modern film. From *La notte* onwards cinema shows us precisely how the precious gifts of doing and being in our daily lives are subtly commodified by circumstance. The cultural marketplace may be resisted but complicity is not always conscious. Yet Sartre's account still misses something of vital importance in film which is implicit in bad faith. Bad faith is capitulation not just to the power which commodifying brings us but to the polar opposite which it always evokes and which is central to the cinema of the double. It is the projecting of the self as a commodified Other, the selling of one's soul to those who reject reason and modernity altogether, the annihilation of self as part of an assault on reason. In this instance bad faith turns its pseudo-critique of modernity into a thirst for revenge.

While the commodified persona tries to sell itself on the marketplace, its alter ego offers itself as a servant to other masters.

It joins the demonic revolt against modernity which, for twenti-eth-century Europe, had its indisputable origins in fascism. Traces of the bourgeois encounter with fascism remain in the bloodstream of the modern cinema, where the fascist monster emerges as the double of the bourgeois citizen, not Promethean but abject in the service of tyranny. The retro-images of the fascist demon in films like *The Damned, Salo, Lilli Marlene, 1900* and *The Serpent's Egg* all show a fascination with demonology which at times verges on the self-indulgent and the kitsch. Modern directors have conveniently blamed many of the forms of decadence which fascinate them on the defunct march of the jackboot. There is of course a strong element of this at its worst, for example, in the sado-masochistic kitsch of *The Night Porter*. But there is something more important. By the end of the 1960s, with new freedoms of sexual and political expression in the cinema there was also the return of the demonic as reverie of Europe's collective past, the obsessive, oneiric imagining of what-has-been, the spectre of fascism as an incomplete project, a time–space imaginary.

It was no coincidence that the retro movement was centred in Italy, for there the break with the fascist past was arguably as incomplete as in any European country. While the new Italian cinema of the war period had been strongly anti-fascist, it had also benefited ambiguously from the patronage of Mussolini's warlike son Vittorio.[2] In the landmark movie of neo-realism *Rome Open City*, the erotic sado-masochism which later lured Fellini, Visconti, Bertolucci, Pasolini and Caviani is already present in the final torture of Rossellini's priest by the Gestapo. By contrast the demythologizing of the fascist era in De Sica's *The Garden of the Finzi-Continis* and Francesco Rosi's adaptation of *Christ Stopped at Eboli* reinstates the legacy of neo-realism against its embryonic modern otherness, its fascination with the enemy which is not only the enemy without (Hitler) but the demon-enemy within (Mussolini). In Rossellini's classic film the German lesbian officer literally seduces her Italian informants into betrayal, and that betrayal has a cryptic erotic attraction for its director which he tries to communicate to his audience. Buñuel, among others, objected strongly to the scene where the tortured priest is in one room and the German officer canoodles with an Italian woman in the other as facile and tactless.[3]

The retro movement was accompanied by articulate and intelligent forms of self-justification. Visconti and Bertolucci both drew on their Freudo-Marxian theories of European history, while Fellini saw vital links between fascism, bombast and a blocked adolescence which he flamboyantly portrayed in *Amarcord* as comic, provincial and ridiculous.[4] Yet the challenge for cinema is to go beyond the dualism of reason and the irrational which all too easily pervades the retro movement. It must challenge a further dualism, that of past and present. Imagining the past becomes a temporal imaginary which co-exists with the present, a feature of the cinema which Welles had established so powerfully in *Citizen Kane*. It is the Wellesian challenge which Bertolucci takes up in *The Conformist* and *The Spider's Stratagem*, the challenge of luminous images of the past which prove so elusive they are both there and not-there, images which either burn the gaze or fade to nothingness. Here the Wellesian tragedy of the American drama is supplanted by a dream of the Italian tragedy. The rise and fall of the single overreacher, Kane, is replaced by the rise and fall of the bombastic and perfidious collective, not just *il Duce*. In Bertolucci's loose adaptation of Borges's story the father is cast in the spitting image of his investigating son as partisan hero turned fascist collaborator. In his more faithful rendering of Moravia's novel, Bertolucci still turns linear narrative into a mosaic of retro fragments, fragments which frame the fascist world of his conformist through a pastiche of prior cinematic images. Time becomes film history, not real history, style and fashion that of the studio, not of the streets.

Space, too, is a re-staging of history as spectacle inspired by the challenge of that other Wellesian masterpiece, *The Trial*. It is Clerici pinned by panning long shots against huge, flat surfaces, walking through corridors towards an advancing camera, or away from one that is tracking backwards in the opposite direction so that movement of camera and character are in permanent contradiction. If Clerici briefly inhabits the vast palatial spaces of heroic fascist architecture with his stiff and rigid walking as a miniature automaton, he is also a seated prisoner in the recording studio where his blind fascist mentor broadcasts, in the Parisian restaurant where everyone dances joyfully without him, and near the end, in the back seat of his car, where, petrified, he witnesses the assassination he has instigated of the Quadris. In all these sequences he is seen through glass, almost pressed against it, unerringly transparent. If Joseph K. guiltily protests his unseen guilt, Clerici is transparent in his betrayal and complicity. If in the images of blindness and the overlong metaphor of Plato's cave he is rendered again and again as spiritually blind, the unseeing collaborator is never himself out of the light. Even when he hides from Mangiello his thuggish minder in the Chinese restaurant, the swinging light-bulb, again from *The Trial* but also from *Psycho*, reveals his frightened face behind the door. Here Bertolucci echoes the Expressionist extremes of the abyss and the tomb, infinity and entrapment; but his rectangular lines and scrupulous adherence to perspective make the oneiric imaginary Mediterranean and not Nordic, classical rather than Gothic. Or rather 'neo-classical'. For, architecturally speaking, Clerici is framed as the agoraphobic prisoner of fascist pastiche. Blind, he is always seen. Purposeful, he is always commodified. Finally he is like the viewer in the cinema, a passive spectator of the murders in the Alpine woods. But these, of course, are the very murders which constitute his special mission. He has thus acted without having acting at all.

Clerici is commodified by choosing to act. He becomes a demon by trying to exorcize his demons. As he sheds the family horrors of child seduction, paternal madness and maternal drug-addiction, he creates public horrors of greater enormity. As he honeymoons in Paris he ignores his wife and discovers in Anna Quadri the woman he really desires. But he can desire her only by idealizing her as the female projection of his *own* desires, as his emancipated double, feminized, bisexual, androgynous, delicate yet powerful, Italian but anti-fascist. Hence the wall-to-wall mirror of the ballet class where Anna's image, in its free and graceful movement, is ubiquitous. Hence the oneiric peeping through the doorway of the hotel room, as Clerici spies her seducing his new bride from the corridor, and where, sensing his hidden watching, Anna defiantly returns his gaze. In watching her caresses, Clerici is watching both a woman who threatens him and a feminized persona of himself. In watching her act of cuckoldry he is watching the ideal emancipation of his own self and the bleak distance it appears from him. Anna is erotic, bisexual, independent, anti-fascist, attributes of which Clerici himself is now incapable. 'Heterosexual', repressed, conformist, amoral, he tries to possess her body to capture her attributes.

But even in seduction she remains the elusive double. The fleeting contact of the body mocks the unaltered distance of the spirit.

Clerici is both the commodified demon and the demonized commodity, the servile slave of Mussolini and the calculating assassin, the prisoner of vast open spaces, the fugitive from desire. Bertolucci spoils the elegant construction of his time–space image by the cheap Freudian melodrama of his glib ending. Once time is out of flash back, once it becomes linear again after the murder of the Quadris and jumps forwards to the moment of Mussolini's downfall, the film is lost. It is lost specifically in the vacuous denunciation of the ageing gay chauffeur who in Clerici's memory of childhood acted as the catalyst of his political neurosis. The film becomes bombastic and empty as Bertolucci's grip on history leaves him, and he changes tone into a denouement of childhood trauma revisited that is closer to *Marnie* than it is to Resnais, Godard or *The Trial*. The sudden switch evokes a bombastic and hysterical emptiness he altogether avoids in *The Spider's Stratagem* where the problem of the fascist past finds no solution in the post-fascist present, where the enquiring hero is and is not his perfidious father. Yet Bertolucci lapses into pure bombast again in the grandiose soap opera of *1900* where Donald Sutherland is a cardboard sadist overplaying blackshirt tyranny while De Niro and Depardieu are allowed to reduce socialist bonhomie to the knockabout levels of Abbott and Costello. Here in the unconscious parody of his own fluid tracking and lyrical cutting, the bombast is unrelenting as the stars of Western cinema, almost none of them Italian, make a mockery of the Italian experience. In this film more than any other one senses that by 1980 the cinematic moment of the modern is over.

The lapse into fascism is the ultimate failure in the modern history of the European bourgeoisie. Clerici capitulates to bad faith too easily, much more easily, for example, than Joseph K. in *The Trial*. In the post-fascist era the resistance is stronger, but the temptations are still there. The demonic and the commodified remain the Scylla and Charibdis of capitalist temptation. They do so this time however as cultural, not political capital. In the Expressionist mode of the moderns the political becomes allegorical. In 1971, drawing on the allegorical idiom of Lang and others in the 1920s, Herzog creates out of his monstrous Basque conquistador, Aguirre a historical parallel to Hitler. The passage downriver to El Dorado on a tributary of the Amazon, an offshoot of Pizarro's expedition, is also the passage to Nazi Götterdämmerung. The passage is chillingly exact. Aguirre deposes the king on the raft and murders his henchman and does so under the cover of a coerced vote among the crew which belongs to the twentieth and not to the sixteenth century, while the Priest–narrator hypocritically refuses to intervene. The journey itself alternates violently between Heideggerian torpor and Wagnerian ecstasy, between the daily discomforts of *dasein* and hallucinated delusions of transcendence. Attacked by Indians, dying of fever, the crew are reduced to a heap of would-be corpses on a helpless raft circling in the rapids, while Aguirre hallucinates his incestuous ascension into the kingdom of El Dorado with his dying daughter. In order to go back thirty years in his poetics of displacement, Herzog goes back four hundred years and replaces the topography of his native Bavaria with the jungles of the Amazon. Thus historical epic as modern allegory becomes two histories and two tyrants for the price of one, with the complex doubling of a time–space image which is far away and long ago, yet uncannily recent and close at hand.

A very different film shows the connecting threat to Lang but one in which the political link has been severed, a sequel to *Metropolis* for the post-fascist age. In Antonioni's *The Red Desert* (1964) the discontent of the workers is not a red peril but a normal event, a predictable strike not a political apocalypse. It is peripheral to the main action while the factory-as-machine-Moloch is no longer deep underground but on the edge of the Ravenna marshes. The link of technology is no longer to politics but to culture. Antonioni naturalizes the studio Moloch-machine into a modern Italian factory with its own topographical schizophrenia. Its interiors are clean, streamlined, hi-tech, transparent. Its exteriors are opaque, angular, polluted, threatening. The inside is an oxygen chamber, the outside a miasma of poisons. Further away the bleached interiors of the city apartments are simultaneously the protective shells of consumer hygiene and the death of the spirit. The vaporous exteriors of a poisoned landscape are the veils over vision and the destroyers of the body. The techno-landscapes of endless funnels and pylons, all jagged horizontals, are visual fields without depth, a brutal flattening of perspective, an angular harness on the eye, a washing-out of all primary colours, an objective correlative to the telephoto lens. This is one of the first major examples of Expressionist coloration in wide-screen film, a fact reinforced by thematic similarities not only to Lang but also to Murnau. Critics often remark on the extreme telephoto shot of the ship glimpsed above the treetops sailing inland as it were sailing overland, on dry land, gliding through the polluted earth. They often fail to notice that it is also a foreign ship from the East bringing disease and death, gliding momentously onwards like the ship which silently brings Dracula to Bremen in *Nosferatu*. Yet Antonioni firmly demythologizes the vampires from the East and the demons in the machine. Ecology instead becomes an analogue for the poisoning of the bourgeois spirit. The faceless and mechanical motion of the machine finds human form in the brute and blank physiognomy of Richard Harris's engineer. In Monica Vitti's portrayal of the hypersensitive Giuliana, the engineer's wife and Harris's lover, demonic possession is transformed into a diurnal neurosis too embedded to disappear but also too banal to become true madness. Neurosis is the lingering, the undulating, the spasmodic, a resistance to ecological fate which resolves nothing.

Throughout Antonioni's tetralogy, Monica Vitti is the icon of female resistance to male perfidy, a perfidy which is at once intimate and cosmic, personal and global, a perfidy which betrays men, women and the world alike. In Bergman's work after *Winter Light* that same resistance becomes an implosive force within the world of woman. But the intimate nature of Bergman's great movies of that period, *The Silence*, *Persona* and *Cries and Whispers*, movies which Bergman himself saw as chamber pieces, should not blind us to their significance. They fix the inner world of women as blinding images on the outer rim of an iconic landscape which merges nature and culture, body and soul. Like Ibsen, Bergman evokes images of Nordic wilderness, echoes of European periphery. Like Strindberg, he explores the collisions of intimacy, the tortured intimacy, that is, of beings wrapped in mutual or collective solitude. *Persona* is his great chamber piece on modernity, its bleached interiors and remote seascapes an oblique view of civilization which strikes at its very heart. *Persona* is intimate, sensual, complex, female. It could equally be read, though, as a parable of the fragilities of social democracy in a post-fascist world, of Bergman's own ambivalent encounter with the psychic hygiene of Europe's most impressive welfare state.

The ironized critique of Sweden's ideology of care is balanced by the dissection of the evasions of actorly performance, and by the enduring guilt of the director's Nazi past. The latter, of course, Bergman documents in his autobiography, his teenage visit to Germany in the 1930s and infatuation with National Socialism, his support of it along with his family at the start of his film career and during the war when Swedish film-makers were deeply divided over the matter. *Persona* has more to do, however, with his immense guilt after the war when he first saw the first documentary pictures of the camps and felt personally implicated in a system perpetrating atrocities he had never dreamed of.[5]

This enduring guilt and its institutional opposite, the social democracy of care, are both crystallized in *Persona*'s rendering of the enigma of the double. Here the spiritual equivalence of self and Other, their equal ontology, makes their artificial separation elsewhere into subject and object, active and passive, seem facile and vulgar. If the double is the subject, then the subject is also the double. More than any other director, Bergman recognized that the very process of doubling is poetically reflexive in the genesis of the film. In *Persona* the actress (Liv Ullmann) playing an actress, Elizabet Vogler, who has a nervous breakdown, is the creation of a film-maker, Bergman, who seeks his feminized persona in the actress-played-by-the-actress, in the character of someone whose task it is to enact personas. Here she does so *offstage*, not on, and does so with destructive consequences when she stamps her persona upon the weak and gullible Sister Alma. For despite the paralysis of her speech Elizabet's acting cannot stop itself. It goes on even when its technical properties are severely impaired. The inspired aesthetic of *Persona* is an infinite regress. For even a breakdown, which renders Elizabet mute and drains her of the power of performing, still ends up as a performance, in many ways one of the most subtle and most powerful of all. The power of silence allows her to devour another woman's psyche.

It would be wrong to see Elizabet's minder, Sister Alma (Bibi Andersson) merely as the naive embodiment of enlightened care, a female apotheosis of an abstract principle, despite her impressive sense of vocation. Bergman after all insinuates an abortive love affair between two women, in which Alma's care is subverted into longing and the patient as actress celebrity, as a 'famous' woman, becomes an icon of desire, the imaginary beloved. The horizontal structure of the hospital room and the bleak hygienic walls with their flat gradations of monochrome are transposed on to the doctor's summerhouse where Elizabet convalesces with Alma's aid. It has the same horizontal structure, the windows covered by white transparent curtains. The room is a bare and bleak place in which few objects appear and even fewer have significance. The streamlined contours of the sea-facing home echo the hospital's bleached surroundings. There is no clutter, no tradition, no past. Everything is in the living moment. Alma's uniform and Elizabet's nightdress, symbols of difference, suddenly disappear. The women wear identical sun-hats, identical swimsuits, identical dresses. They are framed intimately in two-shot in the sunlight as if they were twin sisters, the wide rims of their hats poignantly touching.

Yet they are poles apart, the poles of speech and silence. Elizabet listens while Alma talks, using muteness as a weapon, staging a strategy of minimal gesture, minimal response to her gauche admirer. Spontaneous confessions of sexual experience with teenage boys are teased out of the uncertain Alma through the seductive response of silence to which Elizabet gives subtle and theatrical aura. Once done, Alma senses herself defenceless, robbed of her intimate sexual secrets. Yet the weapon of silence is the mute attention of everyday hearing with no visible stage. The image of the attentive Elizabet in the summerhouse, plain face against plain walls and chairs, is the opposite of the initial shot Bergman has given us of Elizabet as Electra on stage, black-wigged, framed in medium close-up against the spotlights, her face and eyes heavily cosmetic. Deprived of the adornments of the theatre, Elizabet is still mesmeric in the art of passive performance while Alma, the active actor, is tentative, vulnerable, too honest to be compelling. The role-reversal is complete, but not quite. Alma acts but cannot perform. Elizabet performs but cannot act. Everything has changed and yet remains the same.

Elizabet Vogler, whose surname means 'bird-catcher', is a subtle transposition of the other mesmerists in Bergman's film with the same name, particularly Albert Emanuel Vogler, the travelling magician in *The Face*.[6] *Persona* is an exercise in effort-less mesmerism which is also an exercise in the concealment of its own nature. The performance is both a seduction and a masking of the power of seduction which has a 'natural'

expression in nervous illness. The power to perform thus masquerades as the neurotic inertia of the non-performing self and
yet that inertia *is* the void of anguish. Appropriating Alma to
herself is a way of filling it and here it is important that Alma
represents something which Elizabeth lacks, just as, conversely,
the anxious nurse is in awe of her patient's 'celebrity'. The
separation works at multiple levels which are contradictory,
nurse/ patient, spontaneous/calculating, naive/knowing, ration-
al/demonic, anonymous/celebrated, speech/silence and, more
disturbingly, social democracy/fascism. The oppositions thus
suggest the doubling of split *selves* of the two women, rather
than, as some critics think, the split *self* of a single allegorical
figure. The most effective way to read the film is to see Alma
and Elizabet as weakly autonomous beings whose ambivalent
love-affair entails the relinquishment of autonomy. Each tries to
take from the other what she does not have. But the process is
also one of unilateral seduction. Alma is seduced by Elizabet
into the actress's image and the act of seduction is an act of
predation, captured in the vampirish gesture where Elizabet
suddenly bends her head and sucks blood from Alma's forearm.

The subtlety of Vogler's tactics is inseparable from Bergman's
subtle *mise-en-scène* of the two women where each of Elizabet's
masquerades is visually framed as a plausible fantasy of Alma's
imagination. In the night-time sequences at the summerhouse
it becomes impossible to separate the real and the imaginary
because psychologically either is a feasible outcome of Alma's
predicament. Drunk at the end of her intimate sexual confession,
Alma hears off-camera a voice expressing her own desire for
sleep, which she then repeats in her own words. The voice could
be Elizabet's or it could be an imaginary voice inside Alma's
drowsy consciousness. It could be a dream visitation, but the
screenplay specifies that the words come from the actress: 'You'd
better get off to bed, otherwise you'll fall asleep at the table,
says Mrs Vogler in a calm, clear voice'.[7] Yet the refusal of any
shot of Vogler's face was the words come from her lips heightens
the uncanny nature of the scene. The ambiguity intensifies when
Alma awakes at dawn, restless, then returns to bed. Dressed in
a white nightgown, Elizabeth drifts through the grey half-light of
the dawn visible through the doorway into the darkness of the
bedroom. Beautifully backlit, the visit is a ghostly visitation, yet
the deliberate nature of the movement undermines the somnabul-

1 *Marienbad*: the baroque interior as nuclear after-life. Delphine Seyrig, Giorgio Albertazzi.

2 *L'eclisse*: the cool apocalypse. Monica Vitti.

3　*L'avventura*: the gaze as visual assault. Monica Vitti.

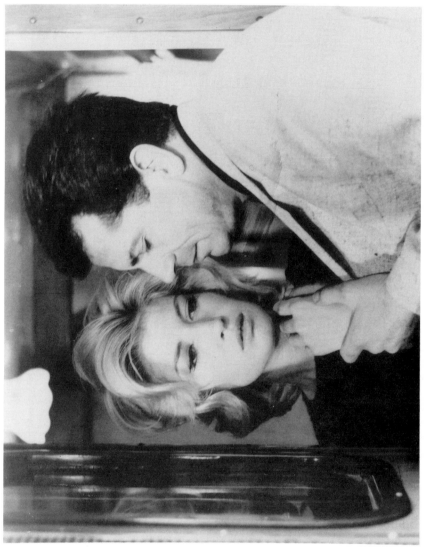

4 *L'avventura*: under the watchful eye of the absent Anna. Monica Vitti, Gabriele Ferzetti.

5   *Persona*: the camera as two-way mirror. Bibi Andersson, Liv Ullmann.

6   *Le Genou de Claire*: eye-level shot/low-angle gaze. Jean-Claude Brialy, Laurence de Monaghan.

7   *Weekend*: the car as destroyer without qualities. Jean Yanne, Mireille Darc.

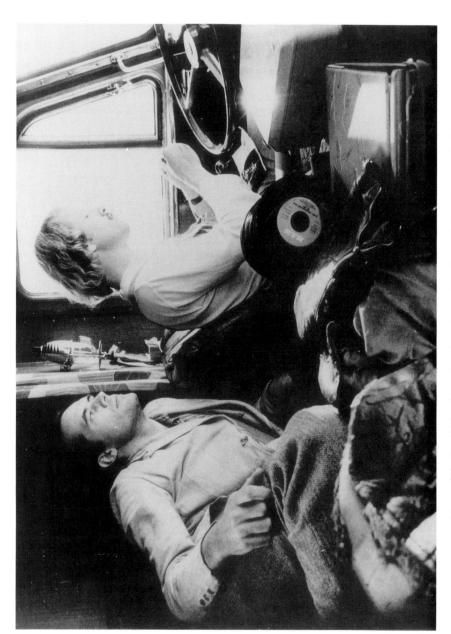

8 *Kings of the Road*: the driver's cab as home. Rudiger Vogler, Hanns Zischler.

ist image. She exits through an adjacent light-filled doorway and then returns to kneel at the bed and caress Alma's cheek with her lips. The sequence can be read as a projection of Alma's subconscious desire for the other woman but also as the charade of a seasoned actress who 'acts out' the desire she has sensed in her weaker companion. In the grey half-light the actress's image and movements work in counterpoint, the former white and ethereal, the latter deliberate and quietly menacing.

Elizabet uses her talent to commodify her own demonology and, in doing so, conceal it beneath the mask of a neurasthenic muteness. Yet her demonism is not something essential to her nature. It exists only in and through the masquerade. It may express an unmistakable desire for domination, yet satisfaction of that desire only increases with its conscious masking. On the other hand, Bergman's picture *is* about the power of conscience, about the contrast between conscience and manipulation, guilt and domination. Elizabet is obliquely self-conscious and self-critical of her failings, yet this is a film in which at times conscience is more repressed than desire. Thus it is conscience, not terror, which bursts forth unexpectedly in the gaze at the horrifying image. This happens twice, the first time in the hospital when, terrified, Elizabet cowers away from the television set bringing pictures from Vietnam of a Buddhist monk setting fire to himself on a Saigon street. The second time occurs in the summerhouse when Elizabet looks at photographs from the Warsaw ghetto of Jews being rounded up by SS troops. The images are familiar ones in the litany of the Holocaust and at first sight it seems as if Elizabet is expressing the revulsion felt by all of us at the spectacle. But in both instances the gaze is ambiguous. It identifies itself with the victims but also identifies itself as the secret source of their suffering. Elizabet feels herself both tyrant and victim, predator and the object of predation. Painfully recalling her desertion of her own son, she identifies, to her horror, *both* with suffering of the Jewish child at gunpoint *and* with the cruel face of the Nazi officer holding the gun. The sensation is unbearable in the sheer power of its guilt and terror. She feels herself to be evil's victim but also evil itself. And in the perverse inversion of appearance and reality in her psyche, guilt is prompted not by the living flesh but by its *represented* image, not the person but the figure in the picture.

Vital here to Bergman's narrative is the precision of sequence.

The dawn visitation scene is followed by the sequence on the beach in which Elizabet jumps up from a perching position out of frame and photographs the camera lens which is filming Alma behind her in long shot. This affirms the complicity of the viewer in the nocturnal visitation and what follows. For earlier in the dawn scene, Bergman cuts from the two women standing by the bed to a shot of Elizabet stroking Alma's hair by cradling her arm around the back of the nurse's neck and leaning intimately sideways so that their cheeks are touching. The sense of looking directly at the camera as if it were a mirror is reinforced by the brushing movement of Vogler's hand. As their heads cradle together, Elizabet brushes Alma's hair in the opposite direction from its parting. This simultaneously suggests two things. It suggests the inversion of the image in the mirror so that instead of us being the mirror into which they look, we are now looking *into* the mirror their images inhabit. It also suggests that Vogler is brushing Sister Alma's hair in the opposite direction to make her nurse look more like *her*, to force an absolute likeness and merging of the two female faces on the darkened screen. Here the complex use of mirroring is every bit as subtle as its use in *Vertigo*, if not more so. Moreover we are made to see their reflection in the mirror, or their looking in the mirror, without seeing the mirror itself so that the 'inversion' of the image has no context. As viewers we are the voyeurs behind the camera lens whose collective gaze Elizabet thrusts back in our faces. On the other hand we are also the mirror-images of the two faces. They are the objects of our gaze. We are the objects of their gaze. They are the objects of each other's gaze. Bergman then cuts to the beach scene in which Vogler photographs us watching Alma in the distance, walks away from the camera to photograph Alma while we look on, then turns around in long shot to photograph us once more, as if to seal not only the act but the whole sequence of spectator complicity. Like it or not, we have become her confederates. The pursuit of the double is a labyrinth of face, mirror, image and figure which constantly repeats itself throughout the film and from which we can never escape.

Like *The Red Desert*, *Persona* turns Expressionist form away from mythology and hallucination into social and psychic realities. These are all the more chilling for being thoroughly naturalized. Elizabet's power of silence is not that of the vampire in the silent cinema, which it echoes, but the mute strategy of a

speaking, calculating actress. Her sudden act of biting at the
broken skin of Alma's forearm is not just the vampirish sucking
of blood but also a ritual gesture of domination, of mental and
bodily appropriation of the Other, woman on woman. It is an
act of both love and hate. Elizabet's threat is material because
she herself is flesh and blood, because she herself is human and
vulnerable. It is the human self not the projected Other which
is the demon. When Elizabet goads Alma into violent defence,
the latter strikes out as the nurse goaded beyond endurance, and
at the end returns, wearing her uniform once more, to her old
identity. Yet she no longer has a 'patient'. For Bergman, neither
woman is truly possessed. Each bears responsibility for her
actions and the consequences of those actions. Elizabet's self-
hatred is a hatred of her own body as *hers*, while Alma, in the
famous interrogation where she accuses Elizabet of neglecting
her son, is also accusing herself as 'Elizabet', as the woman she
still wants to become.

Yet the film *is* about the transfer of identity, the possession
of the soul. Blackwell has perceptively analysed the complex
ambiguities of the seduction fantasy where Elizabet's husband
makes love to Alma with Elizabet looking on.[8] On one level it
is Alma imagining herself as Elizabet, imagining herself in *her*
position in the act of love. At another, it is Alma the lover of
Elizabet, imagining herself in the position of the husband – who
wears dark glasses identical to those Alma has worn earlier
outside in the sun – making love to the beloved. The doubling
is visually complemented by the dual positioning of Elizabet in
the frame. In a tight telephoto shot, Bergman places her first
behind the couple in the background, her face intimately
bisecting their desiring profiles. Then after a sudden cut, he
reveals her in another shot in the foreground at one side of the
love-making pair who in neither shot acknowledge her presence.
In the first shot she appears to be the witness of Alma's desire,
as well as aiding it, uncannily seeing the couple while looking
straight at the camera lens. In the second, where she also looks
straight ahead but past the camera, and *not* back at the couple,
she becomes this time the direct mediator of the spectator's gaze.
At that crucial point, she seems indeed to be the orchestrator of
that collective gaze by making it more reflective. In the first shot
she appears to be an implicated witness *in* the fantasy, in the
act of witnessing. In the second she appears to have orchestrated

the whole fantasy herself through the medium of Alma's imagination, to have 'become' her victim. This is the moment of reflection upon the enormity of what she has done.

The doubling of foreground and background sets up soon afterwards a doubling of camera angles in the sequence where Bergman films Alma's accusation of the mute Elizabet twice over. The accusation by Alma of Elizabet's neglect of her son becomes at the end a form of self-accusation in which Alma condemns her decision to abort her own child. The first sequence starts with an over-the-shoulder medium shot on Elizabet from behind Alma, then cuts to a medium shot on Elizabet from Alma's point-of-view, then to close-up and finally extreme close-up. The second sequence is a set of reverse-angles of the first, exactly replicated, on Alma from Elizabet's point-of-view, similarly cutting to extreme close-up on the nurse's face as the accusation, repeated exactly the second time around, progresses towards its climax. Here in the intricate doubling of *Persona* style and theme are inseparable. They become pure cinematic form, a triumph of the modern cinema. Technically, Bergman probes a weakness in the nature of the spectator's gaze upon the screen, its two-dimensional nature. But the speculator's failure to see frontally and simultaneously the faces of the two women – the normal angle would be a profile two-shot – is more generally a feature of the limits of the visual field of perception. To see the faces of Alma and Elizabet together as we do with such intimacy, that is, confronting each other head on, would mean sitting almost between them and rapidly turning the gaze from one to the other on a plane of 180 degrees, trying in vain, that is, to capture speech and reaction to speech in the same moment. It would be not only to intrude on that intimacy but literally to occupy its visual plane and nullify it at the moment of impact.

The famous merging of the faces of the two women at the climax to the repeated speech is thus a fusion of the visual forms of doubling which accumulate through the film with the unbearable pressure finally breaking Alma's resistance to Vogler's seductive persona. The narrative climax is hence a climax of form. We look simultaneously into the eyes of both women because they have become one, and, in moving us towards this climax, image and story have become one. They too are inseparable. As Alma is 'possessed' by Elizabet we are 'possessed' as spectators by the doubled image of the two women-as-one. Yet Bergman also stresses the resistance to the Other as something resilient, something which can always return, which is never finally broken. Possession is a moment, not a condition and Alma recoils from the disintegration of the self. She reasserts her autonomy. But at a price. Self regained is self transformed, self diminished. The naive impulses of caring, internalized by the welfare, can longer be spontaneous or devoid of scepticism as they once were.

Meanwhile, for Elizabet who constantly hides behind her own persona, the act of possessing the other is also an act of supreme masochism. It invites the retaliation of Alma's anger and rejection. It prompts the humiliation of feeling the nurse's anger as a sentient force, pushing her back on to other roles, other masks, other personas. Meanwhile Alma remains victim to the experience she will never erase. At the end she repeats in the mirror the gesture of pushing back her hair against its parting that Elizabet had earlier made in her dawn visitation. Bergman evokes the earlier shot momentarily in a double exposure giving us Vogler's original stroking superimposed upon Alma's own hand. The demon still haunts, still remains, to taunt the woman it has aged and weakened. Meanwhile Vogler herself goes back to her other roles. In the last reflexive shot of the film we have a low-angle of Bergman the director with Sven Nykvist, his cinematographer, perched high up on a crane in a film studio. In their camera lens is the image of Elizabet upside down in close-up, a replica of the image of Alma lying on the bed which Bergman had used earlier in the film. Elizabet has literally taken Alma into the realm of art without the other woman knowing it, seeming to play the role in a movie of a woman whom she had possessed in actuality, whom she had 'become' in the flesh. The tragedy for Elizabet is that such 'possession' is always temporary. When it fades, as it must do, she is confronted once more by her own emptiness.

In bare outline the story is of a working woman possessed by a celebrity, a servant of the state possessed by the bourgeois patient she cares for. But the act of possessing as an act of class domination would remain banal were it not for the persona of the commodified demon. Elizabet's mute and elaborate masquerade is both the act of a desperate woman and a demonic urge which atones for the residual forms of emptiness in body and soul, self and world. In both the hospital and the doctor's summer house the cold, flat, unadorned interiors of care's institutions become empty vessels of caring, rooms without qualities, purged of excess or ornamentation. They are the streamlined contours of modernity, stark, modernist, brutal, anti-Gothic. *Persona* is the extreme antithesis of that Expressionist masterpiece of demonic possession, *The Cabinet of Dr Caligari*. The bare and bleak walls of Bergman's movie, too uncannily real in their sense of hygiene and cleanliness to suggest any studio design, make all emptiness completely exterior. In no sense are they a distorted projection of a disturbed subjective imagination. They are authentic artefacts of modern architecture and culture, the insitutional rooms we all inhabit. Yet they are also the objective correlatives of Elizabet's emptiness, the emptiness of the demon who cunningly uses her *lack* of being to revenge herself upon the emptiness by which she is surrounded.

In contrast to Elizabet and the modern godless world, Alma is the only authentic presence in the movie. Yet the cultural void of a world in which she feels so fragile, so insecure, eventually weakens her in the face of Vogler's mesmerism. Here the crossover in the film is not so much the swapping of identities which Bergman himself suggested but the creation of a positive out of the meeting of two negatives, the production of evil out of contrasting forms of the void in Elizabet's world, a blankness of soul, but also a bleak and featureless life outside the stage. It might have been a feature, one suspects, of Bergman's own ambiguous relationship to the country in which he lived. Elizabet negates her emptiness by dissimulating, by being a positive force for evil while the empty world around her is given a charged meaning by her intrusion into it. The Sweden of that period, Sweden as the humanist land thriving in 'God's silence', as the country which cares more practically for its citizens than any other, which prides itself upon its reason, is also a country without qualities, dismal, bleak and forlorn. Yet the wilful construction of evil is the wrong response. For Bergman it is a tempting but mistaken solution.

The poetics of displacement in Bergman is both erotic and political. If Elizabet is a feminized version of his own persona, then her spiritual dilemma is equally an outcome of his tortuous politics and his troubled past. An heir to the Expressionist tradition, Bergman avoids the dangers of romanticism which lurk in the displacements in Herzog, and the chamber cinema of

Persona meticulously negates the shrill Wagnerian cry which echoes through the maverick German post-romantic. Moreover, just as *The Serpent's Egg* tried much later to be politically explicit about the chaos of Weimar but failed to create much sense of time or place, *The Silence*, which is never explicit, must be seen as Bergman's retro-masterpiece. In 1963 it could be viewed very convincingly as a contemporary journey through a mid-European nightmare of the Cold War at its height. Yet it can also be seen as a return to an earlier period of Europe preparing for war. Reading off Bergman's early biography it can be seen as the post-Nazi transformation of Bergman's teenage political dream into horrifying nightmare. The journey is the exact opposite of the one Bergman describes as a teenager on a student exchange to rural Thuringia where he was lured by the grand spectacle of a Hitler rally and seduced into a state of ecstasy and a commitment which remained with him beyond the end of the war.[9] Instead the film can be as part reprise of the down side of that fateful visit, a despairing trip through the forbidding streets of Berlin on the day before his return to Sweden. Thus the figure of the young Johan travels through a nocturnal war zone destined not to meet bright noble Aryans who offer the promise of manhood but a senile waiter, solitary tanks in deserted streets and a sinister dwarf-troupe who pose the threat of emasculation.

Bergman's fable, like those of Resnais and Bertolucci, is then and now, past and present, the inseparability of the present and the past. Elizabet's breakdown, her failure to speak, is also Bergman's failure to speak, his paralysis after having supported the wrong side in a war which tore the world apart, a recognition of the horror of his own mistake. *Persona* is an act of expiation but there is no light and uplift in that recognition. Elizabet continues, even in silence, to be a demon. Because both of Bergman's films engage more than the political, because they refuse to be explicit and are so many different things at the same time, they triumph. By contrast, the ingenious puppet-show of Hans-Jürgen Syberberg's *Hitler: A View from Germany* (1977) is too self-conscious and tendentious to capture the enormity of its subject.[10] Conceived as anti-documentary, the antithesis of Riefenstahl's *Triumph of the Will*, Syberberg's complex eight-hour marathon is designed to blame its puppet-Hitler for selling out the spirit of Wagner and German romanticism to the cheap spectacles of Hollywood. In the last decade it seems to have been the other way around. In an age of anabolic steroids and increasing civil violence, Hollywood has at last absorbed the crude remnants of the Nazi ideal for its special-effect, body-count movies. The demon and the machine are combined in cyborg-icons like Arnold Schwarzenegger, Rutger Hauer, Dolph Lundgren and Jean-Claude Van Damme, Euro-Aryans with heavy guttural accents who embody a new spirit of hi-tech anarcho-fascism.

In most respects Syberberg is a reactionary modernist. His strident love–hate relationship with the *Führer*, along with Berto-lucci's very different *1900*, is the nemesis of the neo-modern movement, a pyrrhic victory for the self-indulgent epic which uses modernist technique but succumbs to the shrill sensibilities of romance and loses sight of history. By contrast the more conventional narrative films of De Sica, Rosi and Edgar Reitz, as well as the powerful documentaries of Marcel Ophüls and Claude Lanzmann, remain the enduring legacies of cinema's direct encounter with fascist history over the last twenty years. They, however, have all absorbed the lessons of the neo-modern cin-ema. There is no turning back to a 'classical' realism. Instead they are the legacy of *Nuit et brouillard*, Resnais's first modern masterpiece which had constructed new narrative rhythms to re-present a barbaric history always threatening to be intractable. The complete alternative is Bergman, whose cinema makes few explicit references at all. For although Bergman's films may touch on the retro-movement, they go far beyond its confines to embrace all of the modern condition. Within this universal vision lies their specific power.

7

Commodified Demons II: The Automobile

The automobile has been one of the most powerful machines in our century to link instrumental and symbolic forms of human action. It has the power to move small groups of people, or single individuals, with great rapidity from place to place, depending upon the availability of course of petroleum and good roads. It has also thrived in capitalist countries through forms of competition over makes and models which turn cars into symbolic signs, signs defining the priorities of their owners and to a certain extent their owners' identities. Through the car they drive, people to some extent express who they are. Shape, size, speed and comfort all have material advantages in everyday living. Cars are also forms of self-expression. They connote as well as denote. What applies to saloon cars also applies to sports cars, limousines, motor-bikes, jeeps and pick-up trucks. But the saloon car is the chief repository of the double function and doubled identity of the automobile. Moreover its post-war development has turned it more and more into a consumer item: the styled upholstery of its seats, its heating and air-conditioning and its audio-visual culture, radio, cassettes, telephone, television, stereo – all become a facsimile of living-room culture even for those who have no living-rooms. In teenage dating culture the back seats of automobiles have not just become in folk lore the facsimiles of bedrooms. The automobile also makes possible the trailer or mobile home which in one of Sam Peckinpah's elegies to the West,

Junior Bonner, comes to replace the Western homestead. Fixity of place gives way to mobility of movement. The important thing is to be able to move anywhere and everywhere rather than be just somewhere. The car has now in fact become an integral part of consumer fashion, advertized on billboards and televisions, in magazines and cinemas, until the image of the car has become ubiquitous as the car itself.

There is of course a down side to all this. In the second half of this century the automobile has promised freedom only to imprison us, held out the lure of travel as speed and comfort only to kill us. Aided by its many erratic drivers, it has been responsible for seventeen million deaths in this century and now seriously injures over three-quarters of a million people throughout the world every year.[1] In terms of the economics and culture of advanced capitalist societies, the privately owned automobile has become more and more defined as a necessity. If it has been sold to us as our servant we, in a way, have become its slaves. We have turned it into a god we both love and hate. It is now the central icon of hi-tech mobility on *terra firma*, mass-produced, undertaxed like its gasoline and oversold like its expensive advertising, feted by the endless building of motorways, freeways, parkways which hold out the promise of greater freedom of movement only to transform gridlock into megaproportions. *City of Quartz*, the brilliant study by Mike Davis of the number one car city in the world, Greater Los Angeles, shows how that sprawling metropolis has honed the gridlock to a fine art and produced new definitions of dystopian nightmare for the end of the century.[2]

The *flâneur* of Baudelaire's nineteenth-century Paris has long given way to hurrying consumers and commuters, often on four wheels. It is often dangerous to be a pedestrian, and many cities now have traffic-free precincts to act as a form of protection not only from the deadly physical force of the machine but from the sickening pollution of its exhaust. Yet moving images on cinema and television continue to celebrate the car-cruiser of the open road who speeds through the countryside by day and stalks the city mean streets at night. This is the glamour-icon American cinema above all has given us, a world not of boredom, vitriol, tailbacks and traffic but of freedom, excitement and danger. Against the inspired back-rushing shots of nocturnal branches in Fritz Lang, since copied by Chabrol, we can pit the more immediate gangster raids of *Scarface* or *Bonnie and Clyde*, the daredevil cop chases of *Bullitt* and *The French Connection*, the mainstreet teenage car talk of *American Graffiti*, the spectacular multiple crashes of low-budget Roger Corman, the desert escape-cum-roadscape of *Thelma and Louise*. Here the car is never a truly impersonal force, a disembodied object. It is also a possession. What I want to argue is that American and Western European cinema diverge crucially on this one issue, that of the object owned, the car possessed as ours or mine.

We should see this in a particular context, that of the decline of American car manufacture and of American industry in general. The cinema celebrates the myth of the American car the more its economic status is put into jeopardy. While Japanese cars flood American markets, the Asian cinema hardly concerns itself with the car as icon. While European manufacturers have produced their designer sports cars, their Jaguars, Porsches and Ferraris, and hotted many of their saloons to the delight of all joyriders, the greater speed and performance of European cars is not an iconic feature of the narrative movie. But American cinema's celebration of the American car is not just a defensive manoeuvre. American cinema itself is now at the forefront of the American export market, a form of economic capital predetermined as cultural capital. Its domination of the world market, on television and video screens as well as in cinemas is a major and decisive form of domination – indeed one of the last repositories of Yankee know-now – to be offset against the more competitive television and popular music markets, the greater domination of fashion and advertising by the Western Europeans and of all audio-visual hardware by the Japanese. As if to emphasize the irony of the tie-in of the car and movie culture, Robert Altman in *The Player* has one of his villainous young Hollywood producers driving a black BMW convertible. We may safely assume that such a man is heavily involved in selling the movie myth of the American automobile to the world while disdaining to drive one himself.

What distinguishes the American from the European representations of the car in the cinema? It seems to me that the key criteria are possessive individualism, the open road and the triumph of the heroic machine. The automobile is the thing owned which defines the modern persona, a mechanical extension of the self and the body, a persona invested with magical

properties, a technological form of the will-to-power. The car as
the expressive face of the peripatetic self, the instrument of its
wandering, fits well with the movie camera. In an age when
romance is dead, at times the two seem made for each other.
The love-affair of driver and machine is echoed and matched by
the love-affair of machine and machine. The popular genre of
the 'road-movie' makes its entry in the 1960s with location shooting and the mobile camera. The studio perennial of talking heads
framed against a process screen is dropped in favour of car
mounts placed at any number of angles, high angle chopper
shots and following shots from other automobiles. The camera
moves with the moving object in its lens, as part of the process
of movement in general. This reflexive fix is part of what gives
the car its spectator appeal, making it an ecstatic version of the
body extended in space and time. But to all this possession is
vital, and here ownership is the key. Renting, stealing, bor-
rowing, chauffeuring are all degraded forms of automotive being,
of Heideggerian *dasein*. For the American myth there are in fact
forms of inauthentic being.

Here we must add a further vital distinction. The heroic
machine is usually a car which belongs to a previous decade.
The degraded machine which is stolen or chauffeured belongs,
usually, to the present, a contemporary model. It is not ugly or
despised but simply unmagical, visually a car without qualities.
On the other hand, if it is foreign like the black Mercedes convertible of Richard Gere in *American Gigolo*, it is a clear threat, a
perfect emblem for the noir fall-guy, this year's gleaming model
as a signifier of free fall. Let us then take a few examples from
the past decade of the American cinema. Whatever else they are,
both *Wild at Heart* and *Thelma and Louise* are own-car movies.
The car defines the couple on the run and becomes part of them.
In Lynch's film Sailor breaks his parole but Lula has saved him
his precious snakeskin jacket and they go on the run in Lula's
black convertible. By sharing the driving, they share the identity
of a car which is framed as the speeding prelude to lust, dance,
danger and romance. While on the run in Ridley Scott's picture
Thelma and Louise blow up a massive oil transporter and cause
police cars to crash insanely in hot pursuit. Yet Louise's 1966
Ford Thunderbird convertible remains unscathed through the
havoc it creates as well as providing much needed work for stunt
doubles. While Thelma is tricked, molested, robbed and nearly

raped, her buddy's automobile suffers no humiliation inflicted upon its body.

In the rather different convention of male bonding to be found in Barry Levinson's brother movie *Rain-Man* the iconography of the car is almost identical. Tom Cruise abducts the autistic Dustin Hoffman from an asylum in the mid-West to drive back to California. The bonding of sane and disturbed, hyperactive hustler and mathematical wizard, is established by the white 1949 Buick Roadmaster convertible – limited edition, the one item left to cruise in the will of their avaricious father. But it is Hoffman, not Cruise, who identifies the car while remaining unable in any way to identify his brother. Thus Hollywood mythology goes up yet another notch in its pathos of the machine. In the American road-movie the machine creates profane mayhem but remains itself sacred. From Martin Sheen in *Badlands* to Viggo Mortensen in *The Indian Runner* even the most psychotic outlaws own their cars. Stealing can be at best an interlude. In Sean Penn's retro-movie about a bad brother back from Vietnam, Mortensen steals a Ford Mustang from two pot-smoking trendies at a birthday party, robs a gas station in it, and then removes the evidence by simply torching the car-icon of the late 1960s made famous by Steve Macqueen in *Bullit*. He then resumes the journey home in his own battered 1950s saloon. In a similar vein, when Nicholas Cage is tempted into the blood-spattered heist of *Wild at Heart* by Willem Dafoe, Cage leaves Dern's convertible behind to use Dafoe's machine, thus absolving the former from all evil. Not to be outdone, William Hurt in *Body Heat* temporarily swaps his red sports convertible, both crimson and phallic, for a rented metallic saloon for the murder and disposal of Kathleen Turner's husband. If film noir links passion and murder, as it does so brilliantly here, the iconography of the car also separates them. The phallic machine which prefaces seduction is owned and thus vitally different from the ignoble instrument of corpse disposal which is merely rented from Hertz in downtown Miami.

Underlying the loss of automotive possession is the fear of lost masculinity. If critical theory has always exaggerated the reification of commodities in the culture industry, this is a case where it actually applies. Loss of masculinity is a loss of selfhood, the heroic male petrified into a disposable commodity. The *locus classicus* is without doubt the Schrader/Scorsese collaboration on

Taxi Driver where Robert De Niro, the psychotic Vietnam vet speeding on speed through the seedier streets of Manhattan, is cabbie-cum-voyeur observing the decadent sights he does not want at first to see, but then watching them compulsively. The eye strains to see, the ear to hear, and the back seat is the site of client infamy. If ever someone failed to cultivate what Simmel called 'the blasé attitude', this is it. If ever anyone embodied Deleuze's schizo-culture premissed on the promiscuity of immediacy, this too is it. Lacking possession of his vehicle, De Niro watches without control, inflaming his paranoia back into the culture of the gun, that other Cartesian proof of existence in the maelstrom of American consumerism. Schrader goes further in the movies he has since directed himself, *American Gigolo* and *Light Sleeper*. In both the male anti-heroes are commodities with female bosses, ageing designer toyboys dressed by Armani and dominated by older women. Here metaphysical sickness implodes in the cracking of the image as Gere and Dafoe each face a crisis they cannot handle without the help of their female superiors, Nina van Pallandt and Susan Sarandon, at whose mercy they continue to be. One of Gere's disguises before he reveals himself as a gigolo to his middle-aged clients is to be a chauffeur complete with peaked cap while Dafoe as an upmarket drugs courier is chauffeured from deal to deal around Manhattan in the back seat of the company limousine. The back seat and the chauffeur's cap are signs of deformation, revealing Hollywood's mythical proof of male existence by default. I own/drive, therefore I am.

By contrast, the great 1960s movies of Godard, *A bout de souffle*, *Pierrot le fou* and *Weekend* had already undermined the pride of possessing, of *my* car as opposed to any car. In the ideology of consumerism the object is a prize of possession, yet in consumer practice, as Godard realized, any mass-produced object is disposable, transient, temporary. It is no more permanent than desire itself. If possession is everywhere, it is also nowhere. In *A bout de souffle* (1959) Belmondo is Michel Poiccard, a man of many aliases, a petty thief of cars as much as names, money or anything else. You are what you steal. The opening sequence says it all. When he hotwires a car on the Marseilles waterfront and drives off to Paris without the girl who has acted as his lookout, but in search of the American girl in Paris he wants to take to Rome, we sense that he is doomed to perpetual motion. He is always in between places, people, lovers, so that every lover or city is a stepping stone to someone or somewhere else. The car is an instrument of this nowhere motion, to be chosen for its look as much as its speed, to be stolen simply for being in the wrong place at the wrong time.

On car or foot as he moves through Paris, Belmondo is a commodified demon of modernity, a desiring machine, a hyperactive fragment. At the same time, Godard is the anguished romantic trying as modern *auteur* to exorcize his hero's grand passion for Patricia Francini by all means of ingenuity – the 360-degree pan, the jump-cut, the newspaper headline, the neon sign, the death-cloud of cigarette smoke in the lovers' hotel room. Yet Godard is doomed to fail. Sublimely, he has lost control of his own creation. For in addition to being machine, fragment and demon, Michel is one of life's obsessive lovers. The existential nature of sex, the casual nature of murder and thieving, the attractive perfidy of things American, none can displace the object of his *amour fou*, who is, after all, America in the flesh. In *A bout de souffle* we have one of cinema's great contradictions. One of its most supremely modern films is also one of its most romantic. As in *The Lady from Shanghai* a ridiculous passion thrives on all absurdities which modern life has to throw at it. The femme fatale is not however defined by her glamour, her look, her mystery or her eyes. Jean Seberg remains in the memory for her cropped hair, her awkward walk and her atrocious French.

Just as Welles in *The Lady from Shanghai* does everything he can to mock the passion of Mike O'Hara and Elsa Bannister, Godard tries everything he can to turn us off Michel's romantic quest. In 1960 his car journey north to Paris would have bewildered its audience, a montage of alienation-effects, an action-sequence to mock the essence of melodrama. In quick succession came many things they were not accustomed to expect – the address to the camera, casual insults of hitch-hikers and drivers, reckless overtaking, the shooting of the sun through the tree-tops with the gun found in the glove compartment, the crossing of the line in the mismatch cut between the stolen car and the chasing cops on motor-bikes. The shooting sequence, too, reverses our expectation of murder melodrama, denying climax, focusing not on the act but on its consequence. Thus we have the jump-cut from the close-up of the revolver primed to fire to the brief medium shot of the cop falling behind a tree, then the sudden cut to the panning long shot of Belmondo sprinting into the far distance through an open field. Since the film has so often been copied in so many different ways, the bold mixture of the comic and the serious here is sometimes forgotten. What is existential here becomes in *Bonnie and Clyde* merely cute, undermined by the slow-motion shoot-out at the end of Penn's film, a travesty of New Wave technique which merely emphasizes its betrayal. What is casually murderous and gratuitous in Godard became graphically bloodstained in the American cinema of the 1970s, reclaimed for melodrama with modernist trimmings. For Americans, the anxiety of influence is always skin-deep, which is perhaps why Jim McBride's remake of Godard's film is such a disappointment and cannot even bring itself to have Richard Gere shot by the police as he reaches for his gun at the end of the picture. Besides, in a car-rental culture of standard saloons, the Hollywood of the 1980s is more concerned with something else. It restores the car to its primal state in American mythology of being-possessed-as-image, a sacred icon to be owned because of its special shape, its special colour, its special past.

By contrast, *A bout de souffle* had already captured something Hollywood has never quite managed, the authentically banal experience of the car in the modern age. In place of the romance of the open journey and the straight line, the lure of speed and the danger of the chase, it gives us the slicing up of time, the fragmenting of attention through multiple and simultaneous experience. The car journey is an essay in the seduction and betrayal of attention by speed. Everything the eye sees and searches out in the rushing motion through places and people and other automobiles is doomed to a quick entrance or exit. Or if it is not, it becomes a source of anxiety. Often overtaking is not so much the show of superior speed but desire to annihilate the presence of the automobile in front, to deny it permanent presence in the field of vision. In that respect *A bout de souffle* is *La règle du jeu* taken out of the rooms and corridors of Renoir's chateau and dumped on the city street and the open road. It is a battle-hymn of those impatient with permanence but also despairing of its lack. The stolen car replaces the car owned and shows its lure while denying its glamour. In Godard's film Belmondo goes through several cars which are not his own. Their owners' identities are largely anonymous. The car-fetish becomes impersonal, a feature of the commodity, not the person. In Hollywood, the own-car is eternal in the imagination. In Godard it is predestined for the scrap heap.

Godard has fought his battle against Hollywood in a bold Pascalian wager and been defeated.[3] To lose is to be expected but the slim chances of success, if they materialized, might, he imagined, change the nature of cinema. The modern car movie is unthinkable without him, yet inevitably he has lost his long and at times tortuous struggle. His car-cinema, like that of Antonioni and Wenders, lacks the means of displacing the American Leviathan, but it is a rival which has never gone away and never been completely taken over. If the car is usually stolen or 'borrowed', which is after all the most common form of thieving now in Western societies, Godard also undermines the romance of the willing partner. The difference here with American films of different periods is instructive. Ray's *They Live by Night* (1948) precedes Godard. Malick's *Badlands* (1974) is a truly post-Godardian film. In both films we have loving couples on the run. But in Ray's film Bowie and Keechie are justified outlaws, victims of society and chance alike to whom society has given no real chance. As if to stress their inherent goodness Ray gives us a magical spur-of-the-moment marriage ceremony as their long-distance bus makes a scheduled stop in a small town. The honeymoon is something else. Ray cuts from the quickie ceremony to the specially purchased honeymoon car on the open road, the speeding car in which, one feels, they will literally consummate their union. It is a supremely lyrical moment, romantic, optimistic, defiant, the uncharted space of pure love and the American Dream, before doom catches up with them.

Badlands casually trashes all such hope. The fleeing car consummats not marriage but the cold-blooded murder by Kit, the wooer, of his girl's disapproving father. It follows his burning down of the family house. The murderer may be a James Dean lookalike but Ray's dream of redemption has gone. With Martin Sheen at its wheel, the outlaw car is anything but glamorous, a black, ugly, bear-like apparition which plucks Holly (Sissy Spacek) out of high school and out of childhood into the world of romance poisoned in the bud, an outlaw world of lust in the badlands of South Dakota and love, not sex, in the head. But only Holly's head. Her voice-over 'reads' the story of murder and flight as teenage comic romance while Kit, the casual psychopath, can dance with her to Nat King Cole on the car radio in a darkness lit only by the car's headbeams but has no feeling for any living person. The irony of juxtaposition, her voice, his actions, is humorous but cruel. In Ray's film Keechie reacts with horror to the bank robbery gone wrong but also to society's victimization of her husband–lover. By contrast, Spacek shows no pity for her father or for her lover's later victims. Moral sensibility has degenerated into pure nothingness.

Yet there is a residual likeness in these two vastly different movies. Both girls are hero-worshippers. They stand by their man, much as Laura Dern does in *Wild at Heart* waiting patiently (twice) for Nicholas Cage while he does time and between jail terms fleeing with him to New Orleans and points west to escape her mother's evil clutches. If Malick ironizes such dumb loyalty in place of Ray's despairing vision of hope, Lynch has his cake and eats it. Dern is primarily in love with Cage's body and as an afterthought stands by him through all the slings and arrows of outrageous fortune flying in his direction. Three different kinds of female loyalty, for sure, but all of them anti-noir movies, narratives of transgression which run against the grain of betrayal. *A bout de souffle* is anti-noir for a different reason. It is a daytime movie, self-consciously transparent, mocking all the dark nooks and crannies of melodrama. Yet it ends by contrast with the American road movies in the woman's betrayal of her lover to the police. Jean Seberg is the femme fatale become banal, shorn of all the adornments of myth. Her motive is not at all sinister but quite pragmatic. Her courses at the Sorbonne, her easy life in Paris and her dreams of being a star journalist meeting celebrities all matter more than the passion of a small-time gangster to whom she never really listens and who has stupidly killed a cop. For Michel she is the lure of all things American, but for a middle-class American girl in Paris he is never much more than a sport, a novelty. Her consumerism is much more economical and has no room for romance where his, surprisingly, does. She is more interested in celebrity than passion.

Here Godard is infinitely more subtle than Malick who copies him and parades Martin Sheen as an idolizing James Dean lookalike much as Belmondo is made to adore and imitate Bogart. The difference is that Belmondo does not look like Bogart at all. The power of impersonation, anyway, would cut little ice with Patricia. She craves the presence of real celebrities, not imposters.

Parvelescu, the famous novelist, whose press conference she attends at Orly airport, offers up portentous statements on love and gender she dotes upon uncritically. Previously in bed with Michel their talk has ranged through much the same material but she has failed to take seriously anything her lover has said. Something said to an audience by someone famous is more important than something improvised between the sheets by someone trying to be infamous. Michel offers the wrong kind of notoriety, that of a cop murderer, not that of a controversial artist. Michel can appropriate many of the American objects he desires – the Ford convertible he steals on the streets of Paris, the photo of Bogie which stares down at him from outside the cinema. But he cannot have her in the way he wants, as an object of passion rather than desire. She does not want to go to Rome. She prefers to remain the perennial American in Paris.

Belmondo is an existential outlaw in flight, apotheosis of Gide's *acte gratuit*, whose movement is cyclical. He circulates the boulevards rather than fleeing the city as he later will in *Pierrot le fou*. The sense of circular movement is reinforced by Raoul Coutard's famous wheelchair shots, the frontal tracking of Belmondo without a cut as he walks into the travel agency to see Tolmatchoff and back out again, and, later, similar panning shots in the *Herald Tribune* office and the studio of the Swedish model.[4] This implosive rendering of flight as going nowhere in particular, defying all its American antecedents, is one of the most powerful the cinema has to offer. Michel's greatest heresy, after stealing cars, is refusing the sports car Berruti offers him to escape to Italy just as the cops are closing in. He denies salvation by denying his *modus vivendi*. In the casual shrug which conveys the acceptance of absurd fate, the romantic motive is squashed but never annihilated. Betrayed by Patricia, his residual romance has failed and nothing is left. As we know already, he will choose not the grief that Harry Wilbourne chooses at the end of Faulkner's *The Wild Palms* but the nothingness which has already replaced it.

The bathos of his ending, as he staggers mortally wounded down the middle of the long narrow street only to collapse at the end of it, denies us the romance of death by driving, the heroic escaping crash. But the long continuous tracking shot from behind intimates something else. The moving figure of the wounded outlaw suggests a car out of petrol and out of control which finally lurches to a halt. Belmondo has become the doomed runaway car he uses to steal, and imitated its movement. The car is no longer an extension of the body. Rather the body is an extension of the car, a demon commodified which motors on without it. The image of Belmondo staggering down the street in his bloody shirt is that of a man unbearably vulnerable, stripped naked, exposed, the compulsive driver with the frame of his car torn off him but still slave to its forward motion. The tracking shot from behind of Belmondo's zigzagging process shows us a man literally driving himself into the ground. The man mimics the automobile in the moment that he, like it, is destined for the scrap heap.

In *A bout de souffle* Belmondo is a petit-bourgeois outlaw rejected by a cold and calculating daughter of the American bourgeoisie. Later in *Weekend* (1967) Godard deals with the class he despises as a whole, but as quintessentially French, not American. Like Buñuel his aim is not so much to strike terror at the heart of the bourgeoisie as to seek out an existing terror at the heart of their daily lives. Yet despite his flashy Brechtian devices he lacks the measured distance and deft satirical touch of Buñuel. His critique is always desperate, close to the edge. Distance becomes a defence mechanism, a necessary distraction from desolation, the last refuge of the tortured romantic amidst the chaos of modernity. *Weekend* is powerful because it has no icon. Lacking Belmondo or Karenina, Godard denatures the personality. The infantilism of Jean-Pierre Leaud which cast such a blight on the later movies of both himself and Truffaut, is effectively contained here within a minor role. Jean Yanne, soon to be a naturalized figure in the bourgeois melodramas of Chabrol, and Mireille Darc are perfect foils here for the director's intention. They start where Michel Poiccard left off, as servants of the car, extension-slaves of the speed machine.

Pierrot le fou (1965) is a necessary bridge between *A bout de souffle* and *Weekend*. It shows us the centrality of the car in Godard's imagination, that the car indeed is crucial not only to the movie's theme but to Godard's cinematic art itself. For here, once he abandons the car, art abandons him. In *Pierrot* the movie begins to evaporate when it reaches the coast, despite Coutard's ravishing photography which evokes the landscapes of Matisse. Godard saw the sea as a poetic presence, as the 'presence of nature, which is neither romantic nor tragic'. He also admitted in the same interview with *Cahiers du Cinéma* that 'he wanted to tell the story of the last romantic couple'.[5] But he is the first and last major romantic who makes absolutely nothing out of nature. The romance is already dependent on the motion of the car. Godard satirizes bourgeois car talk at the opening party but his adventure is inconceivable without automobiles, without the Peugeot 404 in which they escape and which Marianne blows up with a pistol shot, without the American car they then steal from off a pneumatic hoist in a garage, and which Ferdinand eventually drives into the sea. But though the sea swallows the car, it does not take over from it. Once it disappears there is a vacuum which the sea cannot fill. The adventure has been taken over by the machine. When the machine is abandoned the sea has no poetic presence to sustain it. Instead Godard works better with the invasion of nature, as in *Weekend*, by the machine, of the countryside by the car. Here again once the couple, this time bourgeois and no longer romantic, abandon the automobile, the film loses its identity.

For Godard the car defines everything. To borrow, wreck and steal is doomed and romantic. To own and be possessive and go on weekend outings is bourgeois. Yet the two are never totally separate. Those who steal and wreck but never own are clearly anti-bourgeois. Those who proudly own and end the crisis of a ruined weekend themselves stealing and wrecking are still bourgeois, but self-destructively so. They have shown their destructive face in crossing to the other side. The automobile out of control is a form of consumer fascism. For Godard the fate of the car unlocks the secret of Marx's prophecy that the bourgeoisie will eventually dig its own grave. In *Weekend* the members of that doomed class wreck the thing they love. In doing so, he implies, they wreck themselves. It is a despairing version of Marx. For Godard's ambivalence over the speed-machine is never exorcized. His love–hate is primordial. The automobile is a work of art but also an agent of destruction. No wonder Godard is reputed to have said in his revolutionary phase that Western capitalism should be abolished but General Motors should be exempt because we all need cars. The 1960s movies are all prophetic not of the car, and capitalism's, destruction but of their enhancement. The car as fate of modernity is clearer in Godard than in any other film-maker. To that extent he is more convincingly futuristic in his car movies than he is in *Alphaville*, his science-fiction dystopia. Here the parody and the technical invention are always strong. But the science fiction effects are hopelessly dated and sci-fi ends up as a cover for covert romance. Anna Karina and Eddie Constantine give us a love-affair with a happy ending almost unthinkable in Godard's bleak parable of contemporary life. Science fiction offers a refuge for romance that the present, and the car, clearly lack.

Weekend deconstructs the automobile 'accident' with an unparalleled savagery and loses its way when it has no more crashed cars to show us. The starting-point of the film is therefore more important than the political rhetoric of its ending. It is a high balcony long shot of a trivial accident between a red Matra and a blue and white Mini below which provokes a violent fight between the two male drivers, the owner of the Matra coupé outraged that a lesser car could stupidly collide with his own. It is not only the affront to one's car-as-possession but also one's sense of owning a *superior* automobile. Unlike most house or car theft where the robbers are never seen, the accident is a visible infraction of property. If the car is an extension of the body, then the dent on the bumper is experienced as a personal injury, a violation of self. The injured party – self-defined – feels the force of the 'crime' and then sees the 'perpetrator'. The accident turns into a ritual of blaming the wrongdoer, though it is often never clear which driver is the wrongdoer and which is the victim. Arguments start when both claim the role of the innocent victim. Godard soon repeats the high-angle long shot from a horizontal plane for a second incident, the ideal framing to make of the 'accident' a comic absurdity with serious consequences. Rolande and Corinne start their weekend journey to Corinne's mother in Normandy by backing into a Renault in the apartment parking lot. They try in vain to bribe the young boy who sees the bump, then boorishly fight off the woman owner who protests at the assault on her precious vehicle. Finally they flee from her irate husband who fires at them with a shotgun. The camera views them distantly as skirmishing insects.

Godard cuts immediately to the famous seven-minute track of a traffic tail-back from a multiple crash in the countryside. In the continuous lateral tracking of the camera, the piled-up traffic is framed as a Balzacian slice of *comédie humaine*. People argue, picnic, play football, cards and chess. Monkeys clamber along the wire roof of a travelling circus truck while a tall llama looks blankly at the camera. An endless artery of trucks and cars leads to a massive multiple pile-up, battered cars and bloody roadside corpses of which no one appears to take the slightest notice. The apocalyptic climax to the shot is a mere blockage on the road for those behind, something to be bypassed at the earliest opportunity as Roland's cheating black convertible shows. The priority in human affairs is made bitterly clear. Injury to the car is a paramount source of indignation. The death of passengers merits barely a glance. Life goes on in a multitude of ways as Rolande jumps the queue by driving on the wrong side of the road. Overtaking, queue-jumping, minor bumps are all an affront to human dignity. Overturned cars and bloodstained bodies are not. Since they cannot be made to feel shame or fear, they do not appear to count.

As in Renoir, Godard's bourgeois couple ignore the signs of their portending fate. In Renoir adultery among servants is still comic even when it threatens to be murderous, so comic the spectator thinks at first it a fate which cannot possibly befall André and his friends. But the gamekeeper's hunting of the poacher through the chateau with a shotgun is a murderous chase they choose to ignore at their peril just as Corinne and Rolande blindly ignore the casualties strewn on the highway. In an ironic coda which still shifts his narrative forwards, Godard then gives a version of the accident as a form of 'class struggle', again echoing Renoir. The title on the screen precedes another car smash, this time between a tractor and a sports car where the bloodied girlfriend of the dead driver berates the bemused tractor-driver with class insults. The couple look on as the incident portends their capture by revolutionaries at the end of the movie. Yet one feels with Godard's picture that their real fate is not the climactic political one he gives us. It comes in the inevitable crash halfway through the movie. It is a crash moreover which turns them into roadside proletarians by depriving them of their sacred automobile. Godard literally gives us a moving parable of downward mobility. Yet the crash of course does not turn them into toiling workers. It turns them into bedraggled hitch-hikers.

In his scrupulous avoidance of melodrama, Godard cuts quickly from the speeding couple, driving cyclists and motorists off the road into a *tableau vivant* of the multiple crash to which they are destined. Only we do not see the crash happen and we do not identify the couple at first in its burning midst. We become aware that they are involved in the chaos only when we hear the distant voice of Corinne coming out of the wreckage to lament the loss of her designer handbag. Later, after their abject failure to abduct Jean-Pierre Leaud's Japanese convertible, they are resigned to becoming hitch-hikers. The speed of the movie changes down abruptly to signify their degraded status as pedestrians, registering states of immobility and whimsical interludes. As a change of mood this is effective. But substance is missing without the automobile. Substance *is* the automobile. We wait for it to return, for the couple to trudge and hitch once more along a highway littered with wrecks and corpses. The movie sets up an addiction to the car and its temporary absence becomes unbearable. Its absence is a vacuum at the centre of Godard's movie. Without it Godard lapses into a whimsy which is often infantile. The various eccentrics the couple encounter in their picaresque journey do not have the edge on the murderous machine. The piano recital in the farmyard with its 360-degree pans, the various theatres of the absurd on route, have a jarring quality of threadbare improvisation. Godard savages the car but is lost when he destroys the thing he loves.

Later, Godard's political interpolations and local revolutionaries are even more embarrassing, rendered with a total lack of conviction which is sometimes too painful to bear. True, his political naivety is less obvious here than elsewhere but even then the despairing romantic barely fleshes out his ideological apparel. In retrospect the film looks like a premonition of the failure of the revolt in Paris soon to come and yet also of the fleeting triumph of its rhetoric in the early 1970s, to which Godard's subsequent films belong. But Godard is not Eisenstein. In Eisenstein's cinema the iconography of revolt depends on the cut and the close-up, the engagement with outraged feelings, with immediate response to the cruel and the unjust. Godard's conscious abandonment of the techniques of montage, his insistence on the long take and the long shot, his pristine refusal of the reverse-angle, diminishes both friend and foe alike. It is brilliantly suited to the savageries of satire but offers no saving grace for humanity at large. It is the Calvinist cinematography of the damned. His workers are wooden, and his local revolutionaries as ridiculous as his car-crazed bourgeoisie. One suspects that Godard in his despair cannot come to terms with the truth at the heart of his vision. Here, despite all Marxist rhetoric, the car outlives the revolution in the modern Western imagination of which his own work, despite its many heresies, is still a part. The apocalypse of revolution remains part fantasy. The apocalypse of the automobile throughout the world has become casually real, the acceptable face of mass consumer carnage and ecological damage. In a premonition of things to come, Godard's French bourgeoisie are no longer Renoir's chateau-bound weak-lings, soon to cave in to their vicious Nazi neighbours. They are the hypocrites of civilization in love with the power and comfort of speed on the open road, redefining the licence to kill.

One of Godard's great legacies to the cinema was his eye for the density of cultural signs. In all his great films – *A bout de souffle, Une Femme est une femme, Vivra sa vie, Pierrot le fou* and *Weekend* – they form the sensuous surround of doomed heroes and heroines, cars, cigarettes, lipstick, bicycles, photographs, mirrors in Paris bars, newspapers, magazines, posters, neon lights. They are material things we consume, disposables which always also point to something else. They are always material and symbolic at the same time, real and fantastic, signifiers and signifieds. They celebrate identity in difference. But they are also signs of the modern, material objects which have multipled in cities of mass consumption throughout the course of the century, fetish signs of fashion, adornment and desire. These signs bear no linguistic or metaphysical essentialism. They are the cultural products of advanced capitalism. Their surfeit, their excess, the many different image-signs on television, in stores, showrooms, magazines and billboards which might display the latest model of a sports car, a drink or a body perfume, are fairly specific to the twentieth century. Thus our current obsession with signs does not unlock the secret of the universe but rather points to an everyday feature of our existence. If we are what we consume, signs increasingly mediate our desire for consuming. They point the way to commodities and in the process become commodities themselves. Our visual and aural fields of perception consume signs just as much as the objects they signify.

The automobile as image-sign continued its career in Antonioni's much derided masterpiece, *Zabriskie Point* (1969), made for MGM in California a couple of years after *Weekend*. Again, revolution is featured here but matters little in comparison with landscape and machine. Luckily it begins the movie and charges it with a loose plot, a catalyst to narrative rather than its culmination. More important than the revolt on the UCLA campus with its constant zoom and re-focusing shots, its real-life rebels and *cinema-vérité* look, is Mark's peripheral role in it as a gun-toting loner, whose weapon may or may not have killed the dead cop. This is the young outlaw in the age of Vietnam, interested not in the rhetoric of campus politics but in the potential of the firearm. The glamour of the car has also gone. Accuracy in the matter of the counter-culture rightly dictates the battered pick-up Mark and his buddies drive through Los Angeles. Here the Italian film-maker plays brilliantly on the alternations of surface and depth. The billboard hoardings and neon signs of the LA boulevards are shot in telephoto. Travelling point-of-view shots of the automobile driver are compiled into swift montage where every image passing him by is too fleeting to have any after-effect. In the interior of his top-floor skyscraper office Lee Allen, however, sees everything around him in deep focus. The flags and buildings outside are as well defined as those inside. Cut off from the city below, the businessman's interior is a place of depth, while down on the boulevards Mark is pressed too close to his passing surroundings to have any perspective upon them.

Later, after the shooting of the cop, where a jump-cut makes Mark's involvement highly ambiguous, the loner's sudden flight demands a different kind of machine. Here Antonioni adds the iconography of the private plane to that of the car, as Mark hijacks a Lilly 7 to escape the police and fly into the desert. He also adds the iconography of the ubiquitous billboard to that of the demon machine. In one moment Mark is framed watching the airport beside a huge hoarding which advertises the getaway family adventure of the passenger flight. The next moment he is illegally entering the airfield. The small plane as consumer possession matches the road-movie's conventional car-or-bike-as-owned. But here, in the Europeanized version of the outlaw tradition brought back by its Italian director to the USA to the great displeasure of his hosts, the plane of course is stolen, not owned. In moving from the battered truck to the stolen plane, Antonioni circumvents the car as icon, and incurs all-American wrath. Yet the image of the 'stolen' car is still at hand. We are never given a reason for Daria's trip to Phoenix until she is well on her journey. A telephone call from Lee to her apartment suggests to us, through the curt male voice on the other end of the line, that she has borrowed her boyfriend's car without permission and taken to the open road. The 'borrowed' car, driving across the desert under Mark's plane, is an ancient 1954 Buick saloon and anything but glamorous. She is roofed and glassed in; no romance of the sleek convertible here.

Yet this chance meeting prompts a courtship from behind glass of a couple who have never met as Mark circles, swoops and daringly buzzes the car below him in the empty desert. It is hi-tech love at first sight. The machine is seen before the figure: the plane before the outlaw in it, the car before the girl. Nor is the episode arbitrary or whimsical, as it would be in most road-movies of the period. Antonioni has already built it up through the iconography of Mark's truck on LA boulevards. The camera catches the back-rushing images of the streets as they become imprinted on Mark's mirrors and windscreen. The outside becomes the inside while, in a supreme instance of visual osmosis Mark's own image is itself imprinted on the windscreen. The inside hence becomes exterior. Distance and separation on the one hand, transference and transparency on the other. The metropolitan boulevards of America's first city of car-culture, a city without true boundaries, project an excess jumble of signs which exist only for the eye in rapid forward motion, not for the eye in static contemplation. At first this is a chaos of iconic surfaces with little meaning or relevance to Mark's own precarious existence. Yet the irony of intention-in-motion is not overlooked. For any desperate action Mark takes there is always some external sign which corresponds to it, however wrongly. The billboard offering up the plane as a means of an escape to a happy holiday for a happy nuclear family is a consumer exhortation Mark will soon fulfil in his own way, with his own idiosyncrasies. The loner in the counter-culture remains a consumer outlaw.

At first sight Daria's lonely journey through the desert in her battered Buick appears to be that of the archetypal hippie of the period doing her own thing. But the circumstances are ambiguous. Her boss, desert property developer Rod Taylor, who asks her on impulse to be her secretary, behaves half the time like a middle-aged seducer and the other half like a concerned father rebuking the prodigal daughter of a rebel generation. The purpose of her journey to the house in Arizona is never specified, and she actually leaves before Taylor gives her the green light, enforcing the image of a prodigal daughter on the run, the uncanny sense that Allen and Daria must have met before, that their strange unnerving relationship has had a previous life. Daria is thus a figure of mystery. At a small town on the edge of the desert, peopled only by old men in a lonely bar and threatening young delinquents hiding in the wrecks of cars on a garbage tip, the boys start suddenly to molest her and force her to flee. Later at Zabriskie Point a cop in dark glasses, oddly reminiscent of the cop who confronts Janet Leigh in the Arizona desert in *Psycho*, makes clear he also has a sexual interest, unaware that Mark is hiding nearby, gun in hand, ready to shoot. Not only for Taylor is she an object of desire. Her journey, on one level, is a journey of exploration, a chance to see Taylor's elaborate desert house near Phoenix built into the side of a cliff. Here there is a double reading of the 'conference centre' which looks and feels uncannily like a home in the desert. In the surface reading, Daria is the hippie commodified as an unlikely businessman's secretary. But once on her journey the brown-skinned Daria never changes her short blue denim dress and its conspicuous Indian belt, not even after the dust and gypsum of love-making in Death Valley. It seems a stylized hippie apparel but the iconography of her figure changes the deeper into the desert she drives. Her figure suggests less and less that of the young hippie woman of her own decade, more and more a young Indian woman of the new West. The journey into the desert, which appears first as an adventure, can then be read as an unspoken homecoming, an ironic echo of Mark's fatal return to LA to meet a predictable fate at the hands of the gun-toting police.

Underlying Antonioni's vision are two contrasting scenarios of the American West. In the first instance we have the artificiality of the vast metropolitan culture of southern California, much of which is built on land which is semi-desert. This is a massive megapolis of hi-tech settlement to be extended further into the desert by Allen's elaborate business plans for holiday homes. Such dwellings are shown in Allen's top-floor LA office in clumsy television commercials framed, at one distance removed, as signs of artefacts which bear little relationship to their environment or its history. Such rational abnormality is shockingly embodied in the visual image of Allen's semi circular glass and sandstone home built into desert rocks, trying to be at one with the look and texture of its surroundings but sticking out like a sore thumb, a testament to the unnatural colonization of nature by consumer comfort. As opposed to the wagon trains of Ford and others rolling west in optimism and hope, this is surfeit settlement of the Arizona desert from the west done with a calculating and rational deadness, the zero-point of civilization.

In the second scenario we have the buried iconography of the classical Western of the Hollywood cinema to which the Italian director is subtly responding, in particular to the cinema of John Ford. The hi-tech courtship in the desert suggests a modern version of a common Western motif, the woman from the East in stagecoach or buggy being feted by the horse-riding Westerner. The plane's freedom-variations which contrast with the straight line of the road-bound car echo the freedom of the horse and the skill of his rider as the buggy ploughs a rutted track in the wilderness. At the end, on Mark's return to the airport at LA, Antonioni inverts those spatial images of the free-flying plane over the desert which had been lyrically sustained by panning, zooms and telephotos, by the most spectacular of travelling shots. Mark's landing is filmed frontally and the plane is pursued on either side by waiting police cars on the tarmac, their marksmen firing revolvers to kill. The iconography is strongly reminiscent of Ford's Indians attacking the stagecoach from both sides in the classic Western of that name and of the sequence in *The Searchers* where Ethan Edwards's revenge posse is ambushed by a group of pursuing Commanches on either side, a deep-focus *mise-en-scène* which creates a startling triptych effect. Here, though, the Indians have become the LA police and, unlike Ford's Westerners, Mark has no miraculous escape. As the plane slews sideways to a halt he is unceremoniously shot dead, no questions asked.

The comparison with Ford is not arbitrary, for the paradigm of *The Searchers* is never far away. In Allen's obsession with Daria there are echoes of Ethan Edwards's quasi-incestuous attraction for Debbie, the captured niece he finally 'brings home' from the Commanche tribe where she has been raised as a native American. The visual similarity of Daria Halprin and Natalie Wood, the look and the clothing, is striking to say the least. The 'search' of Allen for Daria, if it is that, is conducted from his vast office high on the Los Angeles skyline, a sedentary and remote-control search as she speeds across the Californian desert towards Death Valley. Yet when she arrives at his desert home he is already there. Ford's noble horse is replaced by the invisible plane. For Antonioni Death Valley is the modern riposte to Ford's Monument Valley, not Navaho land posing as a settlement of north European farmers as it does in *The Searchers* but just as it is, an uninhabitable terrain attracting only tourists on wheels to Zabriskie Point, whose origins long preceded that of any humans. Antonioni observes as usual some degree of topographical accuracy Ford, dealing in myth, little at all. Give or take a generous detour, Death Valley lies between LA and Phoenix. Monument Valley, however, is nowhere near Texas, while heading north from Texas in the winter, as the searching Edwards does, hardly means ending up in the snows of Alberta.

In Death Valley Antonioni's young couple are gauche and awkward, their talk banal. They are dwarfed by the rugged desert landscape, diminished by its eerie silence. The Italian's non-actors provide an extreme contrast to the Hollywood figure of the Westerner whose presence dominates the landscape out of which he emerges. While John Wayne is ever the professional patriarch of the open range, Mark Frechette and Daria Halprin are amateur nonentities cast for their look, not their voices, figures on no momentous quest, existential rebels playing death-games on impulse in Death Valley. The abiding image in Ford is that of heroic possession. The true Westerner seems to possess the landscape through which he rides just as he owns his horse and his gun. The framing of the figure, the look of the journey, the majestic sweep of the camera, the stirring chords of orchestral strings on the soundtrack, civilize the landscape as also in a more domestic and sentimental way does the modest timber-framed cabin of the settler family where the role of women is especially strong, home as found. In *Zabriskie Point* everything is the opposite. Plane, car and designer rock-dwelling all estrange us from the landscape. All are intrusions. The landscape is silent, the only music the rock music on the car radio. Yet these are also our intrusions, literally the importation of our shared consumer values into a dead landscape. The point is made satirically by the American camper family Mark and Daria see arriving as they climb back up to the outlook point over the valley. Cameras, wheels, T-shirts, junk food are the detritus of civilization necessary to tide the family over their fleeting visit, that brief foray out of their automobile when the camera lens spearheads the tourist gaze before they drive quickly away.

When Daria finally reaches Allen's desert lair, having heard of Mark's death over the car radio, her presence is ambiguous enough to challenge the sentimental domesticity of the Western and emphasize instead the fragility of the American hold over the desert. Allen treats her like a prodigal daughter while the ambiguous look of the Indian maid in the household suggests a recognition of like by like, but perhaps also a feeling of betrayal, the wordless rebuke which might imply that Daria, in accepting Allen's invitation, has betrayed her roots. The connection to the final sequence in the film might then be seen in a different, less transient, light. Here in a multiple-angle explosion sequence the house is destroyed in repeated slow-motion shots. Like the love-in at Death Valley, it is a utopian fantasy, an imaginary triumph of hippie culture against consumer civilization, against the intestines of refrigerators which rise and fall in slow-motion in mid-air. But Daria' dress, her demeanour and her uncanny presence in the household intimate a desire for deeper revenge, that of the Native American against the colonizers of their land.

The Native American is an absent presence and as the film progresses Daria seems to grow back into a deeper role in the film, in culture and in history. If Mark is a makeshift prototype of the doomed romantic hero, the nature of his death and the stronger focus thereafter on Daria suggest otherwise. She has a depth he lacks, which cannot somehow be named. It is something the *mise-en-scène* intensifies through the awkward 'non-acting' of the couple together, a muted and painful hesitancy poles apart from the flashy self-confidence of the American Method idiom in Hollywood. To make it worst for the lover of Hollywood movies, the film's editing severs the main arteries of melodrama. We can think of the disturbing Godardian jump-cut between Mark's gun and the shot of the dying cop during the campus siege, the long shot of Mark himself gunned down and slumped forward in the cockpit of the plane on the runway, his face hidden from view, or of Daria turning her back and walking away from her car as she hears of his death on the radio, watching the cacti wave gently in the wind as the wind in turn catches the back of her hair. We are denied the customary reaction shot of grief.

In the spectacular ending the house is literally blasted out of the cliff, as if after the destruction the rock might eventually be restored to its original nature. The multiple shot montage is a converse movement to the montage of the love-in where Mark's and Daria's bodies try in making love to burrow into the barren soil of the desert, and where their hallucinated vision of other hippie couplings amidst the dust is a vision of the loving community trying to inhabit the uninhabitable. It is a dream vision of collective desire warding off collective death, the polar opposite of the couple's earlier death-games, a time space image of bodies grinding themselves back into an earlier culture and an earlier world. The film had few admirers in the counter-culture despite the director's strong political sympathy, and the reason is obvious. The film makes of the dream vision a vision impossible. But the ending also has an important place in the history of cinema. It provides an uncanny link with the ending of *The Searchers* which it completely inverts. Ford's Western restores the suffering desert homestead to its previous fullness with the return of Debbie, the rescued daughter. In the famous back-track of the final shot John Wayne's return to the wilderness, mission accomplished, is framed by the open doorway, the reverse track moving into the warmth and refuge of the dark interior as Wayne treks back out away from the camera, into the blinding desert sun. In *Zabriskie Point* it is Daria who leaves, Allen who stays. The Anglo-patriarch colonizing the desert with leisure remains behind, the girl escapes. The 'homecoming' has been no homecoming at all. If Ford symbolically reinstates the homestead to the 'rightful place' it possessed before the Commanche massacre, Antonioni blows up the modernist apparition in the rock, removing it from its wrongful place. Here is no point-of-view shot from the interior of the house, similar to that in Ford, of Daria's departing figure. The explosion of the house itself, shot with multiple angles, also defies the fixed point-of-view, the backward look. It starts off as her fleeting vision but then becomes a montage of simultaneous shots of different focal lengths and angles, shots from nowhere-in-particular which advance into the interior of the building with the slow-motion exploding of the fridge and the television. The image of destruction is just as equally her vision or ours.

A rather different response to *The Searchers* is to be found in *Alice in the Cities* (1973), Wim Wenders's first American movie.

Antonioni stood Ford coolly on his head, dehumanizing the mythical uplifting vision of the old West, and instead making the existential moment a source of genuine mystery. It was a strategy which struck a deep chord of resentment among the American critics who hated the movie and tried to bury it. Wenders on the other hand tries to remain true to the Fordian spirit of redemption, but can do so only by returning his characters to their native Germany. Here Philip Winter's 'saving' of Alice is inadvertent, not the result of a compulsive quest but a reluctant undertaking, a purpose which lands in his lap after the desolation of his American journey which lacks any kind of purpose at all. The rhythms of mechanical motion here also transform the Fordian sensibility. It is noteworthy that the automobile plays little part in Ford's cinema, apart from the homely jalopy of the Joad family in *The Grapes of Wrath*. One feels he is ill at ease with modernity, even in his war pictures. *Alice in the Cities*, *Zabriskie Point* and *Taxi Driver*, in which Scorsese and Paul Schrader consciously transcribe the theme of *The Searchers* to New York City, are all movies he would never have dreamed of trying to make. In Wenders's attempt to capture the Fordian sensibility, the automobile and the plane are advances on the horse and the stagecoach which transform that sensibility out of myth and also out of America. The humanization Wenders seeks is possible only by a return to Europe where the United States will once again be a potent myth, not a disenchanting reality.

Here Wenders gives us two different kinds of journey, two different phenomenologies of the car experience, the American and the European. Philip Winter's American trip is a journey of disenchantment. We see him driving alone back north to New York City along the eastern seaboard. Wenders's car shots are flat, featureless horizontals of the straight open road lined by motels, gasoline stations and drive-in diners. It is a shapeless unpeopled world in which Winter maintains a dubious contact with civilization through his car radio where announcers interrupt his favourite tunes, and stuttering television sets in different motel rooms where adverts constantly interrupt old movies. Wenders captures his hero's desolation perfectly in a point-of-view shot from Winter's motel bed in which the malfunctioning television is framed next to the window through which the motel's neon sign glares garishly back at him without meaning. Whereas Antonioni sees in the culture of the American sign an over-determined jumble of excess, for Wenders it is a degree-zero cipher, a desultory blankness. For Antonioni the telephoto shot; for Wenders the normal lens. Predictably, Winter's journalistic assignment is paralysed. He can write nothing about America and his instant Polaroid pictures capture nothing of what he sees.

The German homecoming with Alice, the misplaced daughter of Winter's close friend, re-echoes Europe in a different way. As opposed to Ford and the history of American cinema, it invokes the neo-realists and the history of European cinema. Winter believes in the illusion of the photographic reality until his Polaroid destroys it. Alice is the all-seeing child, the perceiver of the true Real which the hero in his fallen state has forfeited. The film shows the fluid continuum of the neo-realist and the neo-modern, the indeterminate made determinate by the child's sharp inquiry, the shapeless given shape by the luminous gaze of innocence. Yet Wenders plays with delicate irony on the dialectic his film implies. Alice cannot remember the town or region in which her grandmother lives, or describe its streets. She cannot translate the image into the place-name. The search for grandmother's home reveals just how much as a child she does not know. And of course she has already rejected the correct place-name – Wuppertal – which Philip had earlier put to her. She senses the limits of Bruno's own world yet does not know, formally, the topography of her own. It is an adult–child, man–girl relationship in which, as in *Il grido*, each suffers the grainy exasperation of the other's limitations. Wenders has yet to succumb as he does in *Paris, Texas* to the fulsome sentiment of reconciliation between lost father and doting son, a sentimentality absent from his European pictures.

The difference in cars is also crucial. Winter owns a used American saloon in the States which he trades in for $300 towards his air fare. In Germany in the search for Alice's grandmother he rents a modest Renault 4 with expired Eurocheques which pass unnoticed. The American experience differs radically from that of the voyeuristic Travis Bickle in *Taxi Driver* (1976). Winter literally records nothing of the flat, open landscape of freeways and highways through which he moves. Nothing truly attracts. Nothing commands his attention. He is on the open road in the tradition of Jack Kerouac but discovers nothing. In *Taxi Driver*, by contrast, the nocturnal streets of Manhattan are awash with images of hell. For Travis Bickle the yellow cab is a moving platform from which to observe the human Fall in New York City, fights, drugs, whores, derelicts, psychopaths. Bickle has no distance from the immediacy of the city streets, from simultaneous happening. He is the disturbed Vietnam vet unable to cultivate 'the blasé attitude', a victim of the promiscuities of drug-enhanced perception which cannot discriminate events. Instead he is commodified by the yellow automobile which is never his but which seems to be his second skin. If Hollywood's proud all-American owner makes the car the mythic extension of his or her body, then Bickle-as-cabbie is the opposite. He is the human extension of his company's cab, known only, as the title of the picture implies, by his automobile.

Scorsese finds a neurasthenic equivalent in the tense postures of Robert De Niro to match the edgy compulsive quest of John Wayne in *The Searchers*, the maverick desperation of the Confederate rebel compensating for a lost war. But he takes De Niro's quest to rescue child prostitute Jodie Foster to the extremes of dehumanization and gratuitous violence. In Wenders the quest of Philip Winter becomes just as obsessive but understated and humanized by comparison. Scorsese, true to the lure of melodrama, seeks out a literal match to Ford's plot and finds it. De Niro's search for Harvey Keitel, Foster's pimp, is like Wayne's for Scar, Debbie's abductor, a compulsive search for his own double. Wenders's ironies deal, by contrast, in the studied inversion of Ford's themes. In Germany the character of the journey itself is changed through the search. The movie is more like a sequel to Ford which deals with the journey home, and where home is unknown, the implicit motif, as we have already seen, in *Kings of the Road*. In the industrial cities of northern Germany moreover, the motion is not continuous, the vista never a set of open horizontals. The Renault 4 gets sidetracked in back streets, cul-de-sacs, doubling back on its tracks in the nooks and crannies of the city. The American experience, the glide of continuous forward motion into the void, has gone. In its place is the puzzle of the uncanny, mediated by Alice's vague memories. Winter senses that the house is near to hand but cannot find it. America is the land of non-identity, Germany home to the homeless.

In the filmic demonology of the car, *Wild at Heart* (1990) stands half-way between melodrama and the modern, an all-American outlaw movie which borrows heavily from *Weekend* and remakes

Badlands. Touch of Evil and *They Live by Night*. The couple's convertible is black, not white, in an obvious inversion of iconography, but it outlasts murder, disaster and death to witness true love and a final marriage proposal conveyed through Cage's reprise of *Love Me Tender*. Disaster happens to other people and other cars. Lynch pays homage to the wrecks and carnage of *Weekend* but, unlike Godard, always has pathos in mind. The nocturnal wreck on the highway is a tearful romantic elegy which recalls Bruce Springsteen. Sherilyn Fenn, the bloody and dazed survivor of an upturned car full of sprawled corpses, dies in Cage's arms before she has time to be rescued and spill blood all over Dern's convertible. The bank raid, in which Willem Dafoe as the odious Bobby Peru accidentally blows off his own head with a shotgun, is a macabre sequence where the couple's car is conveniently left at their fly-ridden motel and where, anyway, accomplice Isabella Rossellini drives off before the mayhem starts. By and large, the house and the bank, the motel and the hotel, are the territories of evil. The car is the way out, and even the babbling madness of the car radio stations can always be turned into the magic of a transcendental sound. When Dern despairs at the endless news of murders, necrophilia and rotting corpses, Cage can always find a station to bring on the heavy metal riffs of Angelo Badimento's soundtrack. While Sheen and Spacek smooch the dance of death in *Badlands* to the lush sounds of Nat King Cole, Cage and Dern kung-fu to the freaked out megawatt chords of a different generation. But Lynch still has a trick up his sleeve and brings it all back home. The couple stop to embrace in medium close-up before the sequence returns to the long high-angle crane shot which has framed them beside the deserted highway. It leaves the car and couple by the roadside and pans upward in a crescendo, this time, of lush vibrating strings – the other soundtrack – to the golden setting sun. Between death and romance, lust and love, there is always the convertible. E. M. Forster said 'Only connect'. And it does.

8

The Strange Passions of Film Noir

Film noir is a tangent from the main theme of this book but seems a suitable place to end it. For talking about it is a necessary detour. Its beginnings start before the neo-moderns. It ends after they end. It is American. They are largely European. Yet noir cinema contains that Nietzschean element of return we have noted of the modern cinema in general from which it cannot be separated. In its early phase it is a commodified progeny of German Expressionism, made in strictly genre terms mainly by European directors. In the 1970s and 1980s it repeats itself by absorbing the techniques of the neo-moderns, but flourishes in new circumstances where censorship has been relaxed, and where the dark side of American life has meantime spread further afield in all its nocturnal horror. It is thus a by-product of the moderns which in turn bypasses them. Its cycle repeats their cycle, its doubling their doubling. It affirms its difference from the neo-moderns in a number of ways which are distinctly American and which do not easily export. Its will-to-power subordinates its directors to its genre, which is not technically a genre at all, so that noir eventually becomes a genre of genres, where nearly any genre can produce noir movies. On the other hand its will-to-power is seldom reflexive, except where its subject is Hollywood itself. While it is often subversive melodrama, it is doomed to remain melodrama.

There have been two main readings of film noir, both equally valid. The early French study of Borde and Chaumeton, which gave the term a generic meaning, saw it as a cinema of confusion and cruelty in the modern city,[1] darker, more contemporary, more candid and more brutal than the idealized genres of Hollywood to which audiences had been accustomed. This was largely true. In its first half-hour, Howard Hawks's *The Big Sleep* (1946) evokes a sinister though comic world of drug-taking, pornographic photographs, blackmail, murder, homosexuality and casual sex. Produced and edited under the Hollywood Studio Code, however, only murder is made truly explicit. The other forms of behaviour are implied in varying degrees to attract the attention of perceptive viewers while leaving others to watch the picture as a fast, baffling detective mystery with a romantic ending for Humphrey Bogart and Lauren Bacall. At the same time as it evoked the cultural demi-monde of 1940s Los Angeles, it was largely made in the studio and on studio back lots. There was little, if any, location shooting. It has none of the luminous power of the image in Renoir. It was genre Expressionism, diluted to the formula of private eye narrative, adapted with great wit from Chandler's novel, and cut with the functional expertise which is Hawks's trademark. Here the instabilities of motive noted by Borde and Chaumeton accord with nocturnal setting, seedy abode, distorted shadow and low-key lighting. Evil becomes a house style and little else. Film noir is less a genre, more a style with many themes.

Feminist critics, by contrast, have seen film noir as the province of the femme fatale,[2] that ambivalent link between crime and desire fashioned at a time when the morality code had been loosened enough to allow screen adultery, but not enough to overlook its necessary punishment. For many feminists, the figure of the femme fatale was a clear threat to the conventions of the nuclear family and domestic confinement of married women. Yet in many noir pictures the last-minute vindication of morality vitiates the impact of this subversion. In *Double Indemnity* (1944) Walter Neff and Phyllis Dietrichson, alias Fred MacMurray and Barbara Stanwyck, oblige the Studio Code by simultaneously shooting each other in an act of mutual betrayal after Neff's murder of her crippled husband. Moreover the narrative is a controlled nightmare of flashback regret strictly from the male point of view. It starts with its ending. Neff, the wounded transgressor, puts his crimes of violence and passion on to the dictaphone, confessing everything to Barton Keyes, the moral arbiter and company man who is intended to be the conscience of us all. Neff's voice-over singles out the Eve who has lured him to his fall. Subsequent flashbacks oblige by showing her allure. The femme fatale is the discontented woman of a childless marriage, bourgeois, glamorous, bored and dangerous, a clear threat to family life, male sexuality and male ambition. The absent family, as Harvey tells us, is the most usual site of the noir conspiracy.[3]

Greed leads to cruelty, desire to murder. In 1940s noir, both paths of doom are governed by the power of money. In most cases male voice-over leads audiences back into the labyrinths of the past, its authority justified by its deep, hard-boiled timbre, its paranoia justified by retrospective proof of betrayal. Of course, first-person male narrative was by no means the only kind of voice-over in noir cinema. But in that post-war period of Hollywood cinema up to 1950 where voice-over was used with such extraordinary frequency, it was still the most telling. The fall-guy has a voice as well as a look, the power of luring the audience's confidence, setting up the lure of his voice against the look of the woman who seduces and betrays him. The voice-over is not a form of nostalgia seeking to return to the past but an effective way to explain how everything has come to pass.[4] Here the past itself generally catches up with the present, the voice-over narration with the time present of the discourse. In the most bizarre twist on this retro-motion of the noir idiom, William Holden in *Sunset Boulevard* (1950) narrates his fatal entanglement with Gloria Swanson from beyond the grave, or rather from the surface of the swimming pool on which he floats after being shot by her.

Most noir movies fall thematically into the categories of Borde and Chaumeton, or Kaplan. Often they combine both. By contrast, feminist critics like Kaplan have overrated the mystery of character and the ambiguity of motive. True, noir narrative does disorient, but motive and character are usually simplified. There are clear guidelines to worthy male paranoia, the treachery of seductive women and the sadism of footloose hoodlums like the racist Robert Ryan in *Crossfire*. Economy lighting, venetian blinds and the higher ratio of key to fill lighting all add atmosphere for sure, but not much ambiguity. As Wood has remarked, nothing that ever *happens* in their films can ever live up to their menacing look.[5] Voice-over, lookalike characters, and flashbacks within flashbacks within flashbacks ring the changes on the classical narratives of the Studios. But simplistic moral messages still abound and prevail. There are salutary warnings of greed and corruption, envy and untrammelled desire. Stitched-up happy endings then undo a good hour of potentially dangerous story. Of course there are always iconic inversions of the moral code. Colour is the most obvious. The dazzling white dress in the first entrance of the femme fatale has been a predictable stand-by. It was the common property of Barbara Stanwyck, Lana Turner in *The Postman Always Rings Twice,* Jane Greer in *Out of the Past*, Lizabeth Scott in *Dead Reckoning*, Rita Hayworth in *Gilda* and *The Lady from Shanghai*, and more recently Kathleen Turner in *Body Heat*. In many cases of course, white turns to black as the darkness of female motive becomes apparent. The two Turners, Lana and Kathleen, are shown in elegant black mourning outfits for their murdered husbands. As Phyllis Dietrichson, Stanwyck changes to black after her husband's death while her step-daughter appears dressed in white to attract the attention of the unsettled Neff. As Martha Ivers, she changes from white to black when Van Heflin's romantic interest changes to Lizabeth Scott, now dressed in white. In the celebrated funfair shoot-out in the hall of mirrors at the end of *The Lady from Shanghai*, Hayworth, gun in hand, wears formal dark attire to meet her fate. The black dress becomes the uniform of the black heart.

There is no room for doubt here. The femme fatale was a genuine threat, the post-war version of the new woman, officially some man's woman but in reality no one's, substituting desire for domesticity, narcissism for children, wealth for suffering. As such she stands morally condemned, but like many Hollywood transgressors, the glamour of defeat allows vicarious pleasure. This after all is a mythical staging-post between the death of the Protestant Ethic and the hedonism of consumer cultures. But the nature of her defeat is often deeply compromising. In *The Strange Love of Martha Ivers* (1946) there is a sharp echo of *Double Indemnity* when Kirk Douglas, the spurned husband, shoots Stanwyck then turns the gun upon himself. At one level the pair cannot rid themselves of the teenage memory of conniving in the death of Stanwyck's tyrant aunt. At a deeper level, Stanwyck is a being punished as a ruthless and successful businesswoman who wants to make her weak husband governor of the state. The camera constantly frames her towering over Douglas, whom the film punishes for being drunk, cowardly and unable to control his ferocious spouse. It is no consolation that the other possible femme fatale, Lizabeth Scott, is a different kind of threat, young, single, alone in a strange city, father-hating, and a thief to boot. At the end Scott's reunion with Van Heflin, with marriage clearly in the air, helps to draw the sting. In classic noir the female threat is always neutralized in the nick of time.

The most powerful expression of noir narrative comes, therefore, from something deeper than the iconography of the fallen, sensual angel. It comes from the unlikely relationship between passion and paranoia, a deadly combustion of flammable elements in the mobile world of bourgeois sexuality where winning is all. Success, both sexual and social, is the prime gamble in a culture of risk, but the gamble itself brings in its wake a whole host of distrusts, shady deals, broken promises, all sorts of veiled unease concealed by smiles and laughter. The combustion, when it occurs, is a kind of perversity which produces film noir at its most compelling. But it is also rare. It lies beyond the wooden acting, the clichéd dialogue and social stereotyping of much 1940s melodrama. It is no coincidence that the great moments of perversity have their political correlative in the great crises of American public life. They are responses to the threat of the Cold War and the political persecutions of Macarthyism, to the persecution of a defenceless minority. During film noir's rebirth in colour, they belong to the political paranoia induced by Vietnam and Watergate, the paranoia of a profoundly divided nation.

Here we can locate some of the major films in the history of the American cinema. In the first monochrome phase we have, among others, *Sunset Boulevard*, *The Lady from Shanghai*, *In a Lonely Place* and *Touch of Evil*. In the second phase of muted colours, altogether more sparse, we have *Klute*, *Taxi Driver*, *Chinatown*, and *The Conversation*. Here sexuality is always more explicit but eroticism in the central relationship strangely secondary and subdued. There are different reasons for this. In the 1940s the forbidden sexuality fringing the Studio Code meant little open sexuality. In the noir renaissance of the 1970s distrust is more important than eros, and accordingly the element of horror in all these films comes from the systematic perversions of eros which the male protagonist uncovers. Not until the erotic scenes of *Body Heat* in 1982 does freedom from censorship produce a picture which dwells openly upon the mythic powers of direct heterosexual passion, on the hidden *erotic* agenda of fall-guy and femme fatale. *Body Heat*, unlike Rafelson's remake of *The Postman Always Rings Twice*, achieves this while retaining the original noir sensibility. Yet the brief skirmishes of *Double Indemnity* pale by comparison. This is because Kasdan's debut movie is less an *auteur's* triumph and more a matter of the general temptation to transform genre. What Coppola had done so well in *Apocalypse Now*, or Altman in *McCabe and Mrs Miller*, Kasdan then achieved in *Body Heat*. It was, in the curiously impersonal manner of the American cinema, a picture waiting to happen. But it was also a movie about a more stable social world, a country which had forgotten the uncertainties of Watergate during the selfish patriotism of the Reagan era. In *Body Heat* the power of transgression assumes a growth world of finance-capital in which criminal risk thrives, and a legal system which, however casual, still functions in the oppressive summer heat of small-town Florida. It is the film of a decade of returning certainties. Its familiar love triangle is this time a trio of sophisticated predators, narcissists of the me-generation of the 1970s now playing deadly games with flair and self-regard, amoralists of a new age. Yet there is a hardening of the spirit and a new self-assurance. The fragility of the 1970s has largely gone.

Only years earlier, paranoia *was* the central sign of that fragility. The truth, when known, was no way out, no comforting reassurance. It was, on the contrary, an illumination of the depths of perversity. Although 1970s themes were more candid, the tight connection between paranoia and perversity still echoed the earlier syndrome of the Macarthyist era when sex and politics were still under wraps. Then the perverse was only hinted at, a texture, an undercurrent, at times part of the paranoid state of mind of the hero. It could not be witnessed or confessed but was largely submerged, invisible to the eye. What was shown instead was the tip of the iceberg. In the best noir movies the male anti-heroes were the key to this. Many were politically suspect in the new paranoid culture of the Cold War. In *The Lady from Shanghai* Orson Welles is an Irish-American docker who has fought and killed for the Republican Cause in the Spanish Civil War. In *Sunset Boulevard* William Holden is a peripheral screen-writer from the mid-West, down on his luck, and preparing to go home, while Humphrey Bogart's screen-writer in Ray's film, *In a Lonely Place* (1950), is edgy, insecure, paranoid and violent. None of the three is a likeable hero, but none is a criminal either. They occupy a no man's land between good and evil, and they are culturally suspect, always under threat. They are all prime candidates to become 'enemies of the people'.

In the late 1950s, with the completion of the noir series, the male figure shifts into more obvious villainy, witness the ruthless columnist Burt Lancaster plays in Mackendrick's *Sweet Smell of Success* (1957) or the corrupt cop Welles plays in *Touch of Evil*. Here passion, partially flawed in the earlier pictures, becomes fully corrupt and cynical in its new male form. There is a clear descent, a failure to recognize the woman as autonomous, as Other. In the full cut of Mackendrick's movie, not shown at the time, perverse passion is conveyed in the incestuous attraction of Lancaster as J. J. Hunsecker for the younger sister he terrorizes, a one-way infatuation. In *Touch of Evil* perverse passion is reduced even more brutally to the unseen act of gang rape perpetrated on Susan Vargas and later denied, without conviction, by Joe Grandi, drugs baron of the teenage gang. It is casual lust with clear racial overtones, kept sufficiently oblique to get the seal of approval. Opposed in both films to the perverse is of course a Studio version of the normal. Here Mackendrick's film is more conventional. The sister's affair with an affable jazz musician which Hunsecker wishes to stop is a likeable romance for the audience of its time. Welles, of course, risks more. He altogether lampoons love and marriage. Charlton Heston and Janet Leigh act out a cruel parody of the 1950s convention of the newly-wed couple in which Heston as Vargas, the concerned investigator, is blind to the clear dangers facing his new bride. Even with the constraints of the Studio Code one thing is clear in both pictures. Passion without perversity is a non-starter. The perverse comes first and love and marriage are relegated to the second division.

In the earlier films passion does exist without any shadow of doubt. It is more explicit. But it exists only to be betrayed. In the Macarthyite era the culture of distrust was too great for any other outcome. Hence, while never black-listed, Nicholas Ray thought of himself as being 'grey-listed' and that lingering fear of persecution among Hollywood's most talented becomes in noir movies a pervasive distrust. At all times this distrust is implosive, turning friends and allies against each other. The insecurity of the anti-hero in the public world inflates his insecurity in the world of passion. As it implodes someone is always watching. Bogart is watched in *In a Lonely Place* by an old Army pal now in the police force and his eager wife for clues to murderous intent. Welles's ambiguous progress with Rita Hayworth is watched jointly by her husband, his private detective and her lover. Holden's Gothic captivity in Gloria Swanson's mansion is monitored at a distance by more normal members of the industry. Their surveillance refracts our gaze. Our anti-heroes are not watched as powerful and passionate fall-guys seduced by murder, the image that William Hurt decks out so well in *Body Heat*. They are watched for signs of the abnormal, the stupid, the perverse which exist within them, pervisities which go beyond 'normal' temptations of eros and money. Welles's bumbling foolishness in the world of the rich, Bogart's unpredictable and violent paranoia, Holden's capitulation to the ageing, deluded Norma Desmond, his shocking *Liebestod*; all demonstrate a perverse miscueing of social signs, a failure of psychic distance, a naked display of selfhood adrift. The power of the male voice is lost in these degradation rituals. Holden's stern, caustic voice-over cannot save him, while Welles's stage Irishman spews forth confidential blarney in a false Gaelic lilt. In Ray's film, where there is no voice-over, Bogart's deep gravelled voice stands the convention of Philip Marlowe on its head. It is no longer the seasoned and caustic commentary of the incorruptible private eye. It conveys instead the desperate threat of the hunted. It is the sonic match to the gaze of Bogart's haunted eyes, the gaze of a man who yearns to create victims because he himself has become one.

At one level, this fits the campaign of persecution which HUAC had started to instigate in the American film community. Screenwriters were obvious targets, a well-paid cultural proletariat hamstrung by the Studio Code, many of whom had long turned their politics leftward. Subpoenaed, they were threatened with blacklisting and asked to name names, which of course some did. In Welles's picture Mike O'Hara, too, is clearly too socialist for the age. A militant docker but socially naive, he rightly views the rich he serves as sharks who feed off one another. None of our anti-heroes has committed any serious crime but all act as if they were guilty. Welles, as Mike O'Hara, confides to us, 'It's a bright, guilty world'. They also act as if they were martyrs, under wrongful suspicion, unjust threat. It is a combination of the two which is so effective. They behave in Kafkaesque style as if they have committed a crime, are regarded as if they have, but have done nothing more than develop a passion for a particular woman. The guilt is not simply a matter of sexual politics. It is the guilt which springs out of the politics of suspicion in a paranoid nation, and then implodes into convoluted intimacy. If reasonable suspicion no longer exists, neither does reasonable guilt. The anti-hero then lives out the contrary nature of the public realm in a private realm where under the Studio Code explicit reference to the former disappears down a black hole.

Here the power of each of the films comes from the hero's unique intimacy with a woman who is iconically more powerful. By comparison the Stanwyck transparency of conventional noir can be highly limiting. If dark motive is always revealed by the hard stare or the shifty glance, then the female threat is nailed by the audience and consequently diminished. Here the threat of the femme fatale is sustained not by transparent gestures but by the look as enigma, the look of a woman who cannot be fully known, whose nature is never an open book. The mystery of the image, rather than the mystique of the face or the figure, is the important key. Indeed, in each of the few cases where this applies, the role of the woman is more vital to the film's structure of feeling. It shows us there is no nature common to the femme fatale, for such 'nature' simply vanishes. In the films of Welles and Wilder the natures of Elsa Bannister and Norma Desmond are inseparable from the construction of their images. In Ray's film, which is late noir, there is a simple but effective role-reversal. The male point-of-view is replaced halfway through by the female point-of-view. The masculine Bogart is feminized into an homme fatal, while Gloria Grahame becomes a potential fall-girl who resists falling, the very opposite of the gangster's moll she plays in Lang's *The Big Heat*. Here she makes a decisive judgement on Bogart's character, not just on his innocence, and acts accordingly.

The one relatively popular film of the three was *Sunset Boulevard* (1950), partly because it had two vital ingredients for box-office success, an attractive voice-overed hero and a storyline which dissected Hollywood itself. But with the figure of Gloria

Swanson it did something very unusual. It resurrected a silent star especially for the sound cinema, becoming in the process an acerbic comment on Hollywood's history. *The Lady from Shanghai* is equally a reflection on female stardom and with typical Wellesian audacity combines a mystery narrative that is the stuff of melodrama with alienation effects which are deliberately Brechtian. Predictably, Wilder's film is more accessible and more direct. Both, however, highlight the tenuous link which film noir presents between the Expressionist period and the neo-modern narratives of the 1960s. On the one hand, there are genre constraints and a classical action-narrative. On the other, both are undermined as the films progress by the lure of an Americanized Expressionism which goes far beyond the studio style of standard noir cinema. In their adoption of Expressionist structures of feeling to an American landscape, they stand in closer relation to the early plays of Eugene O'Neill than they do to the genre movies of the Studio system. In cinema history they are part of the fragile bridge between the Expressionist and the neo-modern, between, that is to say, the two great modernist challenges to modernity in cinema history.

The focus on extinct stardom in *Sunset Boulevard* is a comment not only on the casualties of the silent cinema in the studio era but also on that other ghost in Hollywood's cupboard, the German cinema of the 1920s out of which so many of its best directors came. Yet Hollywood had not allowed the cinema world to benefit from Hitler's tyranny as best it might. The output of the émigrés was often a grey area in which they clearly made many of the best genre pictures of the sound period but were cut off from country and culture, adapting themselves to a form of exile in which money and technology were on their side but studio policies were often not. Wilder's film encapsulates that dilemma, the chances which existed for fast functional melodrama alongside the casual disregard for film as artwork, the absence in the sound cinema of directors with the stature of Griffith, Stroheim and Murnau. *Sunset Boulevard* is an émigré view of Hollywood, of a place stranger than paradise. Yet part of that strangeness also lies in the legacy Wilder brought with him from central Europe, the passionate attraction to fear and death. It reversed the whole policy of Hollywood Gothic. This was to set the perils of cruel captivity in the haunted mansions of distant Ruritanian lands on studio stages and studio back lots. Wilder places the

Gothic mansion on Sunset Boulevard, using as his location exterior a Spanish-Colonial house of 1920s Los Angeles. If he imports the Gothic spirit from elsewhere, he also brings the Gothic back home. The location is real. It is Hollywood, not Ruritania, that is Gothic.

The culture of Hollywood, its deals, its concepts, its projects, its packages, is that of an eternal present where everything has to be now. It is only television which keeps the Hollywood past alive with repeated showings of old movies which could never get a re-release. In the age before mass television, *Sunset Boulevard* reminds Hollywood of its recent past but also reminds America of its European past. Swanson's Norma fuses both: the Hollywood history of the forgotten silent star, the European legacy of shadow and distortion, captivity and the house of death. In this fusion lies the picture's spectacular success. Swanson combines the image of the vamp with the image of the vampire, and draws them together again when popular cinema had hived them apart. She is not only the ageing seductress, she is also the undead, the extinct star living on into late middle age in the illusion of stardom, her mansion the vast mausoleum of a celebrity's after-life, a narcissist's museum cluttered with photos and mementoes of the star image. In Hollywood mythology a star is born. In Wilder's film the star is undead. She simply refuses to die. Her 'family' dies, but she lives on. Soon after his arrival, Joe Gillis (Holden) witnesses a macabre burial which recalls the coffin of Murnau's *Nosferatu*. Ex-husband Max von Mayerling (Erich von Stroheim), now the faithful servant in the after-life, ceremonially buries the chimpanzee who has been their only 'child' at night in the grounds of the mansion. Norma looks on, dressed in black, lighting the scene with a candelabrum as the coffin is lowered into its tiny grave. The absent family has become a grotesque appendage to absent stardom. Von Stroheim too, of course, is cruel self-pastiche, playing the travestied role of the forgotten silent movie director he himself had been in a bold doubling of Gothic autobiography.

The division in Norma is doubled also by the division between her and the young screen-writer who falls in love with Gillis, the company girl who has grown up in a movie family living near the studio lot and has now turned her hand to the kind of moral melodrama which seems to provide Joe's salvation. She is young, optimistic and innocent, the ideal Hollywood rescue package for the cynical screen-writer down on his luck. Except that Wilder does not allow his kind of film to have the upbeat ending that her kind of film clearly would. The dilemma is in Wilder himself. He is clearly yearning throughout his Hollywood career to find an American identity in the well-made picture, tight, functional, witty and popular. In this of course he succeeded, to a greater extent than Fritz Lang who could never match his achievements in the German cinema. Yet the darker side of Wilder's legacy shows here, the European legacy he could never fully escape. His alter ego Joe Gillis pays with his life for succumbing to the symbolic allure of death personified. The figure of Swanson, with her piercing eyes, her trance-like movements, her fanatic voice and her vampire's fingers, has an Expressionist aura which no earnest and healthy melodrama could ever match. For Gillis, the love-affair is not only subconscious infatuation with death but conscious infatuation with the aura of a stardom which lives on, indestructible. Conversely, for Norma, Joe is not merely a hustling gigolo, a toyboy who can be used to write her back into screen history. His youth nourishes her and sustains her illusions, so that on both sides the bizarre relationship goes far beyond mere instrumentality. In seducing him Norma briefly becomes what she pretends she has always remained. She relives the aura of extinct stardom more fully in her private world, so that even De Mille's discreet rejection of her 'comeback' washes over her. In her imagination she remains the star that she was.

The Lady from Shanghai (1948) is Hollywood's other great reflexive rendering of stardom in the period, equally dark and mordant. Stardom here is hidden, not exposed. Rita Hayworth is an upwardly mobile beauty in the world of the idle rich, a languishing spouse rather than a languishing actress. The 'lady' from Shanghai has clearly risen without trace. In making the picture Welles was only too aware of the spectacular leap into Hollywood fame of his estranged wife. Unlike Wilder, however, Welles takes more chances with his oblique theme. He parodies the compulsions of linear narrative and brutally deconstructs the aura of stardom. His story is as much a mystery as the femme fatale. Both are 'there' as moving images which can be taken any way that we wish. No wonder it was Welles's last big Hollywood picture. Yet studio fears surrounding his 'assassination' of Rita Hayworth are strangely unjustified. The greater the line in parody and the sharper the Brechtian distancing, the more powerful her image becomes. As we have seen already, the accretions of the male gaze in this film go beyond parody into a realm of surreal entrancement. The more compelled the collective gaze, the tougher and yet more vulnerable the female look, a fact that was surely not lost on Hitchcock with his 'cool blondes' of the 1950s. In trying to undermine Hayworth's look, Welles in fact strengthens it. Like *Sunset Boulevard* his is a rare film in the noir canon in which the female look does not falter through any obvious guilt. Even at the moment of death in the spectacular low-angle show where Hayworth tries to claw her way into the earth, the look prevails, haunting, desperate yet utterly powerful, contradicting her fate. It is inspired, fanatical.

To undermine glamour and romance Welles uses a number of imaginative devices, the radio commercial on board the yacht, Grisby's untuned, comic rendering of Elsa's song 'Please don't hold me' and his deranged prophecy of nuclear Armageddon on the cliffs at Acapulco; the much noted embrace of Mike and Elsa in the San Francisco aquarium, watched by giggling school-children and framed against the glass tanks of huge predatory fish; the scene of accusation in the Chinese Theatre where the strange rituals of the stage performance alienate us from the melodrama of Mike and Elsa in the stalls; and finally the shoot-out in the hall of mirrors where each bullet-shattered glass in which Elsa's image is destroyed seems to be replaced by yet another one in which the image is restored and demands to be shot to pieces all over again. In withstanding the assault and battery of virtuoso Welles, the look of Hayworth becomes more luminous. The image crystallizes and Welles, with his manipulative and self-conscious *mise-en-scène*, creates the illusion of the look as autonomous, as something outside of the manufacture of the camera. But the collapse of the real Elsa, fatally shot, amidst the shards of glass, restores the vulnerability of the person beneath the image.

That same vulnerability is present in Gloria Grahame's performance for Ray's *In a Lonely Place* (1950), an identical case of a Hollywood director making a movie with his recently estranged spouse, though concealed this time from the Studio to ensure production and also, perhaps, avoid the kind of adverse publicity Welles had suffered. Yet, right from the start, Grahame's performance moves away from the mystery of image and the look towards the complexity of the person. In Hayworth's look feeling becomes a *tableau vivant* but in Grahame's the look and the personality are fused in naturalistic performance. This marks a decisive break with the 1940s femme fatale. In judging Bogart Grahame has to make a psychological judgement which is a test of character. She has to pass through the culture of suspicion to the other side. As a result Bogart's paranoia is never quite justified by her actions and becomes a self-fulfilling prophecy. His violence only reinforces her suspicions and her willingness to keep in contact with the 'lawful community' which has him under surveillance. Innocent, he acts guilty. Her suspicion in turn feeds his, until trust disintegrates. Innocence thus becomes relative, no longer the easy mark of redemption it had previously been under the Studio Code. Grahame rejects him because she considers him capable of murder, as his violence after the car accident demonstrates. Not what he might have done but what he *might do* becomes the prime consideration. Here Ray is the forerunner of the psychological realism which motivates the pictures of Kazan, Ritt, Kramer and Rossen. At the same time the movie's lesbian subtext, Grahame's unspoken relationship to her masseuse, Martha, whose persuasive services have survived the break-up of Grahame's previous engagement, sustains a certain ambiguity about Grahame's motive and rightfully fuels Bogart's suspicions. Thus the issue is never cut and dried. We shall never know the reason for Martha's phone call at the point of the couple's break-up any more than Bogart himself. Grahame's behaviour here retains a vital tinge of mystery.

Bogart's insecurity is reflexive. It mirrors the Angst of a talented film-maker in a hostile town, fearing political attack and personal isolation. Kolker has called the American cinema of the 1970s a 'cinema of loneliness' but if the term belongs to anyone it belongs to Ray. It continues to find expression in *Johnny Guitar*, where it becomes a political parable hidden in a camp Western starring women in the main roles, and in *Rebel Without a Cause*, where it is transmuted into romantic disenchantment. Both are colour movies which move away from the noir feel of earlier work. Elsewhere film noir moves out of the studios and into location shooting, into the peeling arcades and oil derricks of Venice, California in *Touch of Evil*, or into the noisy and threatening bustle of mid-town Manhattan in *Sweet Smell of Success* (1957). Here the paranoia of the Macarthyist period is refined into specific instances of corruption, of the lawlessness of the powerful in American institutions. Both pictures are forms of revenge by film-makers for the semi-lawless reign of HUAC which had been such a travesty of democracy. Male anti-heroes are no longer victims but oppressors, institutional figures of evil, the crooked columnist and the crooked cop.

The new location movies also create new forms of *mise-en-scène*. Mackendrick and his cinematographer, James Wong Howe, developed new techniques to match the claustrophobia of their exteriors and interiors. They used long lens master-shots for the compression of crowds and buildings and wide-angle shots for close-ups to keep backgrounds constantly in focus. In the night club close-ups they framed Lancaster slightly to the fore of Curtis in every two-shot, so that he always dominates the image. Howe, moreover, had Lancaster fitted with heavy spectacles and shot from a high angle to deepen the eye sockets and turn the face into a skull.[6] As one of the first detailed Manhattan location movies, the Mackendrick film was comparable to Ritt's *Edge of the City*. But its techniques were more advanced and paved the way for the noir reprise of *Klute, Mean Streets* and *Taxi Driver*, where colour is added as a new dimension of claustrophobia, and Manhattan becomes an open prison.

Cinematically Welles was even bolder in *Touch of Evil*. His camera's speed and virtuosity was unprecedented in a Hollywood picture, revolutionizing cinematic space in the noir idiom. Not only is his frontier town Los Robles, a town whose political border is never clearly identified after the film's opening shot. Welles breaks down our sense of place by every single aspect of his time–space image, dispensing with master-shots, reaction shots and static framing. His decentred camera seldom converges with anyone's point-of-view. It has a life of its own which forsakes perspective for perpetual motion, at times mimicking human movement but seldom attempting to imitate the glance of the human eye. The editing juxtaposes perceptual extremes, long shots and close-ups, low angles and high angles, long takes and rapid montage. The Wellesian world is, in his own words, a 'labyrinth' but here it is agoraphobic. Instead of the claustrophobia of studio noir, it offers up the anxieties of unlimited space in darkness, a darkness that is so dimly lit we quickly lose our sense of direction. There are no identifiable borders between countries, between light and darkness, good and evil. Welles's dystopian vision is the antithesis of John Ford's, which he so admired. Instead of the epic grandeur of scenic wilderness where the eye scans the horizon, here the viewer is in free fall. The field of vision is bathed in half-light and shadow but never stands still to offer the solace of easy recognition. We never know where we are at all.

For this reason it is highly ironic that Heath should use *Touch of Evil* as a key example of classic Hollywood narrative in his semiology of the cinema.[7] The key features of such narrative which Heath identifies – closure, economy, intelligibility, suture-editing framed primarily around reverse-angle and point-of-view shots – are all, in fact, strongly undermined by the subversive Wellesian *mise-en-scène*. Heath ignores the obvious studio objections to the movie which arose out of just such a subversion. This conflict is now a vital part of film history. Welles did not have editorial control over the picture, and in 1958 Universal released a ninety-three-minute version of the film with minimal distribution. Needless to say the film had no commercial success. The picture took off only with a showing at the Brussels World's Fair in 1958 and a subsequent two-year run in Paris. It was not until 1975 that a film archivist uncovered a 108-minute version of the picture corresponding more closely to Welles's intentions.[8] The interpolations in this cut, which Welles was powerless to prevent, are all brief 'intelligibility' shots attempting to provide a clearer plot-line, and showing the unease of the studio with the materials they had to edit for theatrical release. If anything, the film becomes the springboard for the transformation of American cinema in the 1970s. In this context, Heath's talk of Wellesian narrative as 'a space where things circulate *a little*' and of 'free play *within its frame*' is patronizing, as if these are the tiny freedoms of a cultural upstart daring to be the author of their own film.[9] No one else at that time in Hollywood could have made such a film. If it were not for Welles the film would not exist, nor would the basis have existed for the modern transformation of classic narrative.

The most damning shortfall of Heath's analysis lies in his literal approach to the film, an approach which blithely ignores its cruel and self-conscious parody of classical convention. He claims that the narrative begins and ends with the kiss of Vargas and his wife, but the whole thrust of the film is to deconstruct this very convention of closure, of the ending as a return to the beginning. The prelude to the first kiss is the planting of the bomb whose detonation interrupts it. The postscript to the final kiss is the killing of Quinlan, moving the film from its fake romantic resolution into grotesque and dissonant tragedy as Menzies shoots Quinlan over the sound of his own voice on the replayed tape denying that he has betrayed him. The spatial and aural confusions of the final sequence after Mike and Susan have left echo the sound overlaps of the sequence prior to the kiss where Vargas has tracked Quinlan and Menzies on the bridge, by holding up his tape recorder as he wades through the water below. The true ending is Quinlan's backward plunge, fatally wounded, from the river bank into the water, and Tanya's final verdict on him. 'He was some kind of a man. What does it matter what you say about people?'[10] Iconically, Vargas, the hero, is no match for Quinlan, the villain, while Susan, the newly-wed, is no match for Tanya, the prostitute. They are both easily supplanted.

Heath views the narrative as an exercise in the restoration of Welles's endangered heroine to purity and safety through the re-assertion of the Law. 'The narrative', he claims, 'must restore the woman as good object.'[11] But Welles mocks the efficacy of the Law at every juncture in the film, a theme he takes up on a more sombre note in *The Trial*. A contemporary audience watching the film would question Grandi's weak disclaimer of the gang rape and read past the fade to black to its actual occurrence during Vargas's search for dossiers on Quinlan's previous cases in dusty archives. It would question Schwartz's assertion that Sanchez has confessed to the killing as in all likelihood confession by torture, no better than Quinlan's planting of fake evidence. It would also read the oblique drugs references as highly plausible, and Susan's discourse as racist and irrecuperable. Instead of restoring the Law and restoring the heroine, the film shatters the Law and taints the heroine. Its structures of feeling are those of the perverse and the unjust. The two mirror each other, and outlast the token vindication of the Law and marriage the film contains. In modern America, for Welles, the perverse and the unjust are never far away. Normality needs them as long as they are out of sight. When they intrude, however, as they do here, it has no defence against them.

The films of Welles and Mackendrick pave the way for the noir films of the 1970s. Their visions of the perverse explore the nadir of male sexuality where the role of the femme fatale is made redundant. Here there are two alternatives. Women are sidelined in many films of the period as Haskell notes,[12] or else, more dramatically, they are cast in a new light as potential victims of a male tyranny which knows no limits. In *Chinatown* (1974) the helpless Jack Nicholson finds out that Faye Dunaway and her sister/daughter are the scarred incest victims of Noah Cross who is protected by corrupt city officials on his payroll. In *Taxi Driver* (1976), Jodie Foster as the child prostitute is the victim of a double-tyranny, that of Robert De Niro, who is sexually obsessed by her, and that of her brutal pimp, Harvey Keitel, who is De Niro's sexual double. In *The Conversation* Harry Caul (Gene Hackmann) sidelines his girlfriend Ann (Cindy Williams) in his continuing obsession with surveillance technology except for the brief period when his paranoia identifies her with the women he has been wire-tapping. In *The Parallex View* reporter Warren Beatty's girlfriend takes second place to his journey into political paranoia, where he fakes the role of the would-be professional assassin he has intended to expose as the murderer of Presidential candidates.

As the femme fatale disappears, the role of the heroic fall-guy changes. He is too weak and buffoonish to be desirable – witness Nicholson in *Chinatown*, or too frantic and obsessive, as Beatty is in *The Parallex View*. He is displaced either by the corrupt patriarch (Hank Quinlan, Hunsecker, Cross), or impersonal corporate power or, conversely, by the dangerous male loner (Travis Bickle, Harry Caul). He is displaced, that is, by the extremes of male power as pure patriarchy or pure marginality. Yet at the same time he cannot avoid complicity in the system. Nicholson and Hackmann both share knowledge of the corruptions of the system from their past work, and old habits die hard. In that respect, the noir movie of political paranoia intermingles black and white. It is Travis Bickle identifying with the populist message of the campaigning politician he intends to assassinate, much as Lee Harvey Oswald did with John F. Kennedy. As Barker has pointed out, this reworking of the moral ambiguities of 1940s noir combines the modern legacy of the new European cinema with the political pessimism of the Vietnam era.[13] It is closer in that respect to the fictions of Thomas Pynchon, Robert Stone or Don DeLillo which evoke the mutual paranoia of political extremes than it is to the hard-edged certainties of the earlier crime thriller.

For all its pyrotechnical editing, Oliver Stone's *JFK* reinstates the virtues of pre-Vietnam melodrama, where there is a clear separation of black and white, good and evil. Stone's moral melodrama is a nostalgia movie which works through the earnest but marginal investigator, which is how, of course, Kevin Costner plays Jim Garrison. Yet if Costner is the moral persona of the moment, he has taken on the mantle from Robert Redford who perfected it in the 1970s. Stone's moralizing has its origins in that other, more conventional strand of political noir, in which Pakula also plays a large part. The alternative to the paranoid attraction of opposites, a new 'normality' which echoes the old morality of the studio hero, is seen in his films *Klute* (1971) and *All the President's Men* (1976). This is the moral man without qualities. As private investigator John Klute, Donald Sutherland is the epitome of small-town blandness. As sanitized versions of Carl Bernstein and Bob Woodward, Dustin Hoffman and Robert Redford are strongly into professional bonding where the crimes of Watergate appear to leave no time for female liaisons. Though women appear as weak links in the chain of cover-up, secretaries more likely to cave in to the pressure of investigation than the male bosses they protect, their interrogators have no nature beyond the role of interrogating the film gives them. In the figure of John Klute there is something even more disquieting, which offsets his incorruptible blandness. His affair with Bree Daniels treads the same route as those of his small-town associates, whose relationships with Bree seem to materialize their own *idea* of sexual perversity in the corrupt city. He is, in a sense, their double, in danger of succumbing to the same temptations of false perception. But he resists temptation and restores the erotic to 'normality', a normality which can sustain itself, however, only by the solving of the murders and the dubious promise of love.

In all these movies corruption is not so much an individual flaw as the core of a complex web of interests in the public domain, and the corrupt are respectable figures of public life. Widespread disillusionment over the Kennedy assassinations, defeat in Vietnam and duplicity at Watergate had finally taken its toll. The powerful could not be trusted and the American cinema now dared openly to say so. The darkness of the noir vision becomes political and its vision consequently mythologizes the new issues of sexual politics. Nowhere is this more clearly seen than in *Klute*, whose sexual ambivalence is central to the history of noir cinema. It repositions the heroine at the centre of film noir. She has the lure of the femme fatale and the situation of a female victim, but is in fact neither. The film also implodes the new split in the male configuration, the split between the perverse and the normal. As opposed to the numbing blandness of the incorruptible Klute, all the perverse desires of Bree Daniels's respectable clients are taken as a sign of their public weakness. They are easily capable of being corrupted. When Bree intones into the telephone 'anything is possible' this acts as the Nietzschean imperative her clients pay to hear from a seductive female voice, an exhortation referring not just to sexual pleasure but to all forms of action. The power her voice and look give to her are supremely narcissistic. As an unemployed actress–model who gets no opportunity to perform on stage or in front of the camera, she performs successfully with her clients. The rituals of her work are highly theatrical, a narrative extension of the failed auditions she has at the start of the movie, and she can bask in the reflected glory of her seductive image. She is her own woman. But her visits to a woman shrink tell us something else. She may be autonomous and confident, but she is also vulnerable, a commodity who puts her life in danger by giving the pleasures men desire and uttering the words they want to hear. The power to manipulate is a genuine counter-power, but finally cosmetic. Male power is never conquered. It remains unstable, and dangerous.

Noir movies have remained part of the underbelly of American myth, denoting the sea-changes in social relations in a much more powerful way than most genre movies. They continue to fill conspicuous absences in the American psyche.[14] The extraordinary power of Kathleen Turner's performance in *Body Heat* comes from her refusal to show weakness, to be caught plotting or to display any kind of guilt. She remains disconcertingly calm and composed as William Hurt gets more and more flustered, performing all the transgressions normally seen as a male preserve with a devastating secrecy which strengthens her erotic power. Finally as Hurt languishes in a Florida jail for his sins, she survives alone with her murdered husband's fortune in South

America. The film's triumphant ending, which literally resurrects her from the dead, atones for an earlier generation of noir movies in which female crime and desire are necessarily punished. We truly feel, watching Kasdan's picture, that the punishment of the woman has lost its mythical *cachet*. But there is something more. Turner is better than Hurt at what has traditionally been a man's game. She knows that, in her words, 'knowledge is power' and acts accordingly, not in imitation of her male protagonists but out of her own definition of self-interest. Her real rival is not Hurt or her husband but her own double, Marianne, the glamorous lookalike Hurt mistakes her for in the garden of her Florida mansion, and whose name she has bought to conceal her criminal past. The figure of the double reinforces the meaning of her own persona. She becomes the sexual Other who cannot be appropriated, who cannot be conquered – a term indeed that no longer has sexual meaning here – or bought off, or punished. The power of women, both erotic and political, refuses to go away. It cannot be dismissed, and it cannot be exorcized.

The turning-point suggested by *Body Heat* rings some interesting changes in the form. In Rafelson's *Black Widow* Theresa Russell, a femme fatale who looks a dead ringer for Turner in *Body Heat* casually devours a multitude of husbands and can be caught only by a member of her own sex. The investigator here is Debra Winger, who, instead of disavowing the beautiful transgressor she obsessively pursues, promptly falls in love with her. In *Sea of Love* (1989) another amorous investigator, Al Pacino, suspects Ellen Barkin of murdering the men she meets through dating ads they place in a New York paper. Barkin, even more sensual than Turner, has all the physical requirements of the femme fatale and when she seduces the suspecting Pacino his fear and desire become inseparable, a death-wish he cannot resist. Yet Barkin is a divorced mother and working woman who has to make her own way in the world. Her sexual power has no dark motive attached, as Pacino wrongly imagines. It is simply the direct expression of her own pleasure. Hence the film plays on the classic expectation of the form, the lure of the woman as dark and treacherous, and then undercuts it with a more plausible and natural explanation. The distrust here, so crucial to all noir narratives, is a crucial failure of perception on Pacino's part alone. It is he, not she, who misrepresents himself, failing to tell her that her new lover is also a police investigator hoping to arrest her for murder. In a novel twist on male paranoia, the dissembling of which he secretly accuses her is stamped all over his own actions. He is the ambiguous and manipulative voyeur who gets lucky and gets laid. Desire and suspicion are inseparable. In fact he is too suspicious of Ellen Barkin to check out the identity of her estranged husband, whom he has already questioned without realizing.

The most powerful literary source of the revived noir idiom is without doubt Jim Thompson, whose existential vision of mistrust and refusal to acknowledge any moral centre to American life have inspired adaptations by Maggie Greenwald of *The Kill-Off*, Stephen Frears of *The Grifters* and James Foley of *After Dark, My Sweet*. All three novels unnerve the reader with their dark vision of the central relationship, which is partly Oedipal and partly criminal, between a younger man and an older woman. In the *Kill-Off* Ray is the servant of a bedridden wife nearly old enough to be his mother, whose malicious gossip destroys the lives of people in a small Jersey town. In *The Grifters* (1989) John Cusack's attraction to Annette Bening comes about through her physical resemblance to Angelica Houston, his own mother, who is also attracted to her 'grifting' son, as he is to her. The link between crime and desire is again made dark, but is also more existential, less a function of deep conspiracy than of casual spur-of-the-moment decisions to play effectively at crime, in which all endings seem as open to chance.

After Dark, My Sweet (1991) is the most accomplished of all the film versions of Thompson's novels because it updates his decentred moral vision to the contemporary world more decisively, this time to south-east California. Shot on location near the edge of the desert, it is supremely painterly, using like *Chinatown* the colours of the landscape to give an exterior feel to noir conspiracy. It sticks closely to the novel in keeping the younger man/older woman relationship so important in Thompson's work. Fay (Rachel Ward) is no longer married but now a widow living alone in a large isolated suburban house with a plantation of decaying date palms. She is in league with a local crook she calls, somewhat ambiguously, Uncle Bud (Bruce Dern) to plan a child kidnapping. The male anti-hero is an ex-boxer, Collie (Jason Patric), now turned desert drifter and evoking the figure of Frank Chambers in Cain's *The Postman Always Rings Twice*, itself remade as erotic noir conspiracy by Rafelson in 1982.

Foley's film uses Collie's voice-over and point-of-view flashback to tell the story of his first encounter with Fay, her employment of him as gardener, and then the botched kidnapping plot which triangulates the mistrust between Patric, Ward and Dern. No one is sure of what the others are planning as a next move.

The relationship between crime and desire is opaque, as too are the surrogate relationships of kin. Bud is 'uncle' and father to Collie, Fay is older sister and lover to him, a relationship with strong maternal overtones, while the presence of the kidnapped boy in the household gives him the fleeting persona of an adopted son, the 'child' of Collie and Fay who is present in the next room during the scene of their first love-making. The absence of biological ties and boundaries sets up an uncanny relationship between the absent presence of the 'family' as an institution and the American culture of distrust, a distrust that is permeable and ubiquitous. The transparent open-plan house in the middle of nowhere becomes after the kidnap the haven of a nuclear family by default, isolated, distrustful, imploding, a quartet of human beings who can hardly bear to be there. The flowing Steadicam shots which move through the open doorways of receptive rooms cut against the static conventions of the enclosed room of 1940s noir. Yet the movements themselves suggest moral uncertainty, anxiety and distrust. When Collie runs back from his trailer to the house to seek out Fay in their first agreed love-match, the camera follows him through all the rooms of the house, charting his expectancy and filming her absence in the same movement, showing the spectator that she has changed her mind and fled.

Like *Body Heat* and *Sea of Love* the picture is a mythic celebration of the contemporary woman's power to survive the male culture of distrust and triumph on her own terms, to triumph without sacrificing desire. All three films combine, therefore, the sense of greater male threat with greater female poise, a more dangerous world with a new and more resilient kind of woman. Interestingly, they also combine unlikely extremes of *mise-en-scène*. They include many of the most erotic scenes in noir history yet counterpoint them with the presence of the ambiguous child. Where the child is the woman's biological daughter, as in *Sea of Love*, she is largely unseen, asleep in another room or cared for by her grandmother. When the relationship is more distant the ambiguity deepens. In *Body Heat* Heather, the young niece of Katherine Turner, stays at the mansion while her uncle is away. One evening she awakes and goes downstairs to become the involuntary witness of an act of fellatio between Hurt and Turner after Hurt's secret arrival. She is the only material witness to the meeting of the couple before the husband's murder. In Foley's film the kidnapped boy, sickly and diabetic, casts a languid eye over the many indecisions of his three captors, whether to turn him in, wait for a ransom or leave him to die. In both cases, the gaze of the surrogate child fixes the adult relationship between crime and desire. The gaze is not that of a secret moral censor to desire but a mediated questioning of where that desire leads. In other words it mediates our questioning as spectators as to where desire must go, and our ungranted wish to separate it out from crime. In that way it censors the link of crime and desire but not desire itself. But it also denies the liberal utopia of eros as redemption from crime, as an illusory guarantor of crime's redundancy in the affairs of the heart.

In the 1980s movement away from the femme fatale, where *Body Heat* is a reprise which ends by destroying the original meaning of the term, the role of the woman is transformed. Marriage dependency becomes an outmoded theme. Distrust becomes existential, the feature of a more brittle culture which breeds the criminal conspiracy rather than vice versa. It is no coincidence that Pacino 'picks up' Barkin as part of an elaborate police sting operation in which he pretends to be someone he is not. It is no coincidence that Hurt, as a sexy but incompetent lawyer, specializes in that American apotheosis of mistrust, malpractice suits, and that Turner targets him as a fall-guy when she finds out that he has been sued by other lawyers over the botching of wills. Absence of trust is everywhere beneath the veneer of casual banter and instant friendship. Here the institutional leads into the personal and back out again. Harvey's 'absent family' is also transformed. There are children without fathers as well as women without children, and there are children as surrogate kin. The child present in the house of desire is a child who 'witnesses' the primal scene but is never the biological offspring of both lovers. In *Body Heat* the niece is fatherless. In *Sea of Love* the daughter is also the child of the estranged husband who murders the lovers consorting with his ex-wife. Pacino, too, wrapped up in his mistrust of female desire, realizes this only as he is about to be attacked. In *After Dark, My Sweet* the kidnapped boy is present during a desire which has preceded his kidnapping but can be consummated only after it, eerily reversing our normal view of adults as creatures who always try to escape children in order to make love. The presence of the surrogate child achieves one final thing. It turns the act of desire into a possible act of conception, and reminds us what the desiring couple lack. If there is a desire which leads to crime, there is also a desire which leads to birth.

If the remakes of noir constantly fill in the absences left by the Studio Code, of those things which many years ago could not be explicitly said, we may feel that we have now reached the point of exhaustion, or plenitude. Surely everything has been filled in. Now we have seen it all. Clint Eastwood's *Bird* (1988), his study of the life of Charlie Parker, reminds us that we have not. Noir movies of the 1940s consistently ignored black Americans but the remakes have done so equally. Where they do feature, as in the case of J. A. Preston, the black detective in *Body Heat*, they are constrained to supporting roles. Eastwood's movie, in a period when directors like Spike Lee, Euzan Palcy and Charles Burnett have challenged the Hollywood establishment, reminds us of what is missing from that earlier period of racial apartheid and prohibition. It is a retro-movie set in the noir period, told in flashback with a distinctly *noir* style. But included in its 'blackness', for perhaps the first time, is something white film-makers have preferred to avoid, the question of pigmentation.

It is not merely that an African–American, Forest Whitaker, triumphs in the main role. It is also that African–American music, conspicuously missing from the musical soundtracks of noir movies, features as theme as well as soundtrack. The movie is about Parker but it is also about modern jazz, the jazz Mackendrick had fleetingly evoked with the casting of Chico Hamilton's quintet in *Sweet Smell of Success* but which had largely been buried by the studios of the day as a non-commercial proposition. The darkness of the streets in *Bird* also has a different connotation, because it evokes something else which went unspoken in films of the 1940s. The main threat to Parker's intense and anxious marriage is not one of his many pecadilloes, as melodrama would normally suggest. The femme fatale as female presence is finally buried, and in her place we have something very different. The femme fatale with whom Bird has a secret assignation on dark, windswept streets is heroin. It is the enemy of desire, not its lure, the white powder which destroys music as much as it destroys the man who makes it. The same point is made in a different way in Paul Schrader's very contemporary Manhattan fable, *Light Sleeper* (1992). Up-market drug dealer Willem Dafoe tries to start over with his ex-wife after both of them have kicked the habit, but she balks at his continual dealing. Like most noir women, however, she flatters to deceive. Yet she is not the film's femme fatale. Dafoe discovers to his horror that she is still hooked and that he unwittingly supplies the narcotics which lead to her death. The femme fatale here is cocaine. Mythically speaking, the white powder in both movies displaces the woman from the vampirish role, but perhaps with hindsight in an age of narcotic culture we might say the displacement is more socially accurate and long overdue. The myth is dead. Long live the myth.

Notes

CHAPTER 1 FILM AND THE PARADOX OF THE MODERN

1 The stress on film as a 'physical redemption' of reality is in Siegfried Kracauer's general study of the cinema, *The Theory of Film: The Redemption of Physical Reality* (Oxford: Oxford University Press, 1960).

2 Peter Sloterdijk goes beyond Adorno in making explicit a Nietzschean critique of modern Germany whose counter-culture repeats itself in different eras before and after national-socialism. 'Cynical reason' is a subversive mind-set which crystallizes first in Weimar Germany and again in the West Germany of the late 1960s and 1970s. Here cynical reason is closely connected to the cyclical theory of Eternal Return, so that it operates in Sloterdijk's historical schema as both the concept and the object the concept designates. See the 'Preface' to *Critique of Cynical Reason* (London: Verso, 1988), pp. xxvi–xxix. Adorno's aesthetics do imply, however, the existence of modern art as a potentially recurrent moment of subversion in the age of modernity. He writes: 'Modern art seeks to obviate the magical commodity fetishism of the disenchanted world by means of its own magical moment, which is blackness. By their very existence works of art postulate the existence of something that does not exist in reality'. Theodor Adorno, *Aesthetic Theory* (London: Routledge

& Kegan Paul, 1984), p. 86. Adorno rejects the mimetic image on film as capitulating all too easily to the demands to the corrupt world of appearances in the culture industry. By contrast, the authentic modern film must attempt the periodic fracturing of the dominant mimetic image. For his rejection of Kracauer and film mimesis, see 'Transparencies in Film' in *The Culture Industry*, edited and introduced by J. M. Bernstein (London: Routledge, 1991) pp. 154–62.

3 Charles Taylor, *The Sources of the Self: The Making of Modern Identity* (Cambridge: Cambridge University Press, 1989), pp. 496–7.

4 Martin Jay dissects the dedramatized apocalyptics of French philosophy's recent revisions of Freud in 'The Psychoanalytic Imagination and the Inability to Mourn', in *Force Fields: Between Intellectual History and Cultural Critique* (London: Routledge, 1992).

5 See Godard's recent remarks at a BFI conference in London, 'Jean-Luc Godard in Conversation with Colin MacCabe', in Duncan Petrie (ed.), *Screening Europe* (London: BFI, 1992), pp. 97–106.

6 See Antonioni's statement to the Cannes Film Festival in 1959 on the screening of *L'avventura*, which is included in 'Two Statements', in Harry M. Geduld (ed.), *Film-Makers on Film-Making* (Harmondsworth: Penguin, 1967), pp. 212–14.

7 Pierre Bourdieu, *Distinction: A Social Critique of the Judgement of Taste* (London: Routledge, 1986), pp. 114–16. Bourdieu's brief glance at the cinema tries to operate a high/low culture distinction to show up the differences in the use of cultural capital among Parisians of different social strata. Ironically, his findings, in 1963, fail to provide any conclusive evidence of clear division between 'art-house' and popular cinema (pp. 270–2).

8 Simone de Beauvoir, *The Second Sex* (Harmondsworth: Penguin, 1990), pp. 790f.

9 See the landmark volume edited by E. Ann Kaplan, *Women in Film Noir* (London: BFI, 1981); also Michael Wood, *America in the Movies* (London: Secker & Warburg, 1975), pp. 97–115.

10 Speaking of Riva's unnamed character in the film, Rivette comments: 'At Hiroshima, she experiences a shock, she is hit by a "bomb" which explodes her consciousness, and for her from that moment it becomes a question of finding

herself again, re-composing herself. In the same way that Hiroshima had to be rebuilt after atomic destruction, Emmanuelle Riva in Hiroshima is trying to reconstruct *her* reality.' 'Hiroshima, notre amour', in Jim Hiller (ed.), *Cahiers du Cinéma, The 1950s* (London: Routledge & Kegan Paul, 1985), pp. 62–4.

11 Maurice Merleau-Ponty *The Phenomenology of Perception* (London: Routledge, 1989), pp. 5f., 132f.; also 'Eye and Mind', in *The Primacy of Perception* (Evanston: Northwestern University Press, 1964), pp. 166f.

12 Vivian Sobchack, *The Address of the Eye: A Phenomenology of Film Experience* (Berkeley: University of California Press, 1992), pp. 88–95.

13 For a discussion of modernist epiphany see Taylor, *The Sources of the Self*, p. 450f.; and John Orr, *The Making of the Twentieth-Century Novel* (London: Macmillan, 1987), pp. 13–14, 44–5.

14 Anthony Giddens, *Modernity and Self-Identity: Self and Society in the Late Modern Age* (Cambridge: Polity Press, 1991), pp. 19–21, 27–32.

15 See, for example, the analysis of *Casablanca* in Umberto Eco, *Travels in Hyper-Reality* (London: Picador, 1987), pp. 197–211. Eco deals with the double reading as an instance of the elevation of a popular movie to the status of a cult among intellectuals. It should be remembered that though this constitutes one starting-point for Eco's version of the 'postmodern' as the intertextual and self-conscious re-reading of the popular, his own attitude is ambivalent. He writes in 1984: 'It will be a sad day when a too smart audience will read *Casablanca* as conceived by Michael Curtiz, after having read Calvino and Barthes. But that day will come', p. 211. That day has come. It is instructive to note that the self-conscious eulogy to the cult American movie originated among the neo-moderns, in particular the critics of *Cahiers du Cinéma* who then went on to become the directors of the French New Wave. See, for example, the *Cahiers* dossier on Nicholas Ray in Hillier (ed.) *Cahiers du Cinéma: The 1950s*, pp. 104–26.

16 Robert Ray, *A Certain Tendency of the Hollywood Cinema 1930–1980*, (Princeton: Princeton University Press, 1985), pp. 129–53.

CHAPTER 2   TRAGICOMEDY AND THE COOL APOCALYPSE

1 The term 'structure of feeling' is used by Raymond Williams, initially to suggest a documentary reconstruction of ways of thinking and feeling in specific historical eras, see *The Long Revolution* (Harmondsworth: Penguin, 1975), pp. 64–78. It was later extended to literary forms of feeling. Williams defines structures of feeling as 'meanings and values as they are actively lived and felt . . . the relations between these and formal and systematic beliefs are in practice variable'. *Marxism and Literature* (Oxford: Oxford University Press, 1977), p. 132.

2 See Stephen Kern, *The Culture of Time and Space: 1880–1918* (London: Weidenfeld & Nicolson, 1983), pp. 287–313; also Randall Stevenson, *Modernist Fiction* (Hemel Hempstead: Harvester, 1992), pp. 128–31.

3 John Orr, *Tragicomedy and Contemporary Culture* (London: Macmillan, 1991), pp. 10–32.

4 Stanley Cavell *Pursuits of Happiness: The Hollywood Comedy of Remarriage* (Cambridge, Mass.: Harvard University Press, 1981).

5 See Frank Kermode's keynote essay on the historical duality of modernism, 'Modernisms', in B. Bergonzi (ed.) *Innovations* (London: Macmillan, 1968), pp. 68–75.

6 On modernity and the avant garde, see the *New Left Review* essays by Perry Anderson 'Modernity and Revolution', *NLR* 144, 1984, and Terry Eagleton 'Capitalism, Modernism and Post-Modernism', *NLR* 152, 1985. Eagleton is right to point out that the pastiche of the postmodern has often been no more than a commodified imitation of the revolutionary avant-gardes of 1917, but the dismissal is somewhat nostalgic. It concedes too much to the postmodern claim to aesthetic novelty and barely conceals a sweeping contempt for the neo-modern, a contempt without which its author might have otherwise recognized the vital importance of neo-modern diffusion into the 'postmodern' (pp. 60–5).

7 Christopher Lasch discusses the resurgence of narcissism in contemporary performative culture in *The Culture of Narcissism* (London: Abacus, 1980), pp. 71–90. The best discussion

of kitsch is, predictably, by Adorno. See *Aesthetic Theory* where he argues convincingly that kitsch is not purely a philistine phenomenon but a thriving parasite upon modern art. 'Kitsch is art that cannot, or does not want to be taken seriously, while at the same time, through its appearance, postulating aesthetic seriousness', p. 435. Thus 'it is useless to draw a fine line between what constitutes art and what is sentimental rubbish (kitsch)', p. 340. The 'postmodern' as defined by Eco comes perilously close to kitsch as defined by Adorno. See also Matei Calinescu *Faces of Modernity: Avant-Garde, Decadence, Kitsch* (Bloomington: Indiana University Press, 1977).

8 Gilles Deleuze, *Cinema 2: The Time Image* (London: The Athlone Press, 1989), p. 5.

9 Pierre Sorlin, *European Cinemas: European Societies 1930–1990* (London: Routledge, 1991), p. 131.

10 On the cultural pessimism of the nuclear age, see Joe Bailey, *Pessimism* (London: Routledge, 1989).

11 Christian Metz, *Film Language* (Oxford: Oxford University Press, 1974), p. 197.

12 Ibid., p. 194.

13 *Cinema I: The Movement-Image* (London: The Athlone Press, 1986), pp. 141–59.

14 André Bazin, *What is Cinema? I* (Berkeley: University of California Press, 1967), pp. 33–8.

15 For a more detailed analysis of Welles's picture as a neo-modern adaptation of Kafka's novel, see John Orr, 'The Trial of Orson Welles', in J. Orr and C. Nicholson (eds), *Cinema and Fiction: New Modes of Adapting, 1950–1990* (Edinburgh: Edinburgh University Press, 1992), pp. 13–27.

16 See Peter Cowie, *The Cinema of Orson Welles* (New York: Da Capo Press, 1983), p. 170.

CHAPTER 3   THE DOUBLE AND THE INNOCENT

1 Paul Coates, *The Story of the Lost Reflection* (London: Verso, 1985), pp. 15–26.

2 In his 1935 lectures Heidegger teases out brilliantly the Nietzschean aesthetic which links the modern artwork and the creative will-to-power. The collective nature of *Gesamt-*

kunstwerk fits ideally with the collective nature of modern film-making, but one senses that for Heidegger as a fanatical national-socialist the concrete exemplar of the delirium or rapture (*Rausch*) in the collective act is the political spectacle of Hitler or Goebbels which the German artwork ought, by implication, to emulate. Heidegger thus sets up the Nietzschean aesthetic in order to betray it. See Martin Heidegger, *Nietzsche*, vols 1 and 2 (New York: Harper Collins, 1991), pp. 92–107. Leni Riefenstahl also subscribes to the *Gesamtkunstwerk* but after the making of *Triumph of the Will* her posture towards national-socialism became more heretical than Heidegger's. Thus in *Olympiad* her images eulogize the figures of non-Aryan athletes, in particular Jesse Owens and the Japanese, and this conscious inversion of the Aryan ideal in her powerful aesthetic of the human body is continued after the war in her unfinished documentary of the Nuba tribespeople of southern Sudan. See David B. Hinton, *The Films of Leni Riefenstahl* (Metuchen, NJ: The Scarecrow Press Inc., 1978).

3　Otto Rank, *The Double: A Psychoanalytic Study* (New York: New American Library, 1979), p. 85. For a general study of the motif see John Herdman, *The Double in Romantic and Post-Romantic Fiction* (London: Macmillan, 1990).

4　'The Uncanny', in *Works* vol. 14 (Harmondsworth: Penguin, 1985), pp. 363–5.

5　'Beyond the Pleasure Principle', in *Works*, vol. 11 (Harmondsworth: Penguin, 1984), pp. 290–4.

6　See Ronald Binns, 'Filming *Under the Volcano*', in Sue Vice (ed.), *Malcolm Lowry: Eighty Years On* (London: Macmillan, 1989).

7　Lotte Eisner, *The Haunted Screen: Expressionism in the German Cinema and the Influence of Max Reinhardt* (London: Thames & Hudson, 1969), pp. 95–100.

8　'Repression', in *Works* vol. 11, pp. 153–6.

9　Jean-Paul Sartre, *Being and Nothingness* (London: Methuen, 1957), p. 38.

10　*Cinema and Psychoanalysis* (London: Macmillan, 1982), p. 110.

11　Noel Burch, *Theory of Film Practice* (Princeton: Princeton University Press, 1981), pp. 117–32.

12　Paul Monaco, *Cinema and Society: France and Germany during the Twenties* (New York: Elsevier, 1976), p. 120.

13 Siegfried Kracauer, *From Caligari to Hitler: A Psychological Study of German Film* (Princeton: Princeton University Press, 1974), pp. 61–76.

14 See the recent remarks on the picture by Wilson Harris, the Guyanese novelist, in 'Tainted Histories', *Sight and Sound*, vol. 1, no. 10, February 1992, p. 31.

15 For an elegant exposure of the limitations of post-structuralism, see Noel Carroll, *Mystifying Movies: Fads and Fallacies in Contemporary Film Theory* (New York: Columbia University Press, 1988). On its limitations for cultural theory in general, see Frank Kermode, *History and Value* (Oxford: Clarendon Press, 1989), pp. 98–146.

16 Peter Brooks points out that, historically, melodrama is a response to the loss of tragic vision. See *The Melodramatic Imagination: Balzac, Henry James, Melodrama and the Mode of Excess* (New Haven: Yale University Press, 1976). Melodrama's search for redemption through its stylistic excesses and its simplified plot-resolutions performs, Brooks suggests, a function similar to that of the talking cure of psychoanalysis, pp. 14–15, 201–2. In this respect, we might argue that it has been the clear popular alternative in the last three decades to the cinema of the neo-moderns. See also Christine Gledhill, 'The Melodramatic Field: an Investigation', in Gledhill (ed.), *Home is Where the Heart is: Studies in Melodrama and the Woman's Film* (London: BFI, 1989), pp. 5–43; and Robert Lang, *American Film Melodrama* (Princeton: Princeton University Press, 1989).

17 In the middle of the neo-modern period, Perkins writes: 'Whenever we talk of the movie's realism we are discussing the artifice as well. It is possible to see the camera as no more than the *convenient* machine that exists to produce the kinds and quantity of still images required by the projector. Conversely, as soon as we recognise the screen image as an illusion *derived from reality* we have to acknowledge the importance of the movie's photographic impact . . . technology has propelled the camera steadily towards increased realism', V. F. Perkins, *Film as Film* (Harmondsworth: Penguin, 1972), p. 43.

18 Robert Carringer has noted that in *Citizen Kane* the multiplane composition of Susan's suicide attempt, usually seen as an example of deep focus, is actually an in-camera matte

shot in which foreground and background are shot se-
parately with a different lens length and then superimposed. *The Making of Citizen Kane* (London: John Murray,
1985), p. 82.

19   Douglas came from a mixed religious background whose
various contradictions seem to crystallize in the trilogy. In
My Childhood and *My Ain Folk*, the *mise-en-scène* with its
stress on the humility of the Bressonian look seems largely
neo-Catholic, but its major theme, this-worldly damnation,
is clearly neo-Calvinist. For a recent discussion of the Scottish
film-maker's life and work, see Eddie Dick, Andrew Noble
and Duncan Petrie (eds), *Bill Douglas: A Lanternist's Account*
(London: BFI, 1993).

20   For a fuller discussion of the relationship between neo-
realism, Catholicism and Bazin's writings, see Hugh Gray,
'Introduction to André Bazin, *What is Cinema? II* (Berkeley:
University of California Press, 1971), pp. 1–15, and Amedée
Ayfre, 'Neo-Realism and Phenomenology' (November 1962),
in J. Hillier (ed.), *Cahiers du Cinéma* (London: Routledge,
1985), *The 1950s*, pp. 182–92.

21   *What is Cinema? II*, pp. 22–37, 47–8. For a fuller discussion
of the 'image-fact' in Bazin, see Robert Kolker, *The Altering
Eye* (Oxford: Oxford University Press, 1983), pp. 46–8.

22   Pier Paolo Pasolini, *A Future Life* (Rome: Associazione Fondo
Pier Paolo Pasolini, 1989), p. 19.

23   'La Strada', in P. Bondanella and M. Gieri (eds), *La Strada*
(New Brunswick: Rutgers University Press, 1991), pp. 203.
For Bazin's comments on Bresson, see *What is Cinema?*
p. 131f.

24   For an assessment of the impact of the HUAC hearings on
Kazan and on Hollywood film-makers in general, see the
articles by Brian Neve 'The 1950s: the case of Elia Kazan
and *On the Waterfront*', in P. Davies and B. Neve (eds)
Cinema, Politics and Society in America (Manchester: Manchester University Press, 1981), pp. 97–119; and 'Fellow Tra-
veller' *Sight and Sound* spring 1990, pp. 117–20.

25   *Cinema I: The Movement-Image*, pp. 146f.

26   Susan Sontag, *Styles of Radical Will* (New York: Delta Books,
1970), p. 165.

CHAPTER 4   THE POWER OF THE GAZE

1   For the central role of the eye in Western art and technology see Don Gifford, *The Farther Shore: A Natural History of Perception* (London: Faber & Faber, 1990), pp. 17–48; and Camille Paglia, *Sexual Personae: Art and Decadence from Nefertiti to Emily Dickinson* (Harmondsworth: Penguin 1991), pp. 62–71, 186–95, 664–6. In her compelling study Paglia is right to stress the role of the cinema as a legitimate heir to the ocular tradition of Western art, but wrong to sideline modernism as a transient and neurotic blip in Hollywood's march to glory. Her metaphorical use of Bergman's *Persona* for the title of her book appears to contradict her general argument.

2   For a detailed comparison of the workings of the eye and the camera see Bill Nichols *Ideology and the Image* (Bloomington: Indiana University Press, 1981), pp. 10–21.

3   *The Consequences of Modernity* (Cambridge: Polity Press, 1991), pp. 57–8.

4   Michael Foucault, *Discipline and Punish* (Harmondsworth: Penguin, 1979), pp. 190–208: also *Power and Knowledge* (Hassocks: Harvester Press, 1984), pp. 162f.

5   *Renoir on Renoir* (Cambridge: Cambridge University Press, 1989), pp. 194–5.

6   The best commentaries on this aspect of Nietzsche's work are Gilles Deleuze, *Nietzsche & Philosophy* (London: The Athlone Press, 1983), pp. 58–72; and Georg Simmel, *Schopenhauer and Nietzsche* (Amherst: University of Massachusetts Press, 1986), pp. 156–60.

7   See the comparison with Hitchcock by Stanley H. Palombo 'Hitchcock's *Vertigo*: the Dream Function in film', in J. Smith and W. Kerrigan (eds) *Images in Our Souls: Cavell, Psychoanalysis and Cinema* (Baltimore: Johns Hopkins University Press, 1987); and John Orr, 'Peter Weir's Version; *The Year of Living Dangerously*' in J. Orr and C. Nicholson (eds) *Cinema and Fiction* (Edinburgh: Edinburgh University Press, 1992), pp. 54–65.

8   *Being and Nothingness* (London: Methuen, 1957), pp. 379–80.

9   Tania Modleski, *The Women Who Knew Too Much: Hitchcock and Feminist Film Theory* (London: Methuen, 1988). Modleski

notes that the mirror-image shot here shows *'from the very outset'* the disturbing nature of Scottie's identification with Madeline, p. 92.

10   Crisp has noted the parallel between events in the film and an incident in Rousseau's *Confessions* that took place near Annecy in 1730, when the author met two country girls in a romantic encounter which ended with a simple kiss on the hand. C. G. Crisp, *Erich Rohmer: Realist and Moralist* (Bloomington: Indiana University Press, 1988), pp. 63–5.

11   Nestor Almendros, *The Man Behind the Camera* (London: Faber & Faber, 1985), pp. 89–91.

12   Peter Wollen, *Readings and Writings* (London: NLB, 1982), pp. 173–4.

13   Paul Virilio, *War and Cinema: The Logistics of Perception* (London: Verso, 1989), p. 71.

14   Ibid., p. 83.

15   For discussion of the film's controversial ending see Gilbert Adair, *Hollywood's Vietnam* (London: Proteus, 1981), pp. 162–8, and Peter Cowie, *Coppola* (London: André Deutsch, 1989), pp. 120–3.

16   For the general logistical problems of the film, which Coppola himself compared to the logistics of the Vietnam War itself, see *Coppola*, pp. 118–200.

17   'Nietzsche, even before elaborating the concept of the will to power and giving it its full significance, was already speaking of a *feeling of power*. Before treating power as a matter of will, he treated it as a matter of feeling and sensibility'. Deleuze, *Nietzsche & Philosophy*, p. 62.

18   Pietro Citati, *Kafka* (London: Minerva, 1991), pp. 126–32.

CHAPTER 5   THE ABSENT IMAGE AND THE UNREAL
OBJECT

1   Jean-Paul Sartre, *The Psychology of Imagination* (London: Methuen, 1972). (Original French title *L'Imaginaire* (Paris: Editions Gallimard, 1939).

2   *Psychoanalysis and Cinema*, pp. 117f.

3   Sartre, *The Psychology of Imagination*, p. 204. Sartre does not discuss the cinema directly but significantly refers to painting which he regards as a material analogue of the painter's

mental image. 'The painting should be conceived of as a material thing *visited* from time to time (every time the spectator assumes an imaginative attitude) by an unreal object which is precisely the *painted object*', ibid., p. 220. Thus the cinema poses the problematic of the unreal object by its own technical transposition of the cinematographic images of the film-maker into edited film as an object viewed from time to time.

4   *Being and Nothingness*, (London: Methuen 1957), pp. 39ff.
5   *The Psychology of Imagination*, p. 208.
6   'Film and the New Psychology', in *Sense and Non-Sense* (Evanston: Northwestern University Press, 1964), p. 58.
7   *Being and Nothingness*, p. 30.
8   Merleau-Ponty, op. cit., p. 59.
9   Gilles Deleuze, *Cinema 2: The Time-Image* (London: The Athlone Press, 1989). Here Deleuze explicates the ontology of the time-image in terms of 'peaks of present and sheets of past', pp. 98ff.
10 See his study of Bergson where he argues that recollection, in Bergson's terms, involves 'a genuine *leap*' into the past, 'the *leap into ontology*'. For Bergson and Deleuze, duration entails differences in kind where space entails difference only of degree. Gilles Deleuze, *Bergsonism* (New York: Zone Books, 1991), pp. 31ff, 56ff.
11 For descriptions of the technical and practical difficulties surrounding the shot see Seymour Chatman, *Antonioni: The Surface of the World* (Berkeley: University of California Press, 1986), pp. 184f.; and Sam Rohdie, *Antonioni* (London: BFI, 1989), pp. 145–7.
12 For a discussion of the *Heimat* tradition in the new German cinema see Thomas Elsaesser, *The New German Cinema* (London: BFI, 1989), pp. 141ff.
13 Wim Wenders, *Emotion Pictures* (London: Faber & Faber, 1989), pp. 114–15.
14 Pierre Sorlin, *European Cinemas: European Societies 1939–1990* (London: Routledge, 1991), p. 185.

CHAPTER 6   COMMODIFIED DEMONS I: THE MACHINE AND THE MASK

1   Jean-Paul Sartre, *Being and Nothingness* (London: Methuen, 1957), p. 49. The complexities of bad faith in Sartre's ontology are discussed by Phyllis Morris, 'Self-Deception: Sartre's Resolution of the Paradox', in H. Silverman and F. A. Ellison (eds) *Jean-Paul Sartre: Contemporary Approaches to his Philosophy* (Hassocks: Harvester Press, 1980), pp. 30ff.
2   Sam Rohdie, *Antonioni* (London: BFI, 1989), pp. 9–11.
3   Luis Buñuel, *My Last Breath* (London: Fontana, 1985), p. 225.
4   See Fellini's remarks on *Amarcord* in Peter Bondanella (ed.) *Federico Fellini: Essays in Criticism* (Oxford: Oxford University Press, 1982), pp. 32–3.
5   Ingmar Bergman, *The Magic Lantern* (Harmondsworth: Penguin, 1988), pp. 119–31.
6   Marilyn Johns Blackwell, *Persona: The Transcendent Image* (Urbana: University of Illinois Press, 1986), pp. 39–40.
7   Ingmar Bergman, *Persona and Shame* (London: Marion Boyars, 1983), p. 59.
8   Blackwell, op. cit., p. 98.
9   See his autobiography, *The Magic Lantern* (Harmondsworth: Penguin, 1988), pp. 119–32.
10   For an impressive and more sympathetic account of Syberberg's work in the context of the German cinema of the 1970s see Thomas Elsaesser 'Filming Fascism: Is History just an Old Movie?' *Sight and Sound*, September 1992, pp. 18–22.

CHAPTER 7   COMMODIFIED DEMONS II: THE AUTOMOBILE

1   John Fordham, 'Is your Journey Really Necessary?' *Independent on Sunday*, 1 December 1991.
2   *City of Quartz* (London: Verso, 1990), pp. 24–8.
3   See James Monaco, *The New Wave* (New York: Oxford University Press, 1976), p. 168. Monaco sees the Pascalian wager as a way of reading Godard's turn to Marxism–Leninism in 1967 in his attempt to create a new political cinema directly challenging Hollywood melodrama.
4   See Dudley Andrews (ed.) *Breathless* (New Brunswick:

Rutgers University Press, 1987). Shot 85, pp. 51–3; Shot 285, pp. 113–15; and Shot 383, pp. 139–40.

5 'Interview with Jean-Luc Godard', *Cahiers du Cinéma* no. 171, October 1965, in *Pierrot le Fou* (New York: Lorimer, 1984), pp. 5–6.

CHAPTER 8   THE STRANGE PASSIONS OF FILM NOIR

1 Raymond Borde and Etienne Chaumeton, *Panorama du film noir americain: (1941–1953)* (Paris: Editions du Minuit, 1955), pp. 1–15.

2 E. Ann Kaplan (ed.) *Women in Film Noir* (London: BFI, 1980).

3 Sylvia Harvey, 'Women's place: The Absent Family of Film Noir' in Kaplan (ed.) *Women in Film Noir*, pp. 29–33.

4 Sarah Kosloff, *Invisible Storytellers: Voice-Over Narration in American Fiction Film* (Berkeley: University of California Press, 1988), p. 63.

5 Michael Wood, *America in the Movies* (London: Secker & Warburg, 1975), p. 98.

6 Philip Kemp, *Lethal Innocence: The Cinema of Alexander Mackendrick* (London: Methuen, 1991), p. 148.

7 See Stephen Heath, *Questions of Cinema* (London: Macmillan, 1981).

8 Terry Comito (ed.) *Touch of Evil* (New Brunswick: Rutgers University Press, 1985), pp. 45–6.

9 *Questions of Cinema*, p. 139.

10 Comito (ed.) *Touch of Evil*, p. 169.

11 *Questions of Cinema*, p. 140.

12 Molly Haskell *From Reverence to Rape: The Treatment of Women in the Movies* (New York: Holt, Rinehart & Winston, 1975).

13 Adam Barker, 'Cries and Whispers', *Sight and Sound*, spring 1990, pp. 117–20.

14 Hence the reference to *Body Heat* as 'pastiche' by Fredric Jameson seems somewhat wide of the mark. Kasdan's movie successfully incorporates its genre history into a clear sense of the America of its own period. It is 'simultaneously' past and present. To see it merely as blank repetition is to miss its mythic force as a social re-presentation of middle-class Americans in the 1980s. The power of the best film noir

comes from a flair for idealizing the social and sexual mores of its period through a good eye for detail. Jameson's attempt to make it illustrate the blank pastiche of the 'postmodern' is thus miscued. See 'Postmodernism and Consumer Society', in Hal Foster (ed.) *Postmodern Culture* (London: Pluto Press, 1985), pp. 111f. For a more convincing though critical view of the movie, see Judith Williamson, *Consuming Passions: The Dynamics of Popular Culture* (London: Boyars, 1986), pp. 171–9.

Select Bibliography

Adair, Gilbert *Hollywood's Vietnam* (London: Proteus, 1981)

Adorno, Theodor *Aesthetic Theory* (London: Routledge & Kegan Paul, 1984)

—— *The Culture Industry*, edited and introduced by J. M. Bernstein (London: Routledge, 1991)

Almendros, Nestor *The Man Behind the Camera* (London: Faber & Faber, 1985)

Anderson, Perry 'Modernity and Revolution', NLR, 144, 1984

Andrews, Dudley (ed.) *Breathless* (New Brunswick: Rutgers University Press, 1987)

Antonioni, Michelangelo 'Two Statements' in Harry M. Geduld (ed.) *Film-Makers on Film-Making* (Harmondsworth: Penguin, 1967)

Armes, Roy *The Ambiguous Image: Narrative Style in the Modern European Cinema* (London: Secker & Warburg, 1976)

Ayfre, Amédée 'Neo-Realism and Phenomenology' in J. Hillier (ed.) *Cahiers du Cinéma: The 1950s* (London: Routledge & Kegan Paul, 1985)

Bailey, Joe *Pessimism* (London: Routledge, 1989)

Barker, Adam 'Cries and Whispers', *Sight and Sound*, spring 1990

Bazin, André *What is Cinema? I* (Berkeley: University of California Press, 1967)

—— *What is Cinema? II* (Berkeley: University of California Press, 1971)

—— 'La Strada', in P. Bondanella and M. Gieri (eds) *La Strada* (New Brunswick: Rutgers University Press, 1991)

Bergman, Ingmar *Persona and Shame* (London: Marion Boyars, 1983)

—— *The Magic Lantern* (Harmondsworth: Penguin, 1988)

Biro, Yvette *Profane Mythology: The Savage Mind of the Cinema* (Bloomington: Indiana University Press, 1982)

Blackwell, Marilyn Johns *Persona: The Transcendent Image* (Urbana: University of Illinois Press, 1986)

Bondanella, Peter (ed.) *Federico Fellini: Essays in Criticism* (Oxford: Oxford University Press, 1982)

Borde, Raymond and Etienne Chaumeton *Panorama du film noir americain: (1941–1953)* (Paris: Editions du Minuit, 1955)

Bordwell, David *Narration in the Fiction Film* (Madison: University of Wisconsin Press, 1985)

Bordwell, David, Janet Staiger and Kristin Thompson *The Classical Hollywood Cinema* (London: Routledge & Kegan Paul, 1985)

Bourdieu, Pierre *Distinction: A Social Critique of the Judgement of Taste* (London: Routledge, 1986)

Brooks, Peter *The Melodramatic Imagination: Balzac, Henry James, Melodrama and the Mode of Excess* (New Haven: Yale University Press, 1976)

Buñuel, Luis *My Last Breath* (London: Fontana, 1985)

Burch, Noel *Theory of Film Practice* (Princeton: Princeton University Press, 1981)

Calinescu, Matei *Faces of Modernity: Avant-Garde, Decadence, Kitsch* (Bloomington: Indiana University Press, 1977)

Carringer, Robert *The Making of Citizen Kane* (London: John Murray, 1985)

Carroll, Noel *Philosophical Problems of Classical Film Theory* (Princeton: Princeton University Press, 1986)

—— *Mystifying Movies: Fads & Fallacies in Contemporary Film Theory* (New York: Columbia University Press, 1988)

Cavell, Stanley *Pursuits of Happiness: The Hollywood Comedy of Remarriage* (Cambridge, Massachusetts: Harvard University Press, 1981)

Chatman, Seymour *Antonioni: The Surface of the World* (Berkeley: University of California Press, 1986)

Citati, Pietro *Kafka* (London: Minerva, 1991)

Coates, Paul *The Story of the Lost Reflection* (London: Verso, 1985)

Comito, Terry (ed.) *Touch of Evil* (New Brunswick: Rutgers University Press, 1985)

Cowie, Peter *The Cinema of Orson Welles* (New York: Da Capo Press, 1983)

—— *Coppola* (London: André Deutsch, 1989)

Crisp, C. G. *Eric Rohmer: Realist and Moralist* (Bloomington: Indiana University Press, 1988)

Davis, Mike *City of Quartz* (London: Verso, 1990)

De Beauvoir, Simone *The Second Sex* (Harmondsworth: Penguin, 1990)

Deleuze, Gilles *Nietzsche and Philosophy* (London: The Athlone Press, 1983)

—— *Cinema 1: The Movement-Image* (London: The Athlone Press, 1986)

—— *Cinema 2: The Time-Image* (London: The Athlone Press, 1989)

—— *Bergsonism* (New York: Zone Books, 1991)

Dick, E., A. Noble and D. Petrie (eds) *Bill Douglas: A Lanternist's Account* (London: BFI, 1993)

Eagleton, Terry 'Capitalism, Modernism and Post-Modernism', *NLR* 152, 1985

Eco, Umberto *Travels in Hyper-Reality* (London: Picador, 1987)

Eisner, Lotte *The Haunted Screen: Expressionism in the German Cinema and the Influence of Max Reinhardt* (London: Thames & Hudson, 1969)

Elsaesser, Thomas *The New German Cinema* (London: BFI, 1989)

—— 'Filming Fascism: Is History just an old Movie?', *Sight and Sound*, September 1992

Faulkner, Christopher *The Social Cinema of Jean Renoir* (Princeton: Princeton University Press, 1986)

Ferro, Marc *Cinema and History* (Detroit: Wayne State University Press, 1988)

Fordham, John 'Is your Journey Really Necessary?', *Independent on Sunday*, 1 December 1991

Foucault, Michel *Discipline and Punish* (Harmondsworth: Penguin, 1979)

—— *Power and Knowledge* (Hassocks: Harvester Press, 1984)

Freud, Sigmund 'Beyond the Pleasure Principle', in *Works*, vol. 11 (Harmondsworth: Penguin, 1984)

—— 'Repression', in *Works*, vol. 11 (Harmondsworth: Penguin, 1984)

—— 'The Uncanny', in *Works*, vol. 14 (Harmondsworth: Penguin, 1985)

Giddens, Anthony *The Consequences of Modernity* (Cambridge: Polity Press, 1991)

—— *Modernity and Self-Identity: Self and Society in the Late Modern Age* (Cambridge: Polity Press, 1991)

Gifford, Don *The Farther Shore: A Natural History of Perception* (London: Faber & Faber, 1990)

Gledhill, Christine (ed.) *Home is Where the Heart Is: Studies in Melodrama and the Women's Film* (London: BFI, 1989)

Godard, Jean-Luc *Pierrot le Fou* (New York: Lorimer, 1984)

Gottesman, Ronald (ed.) *The Cinema of Orson Welles* (Englewood Cliffs, NJ: Prentice Hall, 1976)

Harris, Wilson 'Tainted Histories', *Sight and Sound*, vol. 1, no. 10, February 1992

Haskell, Molly *From Reverence to Rape: The Treatment of Women in the Movies* (New York: Holt, Rinehart & Winston, 1975)

Heath, Stephen *Questions of Cinema* (London: Macmillan, 1981)

Heidegger, Martin *Nietzsche vols 1 & 2* (New York: Harper Collins, 1991)

Herdman, John *The Double in Romantic and Post-Romantic Fiction* (London: Macmillan, 1990)

Hillier, Jim (ed.) *Cahiers du Cinéma: The 1950s* (London: Routledge & Kegan Paul, 1985)

—— *Cahiers du Cinéma: The 1960s* (London: Routledge & Kegan Paul, 1987)

Hinton, David B. *The Films of Leni Riefenstahl* (Metuchen NJ: The Scarecrow Press Inc., 1978)

Jameson, Fredric 'Postmodernism and Consumer Society', in Hal Foster (ed.) *Postmodern Culture* (London: Pluto Press, 1985)

Jay, Martin *Force Fields: Between Intellectual History and Cultural Critique* (London: Routledge, 1992)

Kaplan, E. Ann (ed.) *Women in Film Noir* (London: BFI, 1980)

Kawin, Bruce *Mindscreen: Bergman, Godard and First-Person Film* (Princeton: Princeton University Press, 1978)

Kemp, Philip *Lethal Innocence: The Cinema of Alexander Mackendrick* (London: Methuen, 1991)

Kermode, Frank 'Modernisms', in B. Bergonzi (ed.) *Innovations* (London: Macmillan, 1968)

—— *History and Value* (Oxford: Clarendon Press, 1989)

Kern, Jerome *The Culture of Time and Space: 1880–1918* (London: Weidenfeld & Nicolson, 1983)

Kolker, Robert *The Cinema of Loneliness: Penn, Kubrick, Coppola, Scorsese, Altman* (New York: Oxford University Press, 1980)

—— *The Altering Eye* (New York: Oxford University Press, 1983)

Kosloff, Sarah *Invisible Storytellers: Voice-Over Narration in American Fiction Film* (Berkeley: University of California Press, 1988)

Kracauer, Siegfried *The Theory of Film: The Redemption of Physical Reality* (Oxford: Oxford University Press, 1960)

—— *From Caligari to Hitler: A Psychological Study of German Film* (Princeton: Princeton University Press, 1974)

Kuhn, Annette *The Power of the Image: Essays on Representation and Sexuality* (London: Routledge & Kegan Paul, 1985)

Lang, Robert *American Film Melodrama* (Princeton: Princeton University Press, 1989)

Lasch, Christopher *The Culture of Narcissism* (London: Abacus, 1980)

Merleau-Ponty, Maurice *The Primacy of Perception* (Evanston: Northwestern University Press, 1964)

—— *Sense and Non-Sense* (Evanston, Northwestern University Press, 1964)

—— *The Phenomenology of Perception* (London: Routledge, 1989)

Metz, Christian *Film Language* (Oxford: Oxford University Press, 1974)

—— *Cinema and Psychoanalysis* (London: Macmillan, 1982)

Modleski, Tania *The Woman Who Knew Too Much: Hitchcock and Feminist Film Theory* (London: Methuen, 1988)

Monaco, James *The New Wave: Truffaut, Godard, Chabrol, Rohmer, Rivette.* (Oxford: Oxford University Press, 1976)

—— *Alain Resnais: The Role of Imagination* (London: Secker & Warburg, 1978)

Monaco, Paul *Cinema and Society: France and Germany during the Twenties* (New York: Elsevier, 1976)

Morris, Phyllis 'Self-Deception: Sartre's Resolution of the Paradox', in H. Silverman and F. A. Ellison (eds) *Jean-Paul Sartre: Contemporary Approaches to his Philosophy* (Hassocks: Harvester Press, 1980)

Naremore, James *The Magic World of Orson Welles* (Oxford: Oxford University Press, 1978)

Neve, Brian 'The 1950s: the case of Elia Kazan and *On the Water-*

front', in P. Davies and B. Neve (eds) *Cinema, Politics and Society in America* (Manchester: Manchester University Press, 1981)

Nichols, Bill *Ideology and the Image* (Bloomington: Indiana University Press, 1981)

Orr, John *The Making of the Twentieth-Century Novel* (London: Macmillan, 1987)

—— *Tragicomedy and Contemporary Culture* (London: Macmillan, 1991)

Orr, John and Colin Nicholson (eds) *Cinema and Fiction: New Modes of Adapting, 1950–1990* (Edinburgh: Edinburgh University Press, 1992)

Paglia, Camille *Sexual Personae: Art and Decadence from Nefertiti to Emily Dickinson* (Harmondsworth: Penguin, 1991)

Pasolini, Pier Paolo *Ecrits sur le cinéma* (Lyon: Lyon Presses Universitaires/Institut Lumière, 1987)

—— *A Future Life* (Rome: Associazione Pier Paolo Pasolini, 1989)

Perkins, V. F. *Film as Film* (Harmondsworth: Penguin, 1972)

—— 'In a Lonely Place', in Ian Cameron (ed.) *The Movie Book of Film Noir* (London: Studio Vista, 1992)

Petrie, Duncan (ed.) *Screening Europe* (London: BFI, 1992)

Rank, Otto *The Double: A Psychoanalytic Study* (New York: New American Library, 1979)

Ray, Robert *A Certain Tendency of the Hollywood Cinema, 1930–1980* (Princeton: Princeton University Press, 1985)

Renoir, Jean *Renoir on Renoir* (Cambridge: Cambridge University Press, 1989)

Rentschler, Eric (ed.) *West German Filmmakers on Film* (New York: Holmes & Meier, 1988)

Rohdie, Sam *Antonioni* (London: BFI, 1990)

Ryan, Michael and Kellner, Douglas *Camera Politica: The Politics and Ideology of Contemporary Hollywood Film* (Bloomington: Indiana University Press, 1988)

Sartre, Jean-Paul *Being and Nothingness* (London: Methuen, 1957)

—— *The Psychology of Imagination* (London: Methuen, 1972)

Simmel, Georg *Schopenhauer and Nietzsche* (Amherst: University of Massachusetts Press, 1986)

Sloterdijk, Peter *Critique of Cynical Reason* (London: Verso, 1988)

Smith, Joseph and William Kerrigan (eds) *Images in our Souls: Cavell, Psychoanalysis and Cinema* (Baltimore: Johns Hopkins University Press, 1987)

Sobchack, Vivian *The Address of the Eve: A Phenomenology of Film Experience* (Berkeley: University of California Press, 1992)

Sontag, Susan *Styles of Radical Will* (New York: Delta Books, 1970)

Sorlin, Pierre *European Cinemas: European Societies 1939–1990* (London: Routledge, 1991)

Stevenson, Randall *Modernist Fiction* (Hemel Hempstead: Harvester, 1992)

Taylor, Charles *Sources of The Self: The Making of Modern Identity* (Cambridge: Cambridge University Press, 1989)

Telotte, J. P. *Voices in the Dark: The Narrative Patterns of Film Noir* (Urbana: University of Illinois Press, 1989)

Vice, Sue (ed.) *Malcolm Lowry: Eighty Years On* (London: Macmillan, 1989)

Virilio, Paul *War and Cinema: The Logistics of Perception* (London: Verso, 1989)

Wenders, Wim *Emotion Pictures* (London: Faber & Faber, 1989)

Williams, Raymond *The Long Revolution* (Harmondsworth: Penguin, 1975)

—— *Marxism and Literature* (Oxford: Oxford University Press, 1977)

Williamson, Judith *Consuming Passions: The Dynamics of Popular Culture* (London: Boyars, 1986)

Wollen, Peter *Readings and Writings* (London: NLB, 1982)

Wood, Michael *America in the Movies* (London: Secker & Warburg, 1975)

AMERICAN FILM NOIR

Double Indemnity

Paramount 1944. Produced by Joseph Sistrom; Directed by Billy
Wilder; Screenplay by Raymond Chandler and Billy Wilder based
on the novella by James M. Cain; Photography: John F. Seitz;
starring Fred MacMurray, Barbara Stanwyck and Edward G.
Robinson. 107 mins.

The Big Sleep

Warner 1946. Produced and Directed by Howard Hawks; Screenplay by William Faulkner, Leigh Brackett and Jules Furthman
from the novel by Raymond Chandler; Photography: Sid Hickox;
starring Humphrey Bogart, Lauren Bacall, John Ridgley, Martha
Vickers and Dorothy Malone. 114 mins.

The Postman Always Rings Twice

MGM 1946. Produced by Carey Wilson; Directed by Tay Garnett;
Screenplay by Harry Ruaskin and Niven Busch from the novel
by James M. Cain; Photography: Sidney Wagner; *starring* Lana
Turner, John Garfield and Cecil Kellaway. 113 mins.

The Strange Love of Martha Ivers

Paramount 1946. Produced by Hal Wallis; Directed by Lewis Milestone; Screenplay: Robert Rossen; Photography: Victor Milner; *starring* Barbara Stanwyck, Van Heflin, Kirk Douglas and Lizabeth Scott. 116 mins.

Crossfire

RKO/Dore Schary 1947. Produced by Adrian Scott; Directed by Edward Dymytryk; Screenplay: John Paxton; Photography: J. Roy Hunt; *starring* Robert Ryan, Robert Mitchum, Robert Young and Gloria Grahame. 86 mins.

They Live by Night

RKO 1948. Produced by John Houseman and Dore Shary; Directed by Nicholas Ray; Screenplay by Charles Schnee and Ray from the novel by Edward Anderson *Thieves Like Us*; Photography: George E. Diskant; *starring* Farley Granger, Cathy O'Donnell and Howard da Silva. 95 mins.

In a Lonely Place

Columbia/Santana 1950. Produced by Robert Lord; Directed by Nicholas Ray; Screenplay by Andrew Solt from the story by Dorothy Hughes; Photography: Burnett Guffey; *starring* Humphrey Bogart, Gloria Grahame and Frank Lovejoy. 93 mins.

Sunset Boulevard

Paramount 1950. Produced by Charles Brackett; Directed by Billy Wilder; Screenplay by Charles Brackett and D. M. Marshman Jr; Photography: John F. Seitz; *starring* Gloria Swanson, William Holden and Erich von Stroheim. 111 mins.

The Sweet Smell of Success

Hecht–Hill–Lancaster/UA 1957; Directed by Alexander Mackendrick; Screenplay: Ernest Lehman and Clifford Odets from the novella by Lehman; Photography: James Wong Howe; *starring* Burt Lancaster, Tony Curtis and Susan Harrison. 103 mins (Press Showing) 96 mins (Theatrical Release).

Klute

Warner Bros 1971. Produced and Directed by Alan J. Pakula; Screenplay: Andy K. Lewis and Dave Lewis; Photography: Gordon Willis; *starring* Jane Fonda, Donald Sutherland, Charles Ciotti and Roy Scheider. 114 mins.

Chinatown

Paramount/Long Road 1974. Produced by Robert Evans; Directed by Roman Polanski; Screenplay: Robert Towne; Photography: Richard Sylbert; *starring* Jack Nicholson, Faye Dunaway, John Huston and Perry Lopez. 131 mins.

The Conversation

Paramount 1974. Produced, written and directed by Francis Ford Coppola; Photography: Bill Butler; *starring* Gene Hackman, John Cazale, Allen Garfield and Frederick Forrest. 113 mins.

The Parallax View

Paramount 1974. Produced and Directed by Alan J. Pakula; Screenplay: David Giler and Lorenzo Semple, from the novel by Loren Singer; Photography: Gordon Willis; *starring* Warren Beatty, Paula Prentiss, William Daniels and Hume Cronyn. 102 mins.

All the President's Men

Warner/Wildwood 1976. Produced by Robert Redford and Walter Coblenz; Directed by Alan J. Pakula; Screenplay: William Goldman from the book by Carl Bernstein and Bob Woodward; Photography: Gordon Willis; *starring* Dustin Hoffman, Robert Redford, Jason Robards, Martin Balsam and Jack Warden. 138 mins.

Taxi Driver

Columbia 1976. Produced by Michael and Julia Phillips; Directed by Martin Scorsese; Screenplay: Paul Schrader; Photography: Michael Chapman; *starring* Robert De Niro, Cybill Shepherd, Jodie Foster, Harvey Keitel and Peter Boyle. 114 mins.

American Gigolo

Paramount/Pierre Associates 1980. Produced by Freddie Fields; Written and Directed by Paul Schrader; Photography: John Bailey; *starring* Richard Gere, Lauren Hutton, Hector Elizondo and Nina Van Pallandt. 117 mins.

Body Heat

The Ladd Company/Warner 1981. Produced by Fred T. Gallo. Written and Directed by Lawrence Kasdan; Photography: Richard Klein; *starring* William Hurt, Kathleen Turner, Ted Danson, Mickey Rourke and Richard Crenna. 113 mins.

Black Widow

TCF/Laurence Mark 1986. Produced by Harold Schneider; Directed by Bob Rafelson; Screenplay: Ronald Bass; Photography: Conrad Hall; *starring* Debra Winger, Theresa Russell, Sami Frey and Dennis Hopper. 103 mins.

Bird

Warner/Malpaso 1988. Produced and Directed by Clint Eastwood; Screenplay: Joel Oliansky; Photography: Jack N. Green; *starring* Forest Whitaker, Diane Venora and Michael Zelnikar. 161 mins.

MICHELANGELO ANTONIONI

Il grido

SPA Cinematografica 1957. Produced by Franco Cancellieri; Screenplay: Antonioni; Photography: Gianni di Venanzo; *starring* Steve Cochran, Alida Valli and Betsy Blair. 116 mins.

L'avventura

Cino del Duca 1959. Produced by Amato Penn; Screenplay: Antonioni, Elio Bartolini and Tonino Guerra from a story by Antonioni; Photography: Aldo Scavarda; *starring* Monica Vitti, Gabriele Ferzetti and Lea Massari. 145 mins.

La notte

Nepi-Film, Rome 1960. Produced by Emmanuele Cassuto; Screenplay: Antonioni, Ennio Flaiano, and Tonino Guerra from a story by Antonioni; Photography: Gianni di Venanzo; *starring* Marcello Mastroianni, Jeanne Moreau, Monica Vitti and Bernhard Wicki. 122 mins.

L'eclisse

Intereuropa Film, Cineriz (Rome) 1962. Produced by Robert and Raymond Hakim; Screenplay: Antonioni, Tonino Guerra, Elio Bartolini, and Ottiero Ottieri from a story by Antonioni and Guerra; Photography: Gianni Di Venanzo; *starring* Monica Vitti, Alain Delon and Francisco Rabal. 125 mins.

Blow-up

MGM/Bridge Films 1966. Produced by Carlo Ponti and Pierre Rouve. Screenplay: Antonioni, Tonino Guerra and Edward Bond from a story by Julio Cortazar; Photography: Carlo Di Palma; *starring* Vanessa Redgrave, David Hemmings, Sarah Miles, and Verushka. 111 mins.

Zabriskie Point

MGM 1969. Produced by Carlo Ponti and Harrison Starr. Screenplay: Antonioni, Fred Gardner, Sam Shepard, Tonino Guerra and Clare Peploe; Photography: Alfio Contini; *starring* Mark Frechette, Daria Halprin, Rod Taylor and Joe Chaikin's Open Theatre. 110 mins.

The Passenger

MGM/Cinematografica Champion/Les Films Concordia/CIPI Cinematografica 1975. Screenplay: Mark Peploe, Peter Wollen and Antonioni from a story by Mark Peploe. Photography: Luciano Tovoli; *starring* Jack Nicholson, Maria Schneider, Jenny Runacre, Ian Hendry and Stephen Berkoff. 124 mins.

INGMAR BERGMAN

Wild Strawberries

Svensk Filmindustri 1957. Produced, Written and Directed by

Bergman; Photography: Gunnar Fischer; *starring* Victor Sjöstrom, Bibi Andersson, Ingrid Thulin, Gunnar Björnstrand. 90 mins.

The Face

Svensk Filmindustri 1958. Produced, Written and Directed by Bergman; Photography: Gunnar Fischer; *starring* Max von Sydow, Ingrid Thulin, Åke Fridall and Naima Wifstrand. 100 mins.

Through a Glass Darkly

Svensk Filmindustri 1961. Produced, Written and Directed by Berman; Photography: Sven Nykvist; *starring* Harriet Andersson, Gunnar Björnstrand, Max von Sydow, Lars Passgard. 89 mins.

Winter Light

Svensk Filmindustri 1963. Produced, Written and Directed by Bergman; Photography: Sven Nykvist; *starring* Ingrid Thulin, Gunnar Björnstrand, Gunnel Lindblom and Max von Sydow. 80 mins.

The Silence

Svensk Filmindustri 1963. Written, Produced and Directed by Bergman; Photography: Sven Nykvist; *starring* Ingrid Thulin, Gunnel Lindblom, Jörgen Lindstrom, Häkan Jahberg, Burger Malmsten, the Eduardinis. 95 mins.

Persona

Svensk Filmindustri 1966. Written, Produced and Directed by Bergman; Photography: Sven Nykvist; *starring* Bibi Andersson, Liv Ullmann, Margaretha Krook and Gunnar Björnstrand. 84 mins.

Shame

Svensk Filmindustri/Cinematograph 1968. Written, Produced and Directed by Bergman; Photography: Sven Nykvist; *starring* Liv Ullmann, Gunnar Björnstrand, Birgitta Valberg and Sigge Fürst. 102 mins.

Cries and Whispers

Cinematograph/Svenska Filmeninstitutet 1973. Written, Produced and Directed by Bergman; Photography: Sven Nykvist; *starring* Harriet Andersson, Kari Sylwan, Ingrid Thulin, Liv Ullmann and Erland Josephson. 91 mins.

Scenes from a Marriage

Cinematograph 1973. Executive Producer: Lars-Owe Carlberg; Screenplay: Bergman; Photography: Sven Nykvist; *starring* Liv Ullmann, Erland Josephson; Bibi Andersson and Jan Malmsjö. (Swedish Television in six weekly parts, 11 April–16 May 1973.) Theatrical release: 168 mins.

The Serpent's Egg

Rialto Film, Berlin/Dino de Laurentis Corporation 1977. Produced by Dino de Laurentis and Horst Wendlandt; Screenplay: Bergman; Principal photography: Sven Nykvist; *starring* Liv Ullmann, David Carradine, Gert Froebe and Heinz Bennent. 119 mins.

From the Life of the Marionettes

Personafilm, Munich/Bayerische Staatsschauspiel, 1980. Produced by Horst Wendlandt and Ingrid Bergman; Screenplay: Bergman; Photography: Sven Nykvist; *starring* Robert Atzhorn, Martin Benrath, Christine Buchegger and Riata Russek. 104 mins.

BERNARDO BERTOLUCCI

Before the Revolution (*Primo della revoluzione*)

Iride Cinematografica 1964. Produced by Gianni Amico; Screenplay: Bertolucci and Gianni Amico; Photography: Aldo Scavarda; *starring* Adriana Asti, Francesco Barili, Allen Midgette and Morando Morandini. 112 mins.

The Spider's Strategem (*Strategia del ragno*)

RAI TV/Red Film 1970. Produced by Giovanni Bertolucci; Screenplay: Bertolucci, Marilu Parolini, and Eduardo de Gregorio from the story *Theme of the Traitor and Hero* by Jorge Luis Borges; Photography: Vittorio Storaro, Franco de Giacomo; *starring* Giulio Brogi, Alida Valli and Tino Scotti. 100 mins.

The Conformist (*Il conformista*)

Mars Film, Rome/Marianne Productions Paris 1970. Produced by Maurizio Lodi-Fe; Screenplay: Bertolucci from the novel by Alberto Moravia; Photography: Vittorio Storaro; *starring* Jean-Louis Trintignant, Dominique Sanda, Stefania Sandrelli and Enzo Tarascio. 108 mins.

Last Tango in Paris (*L'ultimo tango a Parigi*)

PEA Cinematografica (Rome)/Les Artistes Associés (Paris) 1972. Produced by Alberto Grimaldi; Screenplay: Bertolucci, Franco Arcalli; Photography: Vittorio Storaro; *starring* Marlon Brando, Maria Schneider, Jean-Pierre Leaud and Massimo Girotti. 129 mins.

1900 (*Novecento*)

PEA Cinematografica (Rome)/Les Artistes Associés (Paris) 1976. Produced by Alberto Grimaldi; Screenplay: Bertolucci, Franco Arcalli, Guiseppe Bertolucci; Photography: Vittorio Storaro; *starring* Burt Lancaster, Robert De Niro, Sterling Hayden, Gérard Depardieu, Dominique Sanda, Stefania Sandrelli, Laura Betti and Donald Sutherland. 320 mins (English version, 248 mins)

LUIS BUÑUEL

Los Olvidados

Ultramar Films SA 1950. Produced by Oscar Dancigers. Screenplay: Buñuel, Luis Alcoriza and Oscar Danzigers; Photography: Gabriel Figueroa; *starring* Estela Inda, Miguel Inclan and Alfonso Mejia. 89 mins.

The Diary of a Chambermaid (*Le Journal d'une femme de chambre*)

Franscope Speva/Cine Alliance/Filmsonor 1964. Produced by Serge Silberman and Michel Sabra; Screenplay: Buñuel and Jean-Claude Carrière from the novel by Octave Mirabeau; Photography: Roger Fellous; *starring* Jeanne Moreau, Georges Geret, Michel Piccoli and Françoise Lagagne. 98 mins.

Belle de Jour

Paris Film Production/Five Film, Rome 1967. Produced by Robert and Raymond Hakim; Screenplay: Buñuel from the novel by Joseph Kessel; Photography: Sacha Vierney; *starring* Catherine Deneuve, Jean Sorel, Geneviève Page, Michel Piccoli, Franciso Rabal and Françoise Fabian. 100 minutes.

The Discreet Charm of the Bourgeoisie (Le Charme discret de la bourgeoisie)

Greenwick Films 1972. Produced by Serge Silbermann; Screenplay by Buñuel and Jean-Claude Carrière; Photography: Edmond Richard; *starring* Fernando Rey, Delphine Seyrig and Stephane Audran. 105 mins.

FEDERICO FELLINI

La strada

Trans-Lux 1954. Produced by Carlo Ponti and Dino De Laurentis; Screenplay: Fellini, Tullio Pinelli and Ennio Flaiano; Photography: Otello Martelli; *starring* Giulietta Masina, Anthony Quinn and Richard Basehart. 107 mins.

8½

Cineriz/Francinex 1963. Produced by Angelo Rizzolo; Screenplay: Fellini, Ennio Flaiano, Tullio Pinelli, Brunello Rondi; Photography: Gianni di Venanzo; *starring* Marcello Mastroianni, Anouk Aimée, Sandra Milo and Claudia Cardinale. 135 mins.

Amarcord

PC Produzione/PECF 1973. Produced by Franco Cristaldi; Screenplay: Fellini and Tonino Guerra; Photography: Giuseppe Rotunno; *starring* Puppel Maggio, Magali Noel and Armando Brancia. 123 mins.

JEAN-LUC GODARD

A bout de souffle (Breathless)

SNC 1959. Produced by Georges de Beauregard; Screenplay: Godard, from a treatment by François Truffaut; Cinematography:

Raoul Coutard; *starring* Jean-Paul Belmondo, Jean Seberg, Daniel Boulanger and Jean-Pierre Melville. 89 mins.

Une femme est une femme

Rome–Paris Films (Paris) 1961. Produced by Georges de Beauregard; Screenplay: Godard; Photography: Raoul Coutard; *starring* Anna Karina, Jean-Paul Belmondo, Jean-Claude Brialy. 102 mins.

Alphaville

Chaumiane/Film Studio 1965. Produced by André Michelin; Screenplay: Godard; Cinematography: Raoul Coutard; *starring* Eddie Constantine, Anna Karina and Akim Tamiroff. 98 mins.

Pierrot le fou

Rome–Paris-Films 1965. Produced by Georges de Beauregard; Screenplay: Godard, from the novel *Obsession* by Lionel White; Cinematography: Raoul Coutard; *starring* Jean-Paul Belmondo, Anna Karina and Sam Fuller. 110 mins.

Weekend

Comacio/Les Films Copernic/Lira Films (Paris) Ascot Cineraid (Rome) 1967. Screenplay: Godard; Photography: Raoul Coutard; *starring* Mireille Darc, Jean Yanne and Jean-Pierre Leaud. 95 mins.

WERNER HERZOG

Aguirre, Wrath of God (Aguirre, der Zorn Gottes)

Werner Herzog Filmproduktion/Hessischer Rundfunk 1972. Written, Produced and Directed by Herzog; Photography: Thomas Mauch, Francisco Joan, Orlando Macchievallo; *starring* Klaus Kinski, Helena Rojo, Ruy Guerra and Peter Berling. 93 mins.

Stroszek

Werner Herzog Filmproduktion/ZDF Mainz 1977. Written, Produced and Directed by Herzog; Photography: Thomas Mauch, Ed Lachmann, Wolfgang Knigge and Stefano Guido; *starring* Bruno S, Eva Mattes and Clemens Scheitz. 108 mins.

Nosferatu (Nosferatu – Phantom der Nacht)

Werner Herzog Filmproduktion/Gaumont Paris/ZDF Mainz. Produced by Herzog; Screenplay: Herzog, based on the novel *Dracula* by Bram Stoker; Photography: Jörg Schmidt Reitwein and Michael Gast; *starring* Klaus Kinski, Bruno Ganz and Isabelle Adjani. 107 mins.

ALFRED HITCHCOCK

Notorious

RKO 1946. Produced and Directed by Hitchcock; Screenplay: Ben Hecht from a story by Hitchcock; Photography: Ted Tetzlaff; *starring* Cary Grant, Ingrid Bergman and Claude Rains. 101 mins.

Rear Window

Paramount 1954. Produced and Directed by Hitchcock; Screenplay: John Michael Hayes from a story by Cornell Woolrich; Photography: Robert Burks; *starring* James Stewart, Grace Kelly, Wendell Corey, Thelma Ritter and Raymond Burr. 112 mins.

Vertigo

Paramount 1958. Produced and directed by Hitchcock; Screenplay: Alec Coppel and Samuel Taylor, from the novel by Pierre Boileau and Thomas Narcejac, *D'entre les morts*; Photography: Robert Burks; *starring* James Stewart, Kim Novak and Barbara Bel Geddes. 120 mins.

Psycho

Paramount 1960. Produced and Directed by Hitchcock; Screenplay: Joseph Stefano, from the novel by Robert Bloch; Photography: John L. Russell; *starring* Janet Leigh, Anthony Perkins, Vera Miles, John Gavin and Martin Balsam. 109 mins.

The Birds

Universal 1963. Produced and Directed by Hitchcock; Screenplay: Evan Hunter from the story by Daphne du Maurier; Photography:

Robert Burks; *starring* Rod Taylor, Tippi Hedren, Suzanne Pleshette and Jessica Tandy. 120 mins.

Marnie

Universal 1964. Produced by Albert Whitlock; Screenplay: Jay Presson Allen, from the novel by Winston Graham; Photography: Robert Burks; *starring* Tippi Hendren, Sean Connery, Diane Baker and Martin Gabel. 120 mins.

DAVID LYNCH

Blue Velvet

De Laurentis 1986. Produced by Richard Roth; Screenplay: Lynch; Photography: Frederick Elmes; *starring* Kyle MacLachlan, Isabella Rossellini, Dennis Hopper, Laura Dern and Dean Stockwell. 120 mins.

Wild at Heart

Polygram/Propaganda 1990. Produced by Monty Montgomery, Steve Golin, Joni Sighvatsson; Screenplay: Lynch; Photography: Frederick Elmes; *starring* Nicholas Cage, Laura Dern, Willem Dafoe, Diane Ladd, Crispin Glover, Isabella Rossellini and Harry Dean Stanton. 120 mins.

TERENCE MALICK

Badlands

Edward Pressman/Warner 1974. Produced, Written and Directed by Malick; Photography: Brian Probyn, Taki Fujimoto, Steven Larner; *starring* Martin Sheen, Sissy Spacek, Warren Oates and Ramon Bieri. 94 mins.

Days of Heaven

Paramount/OP 1978. Produced by Bert and Harold Schneider; Screenplay: Malick; Photography: Nestor Almendros; *starring* Richard Gere, Brooke Adams, Sam Shepard and Linda Manz. 95 mins.

BOB RAFELSON

Five Easy Pieces

BBS/Columbia 1970. Produced by Burt Schneider; Screenplay: Adrien Joyce (Carole Eastman); Photography: Laslo Kovacs; *starring* Jack Nicholson, Karen Black and Susan Ansprach. 98 mins.

The King of Marvin Gardens

BBS/Columbia 1972. Produced and Directed by Rafelson; Screenplay: Jacob Brackman; Photography: Laslo Kovacs; *starring* Jack Nicholson, Bruce Dern, Ellen Burstyn and Julia Anne Robinson. 104 mins.

ALAIN RESNAIS

Nuit et brouillard (Night and fog)

Como/Argos/Cocinor 1955. Produced and Directed by Resnais; Screenplay: Jean Cayrol; Photography: Ghislain Cloquet, Sacha Vierney. 31 mins.

Hiroshima, mon amour

Como/Argos/Daiei, Tokyo 1959. Produced by Sacha Kamenka, Shirakawa Takeo, Samy Halfron; Screenplay: Marguerite Duras; Photography: Sacha Vierney, Michio Takahashi; *starring* Emmanuele Riva, Eiji Okada and Bernard Fresson. 91 mins.

L'Année dernière à Marienbad (Last Year at Marienbad)

Terra Film/Société Nouvelle des Films, Cormoran/Précital/Silver Films/Cineriz 1961. Produced by Leon Sanz; Screenplay: Alain Robbe-Grillet; Photography: Sacha Vierney; *starring* Delphine Seyrig, Giorgio Albertazzi and Sacha Pitoëff. 94 mins.

Muriel, ou le temps d'un retour

Argos/Alpha/Eclair/Films de la Pléiade/Dear Film, Rome 1963. Produced by Philippe Dussart; Screenplay: Jean Cayrol; Photography: Sacha Vierney; *starring* Delphine Seyrig, Jena-Pierre Kerien, Nita Klein and Jean-Baptiste Thierrée. 116 mins.

Providence

Action/Société Française de Production/FR3/Citel Films, Geneva 1977. Produced by Philippe Dusart; Screenplay: David Mercer; *starring* Dirk Bogarde, Ellen Burstyn, John Gielgud, David Warner and Elaine Stritch. 110 mins.

ERIC ROHMER

Ma nuit chez Maud (My Night at Maud's)

Les Films du Losange 1969. Produced by Barbet Schroeder and Pierre Cottrell; Screenplay: Rohmer; Photography: Nestor Almendros; *starring* Jean-Louis Trintignant, Françoise Fabian, Marie-Christine Barrault and Antoine Vitez. From the series *Contes Moreaux*. 110 mins.

Le genou de Claire (Claire's Knee)

Les Films du Losange, 1970. Produced by Pierre Cottrell; Screenplay: Rohmer; Photography: Nestor Almendros; *starring* Jean-Claude Brialy, Aurora Cornu, Béatrice Romand, Laurence de Monaghan and Michèle Montel. From the series *Contes Moreaux*. 105 mins.

La femme de l'aviator (The Aviator's Wife)

Les Films du Losange 1980. Produced by Margaret Menegoz; Photography: Bernard Lutic, Romain Windig; *starring* Philippe Marland, Marie Rivière and Anne-Laure Meury. From the series *Comédies et Proverbes*. 103 mins.

Pauline à la plage (Pauline at the beach)

Les Films du Losange/Les Films Ariane 1982. Produced by Margaret Menegoz; Photography: Nestor Almendros; *starring* Amanda Langlet, Arielle Dombassle, Pascal Gregory and Feodor Atkine. From the series *Comédies et Proverbes*. 95 mins.

FRANÇOIS TRUFFAUT

Les Quatre Cents Coups (The Four Hundred Blows)

Films du Carosse/SEDIF 1958. Written, Produced and Directed by Truffaut; Photography: Henri Decae; *starring* Jean-Pierre Leaud, Claire Maurier and Albert Remy. 94 mins.

Tirez sur le pianiste (Shoot the Pianist)

Films de la Pléiade 1960. Produced by Pierre Braunberger; Screenplay: Truffaut and Marcel Moussy from the novel by David Goodis, *Down There*; Photography: Raoul Coutard; *starring* Charles Aznavour, Nicole Berger and Marie Dubois. 80 mins.

Jules et Jim

Films du Carosse/SEDIF 1962. Produced by Marcel Berbert; Screenplay: Truffaut, Jean Gruault from the novel by Henri-Pierre Roche; Photography: Raoul Coutard; *starring* Oskar Werner, Jeanne Moreau and Henri Serre 105 mins.

PETER WEIR

Picnic at Hanging Rock

Picnic Productions/Australian Film Corporation 1975. Produced by Hal and Jim McElroy; Screenplay: Cliff Green, from the novel by Joan Lindsay; Photography: Russell Boyd; *starring* Rachel Roberts, Dominic Guard and Helen Morse. 115 mins.

The Last Wave

UA 1977. Produced by Derek Power; Screenplay: Peter Weir, Tony Morphett, Petra Popescu; Photography: Russell Boyd; *starring* Richard Chamberlain, Olivia Hamnet and Frederick Parslow. 108 mins.

The Year of Living Dangerously

MGM/McElroy and McElroy 1982. Produced and Directed by Weir; Screenplay: Weir, David Williamson and C. J. Koch from the novel by Koch; Photography: Russell Boyd; *starring* Mel Gibson, Sigourney Weaver, Linda Hunt, Michael Murphy, Bill Kerr. 114 mins.

ORSON WELLES

Citizen Kane

RKO/Mercury Productions 1941. Produced and Directed by Welles; Screenplay: Welles and Herman J. Mankiewicz; Photography: Gregg Toland; *starring* Orson Welles, Joseph Cotten, Everett Sloane and Dorothy Comingore. 119 mins.

The Lady from Shanghai

Columbia 1948. Produced by Harry Cohn; Screenplay: Welles, from Sherwood King's novel *If I Die Before I Wake*; Photography: Charles Lawton Jr; *starring* Rita Hayworth, Orson Welles, Everett Sloane and Glenn Anders. 86 mins.

Touch of Evil

Universal 1958. Produced by Alfred Zugsmith; Screenplay: Welles from Whit Masterson's novel *Badge of Courage*; Photography: Russell Metty; starring Orson Welles, Charlton Heston, Janet Leigh, Akim Tamiroff, Marlene Dietrich, Joseph Calleia and Dennis Weaver. 118 mins.

The Trial

Paris Europa Productions/FI-C-IT/Hisa-Films 1963. Produced by Alexander and Michael Salkind; Screenplay: Welles, from the novel by Franz Kafka; Photography: Edmond Richard; *starring* Anthony Perkins, Jeanne Moreau, Romy Schneider, Orson Welles, Elsa Martinelli and Akim Tamiroff. 119 mins.

WIM WENDERS

Alice in the Cities (*Alice in den Städten*)

Filmverlag der Autoren/WDR Cologne 1973; Produced by Peter Genée; Screenplay: Wenders and Veith von Fürstenberg; Photography: Robby Müller, Martin Schäfer; *starring* Rüdiger Vogler, Yella Röttlander and Lisa Kreuzer. 110 mins.

Kings of the Road (Im Lauf der Zeit)

Wim Wenders Filmproduktion/WDR Cologne 1976. Produced, Written and Directed by Wenders; Photography: Robby Müller, Martin Schäfer; *starring* Rüdiger Vogler, Hanns Zischler, Lisa Kreuzer and Marquard Bohm. 176 mins.

Paris, Texas

Gray City/Road Movies/Pro-Ject Film/Argos 1984; Produced and Directed by Wenders; Screenplay: Wenders and Sam Shepard; *starring* Harry Dean Stanton, Natassja Kinski, Bernhard Wicki and Dean Stockwell. 148 mins.

Index